MW01169478

SEVENTY THOUSAND
WORDS BETWEEN STRANGERS

JESSE ISAACS

SEVENTY THOUSAND
WORDS BETWEEN STRANGERS

TATE PUBLISHING
AND ENTERPRISES, LLC

Seventy Thousand Words Between Strangers
Copyright © 2013 by Jesse Isaacs. All rights reserved.

No part of this publication may be reproduced, stored in a retrieval system or transmitted in any way by any means, electronic, mechanical, photocopy, recording or otherwise without the prior permission of the author except as provided by USA copyright law.

The opinions expressed by the author are not necessarily those of Tate Publishing, LLC.

Published by Tate Publishing & Enterprises, LLC
127 E. Trade Center Terrace | Mustang, Oklahoma 73064 USA
1.888.361.9473 | www.tatepublishing.com

Tate Publishing is committed to excellence in the publishing industry. The company reflects the philosophy established by the founders, based on Psalm 68:11,
"The Lord gave the word and great was the company of those who published it."

Book design copyright © 2013 by Tate Publishing, LLC. All rights reserved.
Cover design by Ronnel Luspoc
Interior design by Caypeeline Casas

Published in the United States of America

ISBN: 978-1-62746-824-4
1. Biography & Autobiography / General
2. Family & Relationships / Love & Romance
13.10.09

DEDICATION

To my loving wife, Gia, the one who *didn't*
get away, and to our two beautiful little girls,
Ashley Jane and Lexi Michelle.

PROLOGUE

Sitting in my apartment with little to do and feeling a bit lonely, it had been quite a while since I'd been in a relationship—a serious relationship, I should say. As most people who still live in the town that they grew up in, going to the bar was like revisiting high school. All the same faces acting pretty much as they did in high school. To this day, I couldn't tell you what made me do it, but I decided to post a profile on an online dating website. This was far back enough where it wasn't so commonplace to do something like that. In fact, most people who did have profiles on internet dating sites rarely admitted it.

I'd be lying if I said that I took it seriously. I didn't expect anything to come of it, nor did I expect to meet anyone worth talking to. With this in mind, I created my "About Me" page and tried my best to keep it as ridiculous as possible—for many reasons. First off, looking back on it I think that by making my profile somewhat of a joke, it helped me to justify doing it in the first place. Second, I figured that only the right person would get my sense of humor, and if that person did come along and found it funny, well then who knows? Maybe we could have some kind of connection. With that being said, the paragraph where you're supposed to give a brief history about yourself read as follows:

> At the age of four months I was left on the doorstep of a ficticious 17th century poet. I lived, by myself, on this doorstep until the age of 23; surviving only on pebbles and puddle water. I am now involved with a not-for-profit organization that provides lap dances for poor and underprivledged children.

Needless to say, I was certain an introduction like that would either turn off the girls who were too tightly wound or appeal to girls with a good sense of humor. I never expected that anyone would actually believe such a preposterous prologue. However, much to my surprise, many people did. Pamela was not one of them.

What you are about to read is a compilation of conversations that took place over the course of about a week between me and a girl that I met on Match: Pamela. Never in a million years did I think that two people would be able to build such an intense relationship in such a short amount of time and having never met one another in person. Well it did happen and you're about to read exactly how it all unfolded.

In an effort not to give away the ending, I'll simply leave it at this: Love can and will strike you when and where you least expect it; and when it happens, you'd better be ready for it, because if you're not—well—read on.

To Pamela, by Microsoft Word word count, this is 274 pages and about 70,000 words, and we did it all by ourselves in about a week. It would take you forever to read all this, so I will sum it up for you: "We like each other."

THE FIRST CONVERSATION—EVER

GatorCandie: So my nickname for you is "doorstep guy"

BDR 529 IL: ok...why is that?

GatorCandie: "left on a doorstep, bla bla"

BDR 529 IL: oh... yah... I'm glad you can find humor in my misfortune

BDR 529 IL: lol

GatorCandie: that's where I find most of my humor. Not just your misfortune...

GatorCandie: there's a little bit of misery everywhere you look

BDR 529 IL: oh... dont get me wrong... the misfortune of others is hilarious

GatorCandie: ...just not your's... haha

BDR 529 IL: exactly

BDR 529 IL: now you're on the trolley

GatorCandie: my misery is not so funny either, actually

GatorCandie: keep that in mind

BDR 529 IL: ok... your's and mine... off limits.

BDR 529 IL: everything else goes

GatorCandie: except when it's especially funny, then it MIGHT be ok

GatorCandie: like if I slip on ice?

BDR 529 IL: or a banana peel

GatorCandie: oh, that's old news

BDR 529 IL:	you wouldn't believe me but a friend of mine actually did slip on a banana peel
BDR 529 IL:	he was getting out of the passenger side of the car, went down, I asked what happened, he said, "you wouldn't believe it"
GatorCandie:	I'd believe me if you really wanted me to. In front of lots of people? That's key.
GatorCandie:	I slipped on a sock monkey once, that's close.
BDR 529 IL:	oh…dont get me started on sock monkeys
GatorCandie:	sore subject?
BDR 529 IL:	well…it might be if I knew what sock monkeys were
GatorCandie:	wants to directly connect.
BDR 529 IL:	is now directly connected.
GatorCandie:	hideous things, really
BDR 529 IL:	oh…those should be removed from existance
GatorCandie:	they're kind of like cockroaches. They won't go away.
BDR 529 IL:	although that lipstick kind of does it for me
GatorCandie:	Playschool/firetruck red?
BDR 529 IL:	yep… mmm mmm mmm
BDR 529 IL:	so… why are you up so late??
BDR 529 IL:	you should be in bed young lady
GatorCandie:	I know. Would you like to hear my story?

BDR 529 IL:	of course I would
GatorCandie:	My friend from high school (best friend) is in North Carolina. She does tattoos for a livin' and stays up late and gets up late. Therefore, if I want to chat about nothing in particular, it happens at around 11 or 12. Sometimes we are very funny so I end up doing this sort of thing. But it can't happen very often because I have to get up early. That's my story.
BDR 529 IL:	it's a touching story
GatorCandie:	I'm crying just telling it. I laughed, I cried, it became a part of me
BDR 529 IL:	ha
BDR 529 IL:	so… you seem good… wanna get married??
GatorCandie:	nah, not yet
BDR 529 IL:	ok…well… if you marry me within the next 10 minutes, you get this amazing tearless onion chopper
GatorCandie:	Why, is this a race against time or a bar bet? I'll help in any way I can.
BDR 529 IL:	nah…. just want an excuse to go to Vegas
GatorCandie:	and a puppy? Oh say you will!
BDR 529 IL:	puppy??? Who do I look like… Lorenzo DeMedichi??
GatorCandie:	I'm not that easy.
GatorCandie:	It'll take more than a puppy and a Lorenzo DeMedichi look-a-like to get me to cook onions for you.
BDR 529 IL:	Why does it always have to be about the onions with you??

GatorCandie:	That's where I got my training, and sometimes I get stuck.
BDR 529 IL:	ahh
BDR 529 IL:	so…. what do you do in Upstate New York???
GatorCandie:	this and that. Repair computers, compose resumes for profit, cook puppies, sell cell phones, do outsourced business work for small businesses
BDR 529 IL:	you repair computers? That's horrible!!!
BDR 529 IL:	you should be ashamed
GatorCandie:	Well, I tinker around with the computers and I stir occasionally with the pups
BDR 529 IL:	you should try stirring with the computers!!
GatorCandie:	I should be smashing them
BDR 529 IL:	see…this could work out cause I actually de-compose resumes for profit
GatorCandie:	with some sort of acid?
BDR 529 IL:	I use a combination of bleach, applesauce and hobo sweat
BDR 529 IL:	breaks those resumes down so fast your head would spin
GatorCandie:	where do you get the applesauce?
BDR 529 IL:	the hobos usually have some stuck between their toes
GatorCandie:	As long as I can still charge for them. It can be like the dollar on the string
GatorCandie:	ha
BDR 529 IL:	or like the itchy and scratchy cloning and killing machines right next to each other

GatorCandie: haha, never saw it, but I like it

BDR 529 IL: yes…very efficient

GatorCandie: you can be itchy

BDR 529 IL: ok…. it's a deal

GatorCandie: and I'll watch

BDR 529 IL: you like to watch, aye??

GatorCandie: Yeah, then sometimes I jump in if it's interesting enough

GatorCandie: So what's your story Pebblo? You already know lots about me

BDR 529 IL: I own a company that manually masturbates horses in captivity

GatorCandie: liar, horses don't need that

BDR 529 IL: well… they dont need it but they like it

GatorCandie: or is it for the employee's benefit?

BDR 529 IL: I'm an animal lover… what can I say

GatorCandie: love is grand. Really grand sometimes I guess

BDR 529 IL: nah… the real story is…

GatorCandie: I will listen

BDR 529 IL: I own some property in New York…. down here and up there in your neck of the woods. And….well… I do a bunch of other stuff here and there… like… my brother and I re-build cars, boats…. blah blah blah

GatorCandie: re-build cars?

GatorCandie: like what?

BDR 529 IL: well…. the last car I bought was a 1968 Cadillac convertible

BDR 529 IL:	and an Alfa Romeo Spider convertible
GatorCandie:	a restorerer
GatorCandie:	ooh love Alfa Romeos
BDR 529 IL:	yeah… it's a cute little car
GatorCandie:	I am a fan of cars.
BDR 529 IL:	the only probem is, everytime we finish one, I want to keep it
BDR 529 IL:	so… I now have 9 cars
BDR 529 IL:	lol
GatorCandie:	I bet. haha!
GatorCandie:	whatcha got?
GatorCandie:	short list it
BDR 529 IL:	well… let's see… a BMW 740il (not restored, just a car), a BMW 318is, a 1981 caddy limo, a caddy coupe deville, the caddy coupe deville convertible, the alfa convertible, a dodge truck….
BDR 529 IL:	ummm…. a few others… and there is a 60's Jaguar on the way (hopefully)
GatorCandie:	I hear a sesame street song coming on… One of these things is not like the others… A Dodge truck.
BDR 529 IL:	yah…. well…. its good for winter. I used to have a drab green army truck, but it's gone now… tear
GatorCandie:	Thats pretty cool about the Alfa
BDR 529 IL:	God rest its sole

BDR 529 IL:	yeah…Alfas are cool looking cars but they are built horribly. Probably the worst I've ever seen
GatorCandie:	how do you feel about Jags?
BDR 529 IL:	I love Jags
BDR 529 IL:	The Jaguar XKE convertible is my favorite car
GatorCandie:	So you're a wrench?
BDR 529 IL:	no, not really. My brother is a good mechanic. He has a shop. So I buy em and design the restoration, locate the parts, which are often very hard to get, and he does most of the mechanical work
GatorCandie:	That's awesome. They're sweet looking but I hear a rumor they're a tad unreliable.
BDR 529 IL:	totally unreliable but beautiful.
GatorCandie:	Ok, totally
GatorCandie:	Like Ferraris. I've seen a few of them at the side of the road
BDR 529 IL:	kind of I suppose, but I've never worked on a Ferrari
BDR 529 IL:	I've driven one but never owned one
BDR 529 IL:	so… what kind of car do you have?
GatorCandie:	I'm big into F1 racing
BDR 529 IL:	a rag top I know—from your profile, but what kind?
GatorCandie:	Volkswagen Cabrio. I've had one for 13 years (not the same one) ha. I love it, except the power thing.

GatorCandie:	And the no respect thing
BDR 529 IL:	awww... a Cabrio is a cute car. I just sent you a picture of the Caddy
GatorCandie:	Nice color. Good for a sock monkey maybe
GatorCandie:	Cabrios ARE totally adorable. Thus no respect, ha
GatorCandie:	I've had the opportunity to drive a mean looking lifted Silverado and the difference is vast
BDR 529 IL:	:-)
BDR 529 IL:	I can't see you in lifted truck
GatorCandie:	Actually, you have.
BDR 529 IL:	I have??
GatorCandie:	It is pretty funny, it being all redneck and me being all...not
GatorCandie:	In one of my profile pictures I'm sitting in the passenger seat of that truck.
BDR 529 IL:	lemme look
BDR 529 IL:	oh... but you can't tell what it is. ahhh... a sneaky player.
GatorCandie:	that's true, that's me
BDR 529 IL:	so... how's the weather in Buffalo these days? I'm coming up there next Tuesday
GatorCandie:	Um, come on in the weather's still ok. Little sunshine, little rain today. Actually it was cool; there was a sun shower at about 2pm.
GatorCandie:	So facial hair or none?
BDR 529 IL:	5 o'clock shadow
GatorCandie:	So do you live in NYC or suburbs?

BDR 529 IL:	north of the city... about 25 minutes... a suburb called Rockland County
GatorCandie:	I live in a rail car with my applesauce.
BDR 529 IL:	do you know... I have a good job for you
GatorCandie:	goody!
GatorCandie:	I grew up on Long Island so
BDR 529 IL:	cool... my uncle has a house out there. He lives in the water in Cutchague
BDR 529 IL:	on a little floating tire. On the water not in the water.
GatorCandie:	IN the water, ha. Spluttering.
BDR 529 IL:	haha.... no... he has a nice house with a dock. Its great. I would love a house on the water
GatorCandie:	When I was growing up I always thought I wanted a house on the North Shore.
BDR 529 IL:	That's where he is. North Fork just below Orient Point
GatorCandie:	Gorgeous.
GatorCandie:	hey fork you too
BDR 529 IL:	yes ma'am
GatorCandie:	I had to
BDR 529 IL:	...understood
BDR 529 IL:	so... no boyfriend for you? How does a cool chic like yourself have no boyfriend??
GatorCandie:	interesting question. What makes you think I'm cool?
BDR 529 IL:	believe me... I've talked to some girls for hours and I can tell in 5 seconds that you're cool

GatorCandie:	aww do you mind if I cry for just a sec? :-)
BDR 529 IL:	make it snappy
GatorCandie:	haha
BDR 529 IL:	hahaha
GatorCandie:	I'm coming out of a seriously long-term relationship. It's been about a year since the "END", so I'm flying under the radar just a bit.
BDR 529 IL:	gotcha
GatorCandie:	et vous?
BDR 529 IL:	eh… nothing serious
GatorCandie:	same story. For me, I mean. Nothing serious.
BDR 529 IL:	yeah… pretty much. I was in a long-term relationship a few years ago and since then I haven't found anyone that I've clicked with
GatorCandie:	but seriously, I'm kinda special and therefore
BDR 529 IL:	and by click I mean talk Swaheelie
BDR 529 IL:	oh who am I kidding… I can't even spell Swahelie
GatorCandie:	my clock hasent been clicking in any language, ha
GatorCandie:	Swahili my friend
BDR 529 IL:	ahh… I can't spell it but I can click it like the wind
BDR 529 IL:	your clock hasnt been clicking? Maybe you need new batteries
GatorCandie:	click, Lassie! Good boy, click!
GatorCandie:	double as in double your money, double your pleasure, doublemint gum

GatorCandie:	sorry, thats my nervous click
BDR 529 IL:	yeah… I stab whinos. We all have our quirks.
GatorCandie:	Stab them with what?
BDR 529 IL:	just a little stick
GatorCandie:	a pointed stick?
BDR 529 IL:	I don't break the skin but its terribly annoying for them
BDR 529 IL:	yes… a pointed stick. haha
GatorCandie:	I didn't think they could even tell
BDR 529 IL:	most of 'em can't, but if you catch 'em early in the afternoon, they notice
GatorCandie:	haha!
GatorCandie:	I really am laughing pretty hard, and even the whinos could tell if their rheumy eyes were watching
BDR 529 IL:	hahaha
BDR 529 IL:	wow… 3am. You know… usually, if Im not in bed by 11 o'clock I go home
GatorCandie:	oh, is that how it is?
BDR 529 IL:	lol… that's an old Dean Martin line
BDR 529 IL:	I can't take credit for it
GatorCandie:	yeah, I got it… I wouldn't, haha
BDR 529 IL:	well… I am wearing a golf hat… so, ya know.
GatorCandie:	well you're pretty funny
BDR 529 IL:	why thank you. You're pretty funny yourself
GatorCandie:	I usually harken back to Rodney Dangerfield. When I'm in my car. And I wish I had a sub

machine something or other mounted to the hood of my car

BDR 529 IL: you know what I find really annoys other drivers for some reason… when you give them the thumbs down and a dissapointed look. It works much much better than the finger. Makes them think about what they've done

GatorCandie: I never give the finger. I shake my head like I'm dissappointed

BDR 529 IL: yes… so we're on the same page. Try and incorporate the thumbs down. It's a nice touch

GatorCandie: Sometimes I hit the rumble strip for good measure if I'm behind someone though

BDR 529 IL: oh how I love that rumble strip

BDR 529 IL: my God… don't yell at me

GatorCandie: I just sent you a picture. It's my fantasy rumble strip face

BDR 529 IL: very impressive

GatorCandie: My fanatasies are… different.

GatorCandie: haha

BDR 529 IL: I have quite an interesting fantasy, as you only have one chance to do it.

GatorCandie: tell me.

BDR 529 IL: It's too late for such a story. Another time, I promise.

GatorCandie: I agree about it being late and if I weren't a responsible adult I might blame it on you.

BDR 529 IL: hahaha

GatorCandie:	But I'm over that, so let's catch each other again?
BDR 529 IL:	ok… will you be on tomorrow?
GatorCandie:	Well, I will be online tomorrow but I will be working during the day but can say a quick hello. I'm not usually on this late.
GatorCandie:	or early, depending on how you look at it.
BDR 529 IL:	ok, well… I'm online a lot so message me if ya see me and I'll do the same
GatorCandie:	k. nice to meet you. What's your name sailor?
BDR 529 IL:	It's Jesse
BDR 529 IL:	and yours is Pamela?
GatorCandie:	Really? Yes. Pamela. I won't ask you how you know, but I would love to know. It's probably something obvious.
BDR 529 IL:	hehehe… it's attached to your email header
GatorCandie:	Cool, along with my last name. Please dont be a stalker, haha.
BDR 529 IL:	haha… dont worry…. I keep my stalking to a minimum
GatorCandie:	If you want, hang on to my cell and call me if you cant find me online 716-555-1212
BDR 529 IL:	ok… mine is 845-555-1212
GatorCandie:	k. have sweet dreams :-)
BDR 529 IL:	you too cutie
BDR 529 IL:	goodnight
BDR 529 IL:	:-)

THE SECOND CONVERSATION

BDR 529 IL: Hi!

Auto response from GatorCandie: …gurgle….

BDR 529 IL signed off at 7:40:31 PM.

BDR 529 IL signed on at 7:58:28 PM.

BDR 529 IL: Wow… still working??

Auto response from GatorCandie: …gurgle….

BDR 529 IL signed off at 8:01:15 PM.

BDR 529 IL signed on at 9:58:28 PM.

GatorCandie: Go easy on me Tiger…I just woke up :-)

BDR 529 IL: hehehe… hey cutie. How was your day?

GatorCandie: it was great! It was even better after I laid down at about 6pm to "rest…" fast forward to 9:30…

BDR 529 IL: ha. Well, at least you're fully rested

GatorCandie: What a strange feeling… Going to sleep when its light out and getting up when its dark.

BDR 529 IL: oh my. Are you sure you're not a vampire?

BDR 529 IL: or a crystal meth addict?

BDR 529 IL: or a vampire ON crystal meth??

GatorCandie: neither…then again… hey brb in a few darlin', I must attend to basic necessities.

BDR 529 IL: gotcha …I'll be here

I waited a few minutes for her to return. The instant messenger that we were using gave the user the ability to see when the other person was typing a message. Of course, that function had to be turned on through the preferences panel and it was a bit convoluted. I knew how to use it and she didn't, which at the time, seemed like a cool upper hand to have, if you want to consider it an upper hand. More of a conversational advantage, really.

BDR 529 IL:	everything go ok? ;-)
GatorCandie:	Yeah, just had to do a bit of crank and drink a cat. You know how it is…
BDR 529 IL:	oh yeah… same old crank and cat juice here too
GatorCandie:	hmmm… I wonder how it would be if fed the crank to the cat then drank its blood?
GatorCandie:	so many options!
BDR 529 IL:	ha
GatorCandie:	I just had to do the usual baloney, like eat something (applesauce). It was a pain this time though. The railyards aren't yeilding what they used to.
BDR 529 IL:	I'm so out of it. I'm hungry too, but I'm pretty sure there's nothing to eat
GatorCandie:	I'm sure theres some mustard, ketchup and maple syrup… you could do something with that couldn'tcha? It's not 11:00 yet… Are you home already?
BDR 529 IL:	I was at the marina all day… then got home at about 8 or so
GatorCandie:	Playing?

BDR 529 IL: I guess so. I was doing some work on the boat (polishing some wood. Then I went for a little cruise

GatorCandie: "The incomparable beauty and quaint charms of Rockland County offer peaceful, pastoral countryside spiced by river villages, historic sites and, arguably, the world's most beautiful river valley".*Quoted from the Rockland County Department of Tourism

GatorCandie: Do you like that? I just thought of it and I'm thinking of suggesting it for their tourism website.

BDR 529 IL: "pastoral countryside"

BDR 529 IL: lol

BDR 529 IL: haha… I think they might be interested. Give 'em a shot!

GatorCandie: I, however, was NOT down at the Marina all day. I was working on my first Worker's Compensation claim!

BDR 529 IL: Sounds like fun… I usually work on my workman's compensation claims on the weekends

GatorCandie: Luckily I had the foresight to hit Boston Market before I got home. Do you have employees?

BDR 529 IL: I was kidding about the workman's compensation claims. I have a few guys who do work for me but they are all freelance

GatorCandie: Free Lance sounds like the title to a boring movie. I have a friend named Lance and I'm imagining a drunken night of prostitution,

	drugs and stolen cars culminating in a 3am phone call.
BDR 529 IL:	hahaha
GatorCandie:	Where I say, "Lance who? huh? Wrong number, buddy."
BDR 529 IL:	haha
BDR 529 IL:	do you know what briny water is?
GatorCandie:	salty??
BDR 529 IL:	it's when you go from the ocean to a river and once you get far enough up the river, the water becomes less salty or briny. Anyway… my brother was talking about the briny Hudson to someone—you know, the Hudson River. I caught half the conversation and thought they were talking about an actor
BDR 529 IL:	sounds like a good actors name to me—"Briny Hudson"
GatorCandie:	It sounds like it could be someones porn star name.
BDR 529 IL:	yeah… I was considering it for me if I ever got into the porn business
GatorCandie:	Did you ever do that porn star name thing?
BDR 529 IL:	yep… I would be Kane Kensington
GatorCandie:	Sapphire Craydon
BDR 529 IL:	wow…it really does work. Who whoulda thunk it?
BDR 529 IL:	middle name and street address?
GatorCandie:	pets name and street
BDR 529 IL:	ahh

BDR 529 IL:	whats your middle name?
BDR 529 IL:	…now that you know mine
GatorCandie:	Christine
BDR 529 IL:	pretty
BDR 529 IL:	so…do you have a busy day tomorrow?
GatorCandie:	~ Jesse Kane
BDR 529 IL:	that's me
GatorCandie:	Jesse Kane Fairfax?
BDR 529 IL:	no…. Jesse Kane Isaacs
GatorCandie:	Wow that's alot of name to live up to. Very white.
GatorCandie:	Pamela Christine Souther is just about the same deal.
BDR 529 IL:	haha… well… my friends call me Tito Angelo Lopez
GatorCandie:	I used to date someone a long time ago with the last name Lopez (he was white though) and my mother used to call him spic and span.
BDR 529 IL:	oh no. That's horrible!
BDR 529 IL:	lol
GatorCandie:	So why are you Tito? An earlier singing career?
BDR 529 IL:	lol… no… I just made that up
BDR 529 IL:	actually, I play in a band and I go by the name stage Uncle Louie
GatorCandie:	um, Gullible Pamela alert. Do you really play in a band?

BDR 529 IL:	Yes, I play the drums. The band is named Among Other Things
GatorCandie:	I googled you, didn't see anything. What does your band do? Not weddings, I'm sure.
BDR 529 IL:	lol... not lately...
BDR 529 IL:	we play local bars and clubs in NYC here and there
BDR 529 IL:	www.amongotherthings.net

This website (and band) no longer exists. I did play in this band with three of my close friends from high school. We were pretty good and even recorded an album. All of the makings of a true rock and roll band were present—we were all good musicians, heavily abused alcohol and hated each other. Sadly, the band is gone but the memories and a few random recordings still remain. I could go on and on about the trials and tribulations of Among Other Things but that's for another book.

GatorCandie:	I used to love being near the city.
BDR 529 IL:	I can send you a CD if ya want
GatorCandie:	Of course, I would love that! Um... are you any good?
BDR 529 IL:	2201 Alpine Ave??
BDR 529 IL:	hehehe
GatorCandie:	Not by a long shot, smartie stalker guy.
BDR 529 IL:	lol... hey, you googled me so I just retaliated!
GatorCandie:	I used to live at 2201 Alpine, not anymore. My ex lives there.
BDR 529 IL:	oh... gotcha
GatorCandie:	You googled me?
BDR 529 IL:	no. I "anywho'd" you

BDR 529 IL:	anyway... If I were you I would speak to the girl at 2201 Alpine... She's parading around as you
GatorCandie:	I only googled your band
GatorCandie:	wow, I googled myself and there I am, parading around like I'm me or something.
BDR 529 IL:	you should be ashamed.
GatorCandie:	I am, because I also have no clothes on!
BDR 529 IL:	ooo la la
GatorCandie:	just kidding, not really
BDR 529 IL:	darn
GatorCandie:	I am now living at 226 Durrant Avenue, which should also be in "the book" so to speak.
GatorCandie:	Have you been familiar with the music scene in NYC?
BDR 529 IL:	yes...pretty much
GatorCandie:	Then you should know of my favorite band and artist...
GatorCandie:	Soul Coughing (no more) and Mike Doughty
BDR 529 IL:	sure... I have Soul Coughing in my car
BDR 529 IL:	haven't seen them live though
GatorCandie:	They were great, but they're gone. I had/have all of their stuff. Someone broke into my car and ripped my stereo out.
GatorCandie:	And they took my CD visor and wallet.
GatorCandie:	So my signed Mike Doughty CD is gone :-\
BDR 529 IL:	awww

GatorCandie:	Hey, I only had one car/stereo, haha. It was a super nice stereo unit too. Just a good excuse to get a better one though. I'm thinking of getting a hard drive unit.
BDR 529 IL:	I just got one for the Caddy. I hate getting newer looking stereos for old cars, so I found a place that makes reproduction stock stereos with all digital internal parts
GatorCandie:	Wow, cool. Who makes it?
BDR 529 IL:	I'd have to look it up. It's a place about 30 miles from here. I don't think they are a very big company
GatorCandie:	That's really neat. Did you ever think about all these little niches that get filled by people? I mean, there are busy unique people everywhere.
BDR 529 IL:	Yes... and inside that radio are little nuts and bolts that a WHOLE other company makes... and thats all they do... and then... there is another WHOLE company devoted just to making the cardboard boxes that the nuts and bolts go in
GatorCandie:	uh oh, sounds like someone's making fun of me... haha
BDR 529 IL:	No, I'm being serious
BDR 529 IL:	I've often thought about how many different industries are involved in the making of just one product
GatorCandie:	really? Cool. I know. In a previous life I was a corporate recruiter and got to see all kinds

of different companies living busy worker bee lives.

GatorCandie: There's a manufacturing company in my area and they sell those vending units that have the grabby thing with the stuffed animals in it, all over the world. They gave me a tour and said that in Russia they put packs of cigarettes in them.

BDR 529 IL: wow... that's odd

GatorCandie: I know it. But cool. Think about all the different vendors just that one little company has. People like me, finding more people to work for them, you know? Yeah the cigarette thing kind of popped my eyes a bit.

BDR 529 IL: Yeah. It's amazing, when you think about it, that anything gets done at all

GatorCandie: haha. Well its all because a very few of the people are driving the rest.

BDR 529 IL: yes, this is true

GatorCandie: So what did you eat for dinner?

GatorCandie: Mustard ala King?

BDR 529 IL: nothing... I had a Subway sandwich for lunch

GatorCandie: awww. I'll have some Chinese sent over.

BDR 529 IL: what a good girl you are. Chinese people or Chinese food?

GatorCandie: Chinese food, but, um, it might be a bit late actually. Maybe next time?

BDR 529 IL: It's a date.

GatorCandie: I am a good girl, actually.

BDR 529 IL: oh really? How so?

GatorCandie: I'm like that. Like try to think of nice things to do for people. When I'm not all cranked out, that is. I think that's good.

BDR 529 IL: awww... that's nice... and of course I can't expect you to do good things on a crank binge

GatorCandie: I think of things when I'm sitting on the docks, with the boombox, nodding out. You know.

BDR 529 IL: yeah... that's when I do my best thinking too

GatorCandie: Then I get sudden bursts of manic energy, trying to get my karma levels back to where they should be

GatorCandie: Seriously, I'm not particularly on drugs. I just pay attention.

BDR 529 IL: hahah

BDR 529 IL: can you buy back karma at the end? Like a balloon payment?

GatorCandie: I actually blow through my karma at alarming speeds and try to buy it back from the guy who does my dry cleaning.

BDR 529 IL: wow... does he have good prices?

GatorCandie: I'm not sure what would happen if I hit the end and had nothing but a bunch of drycleaning deductions and bad deeds that needed settling.

BDR 529 IL: I'm sure you could flash those big blue eyes and get away with murder

GatorCandie: Maurice? He's ok.

GatorCandie: Maurice and I have bonded since he put those bra cups in my dress, haha.

BDR 529 IL:	that magnificent bastard
GatorCandie:	I actually don't let myself get away with much, since I have a tendency to be straightforward. I guess I could. My looks do provide me with advantages.
GatorCandie:	Yeah he stuck me with a pin!!
GatorCandie:	My foot bonded with his butt.
BDR 529 IL:	good work. I'm proud of you
GatorCandie:	Pamela "violence is my middle name" Souther
BDR 529 IL:	is that Latin for Christine?
GatorCandie:	Violencia, actually, which is the Greek for Key, which is the Croation for Christ, which is essentially Christine.
BDR 529 IL:	I should have known… it was right there in front of my face
GatorCandie:	All you have to do is pay attention.
GatorCandie:	haha
BDR 529 IL:	pay attention… great… how much does that cost?
GatorCandie:	just a few sheckles
BDR 529 IL:	oh, ok. Deal!
BDR 529 IL:	So, do I get the pleasure of your company on Tuesday night?
GatorCandie:	Are you bringing the crank and prostitutes? Just checking my understanding…
GatorCandie:	Maybe I should have been serious instead.
GatorCandie:	And said yes.
BDR 529 IL:	well, I'll bring the crank but the plan was to rob you, kidnap you and make you my sex

slave, but don't worry, it won't be just me abusing you. I will rent you out to others so you don't get too bored. And the best part is, I'll keep the crank coming—Which we all know is the most important thing

GatorCandie: Do you think if you film it I'll become a big Hollywood star?

BDR 529 IL: well… you just might. We'll have to try a few different backdrops you understand. This might take a while

GatorCandie: I don't think I like the way you're planning this "date." It sounds like you're the one making all the money on this deal.

BDR 529 IL: hey, you get the crank, remember?

GatorCandie: I'm sorry. I'm so ungrateful. That's what it really comes down to.

BDR 529 IL: exactly…. NOW you're thinking like a Hollywood star

GatorCandie: It can't be all about me, no matter how badly I want it to be. Will you at least pay for my breast augmentation? I mean, down the line, if I'm not dead.

BDR 529 IL: Well, if I can't figure out how to do it myself, then yes, I will pay

GatorCandie: haha! Yeah, give it a shot yourself first.

BDR 529 IL: how about instead of the crank, porn and botched surgery, we just order some drinks and abuse room service for a while

GatorCandie: If you are willing to set your expectations a notch or two below sex, that's fine with me. Or did I misunderstand your intentions?

BDR 529 IL: hmmm... what's below sex?

BDR 529 IL: lol.... no, I don't expect sex from you, silly. Of course you'll probably be overcome by my charm anyway.

BDR 529 IL: Don't get the wrong idea. I got a big 2 level suite. I don't expect you to sit on a hotel bed with me for 2 hours. There's plenty of room for you to try and escape from my inapropriate advances.

GatorCandie: I don't date a lot and I have been out of the whole dating etiquette thing for a long time. Can't you tell? haha

BDR 529 IL: yeah, well... same here. I figured we could hang out in the room, because, well.... I hate bars and the room is pretty cool... in a really tacky hotel kinda way

GatorCandie: I have a funny room service story.

BDR 529 IL: ok... let's hear it

GatorCandie: Which hotel are you staying at?

BDR 529 IL: Adams Mark

GatorCandie: Cool. Ok, the story.

GatorCandie: My girlfriend and I took a road trip to NYC and decided to stay at the Waldorf. Her husband made the reservation and got us a queen sized bed, which is definitely his sense of humor...

BDR 529 IL: so far so good

GatorCandie: And we ordered room service right after I got out of the shower. While we were waiting, Erica took a shower so there we are,

hanging out and talking in our robes when
the guy comes.

GatorCandie: He was SO flustered when he put the tray
                 down it was silly.

BDR 529 IL: hey… didn't I see this on Cinemax last night?

GatorCandie: Then all of the sudden, out of nowhere, this
                 heavy beat disco music started playing.

GatorCandie: It was just a coffee tray for Christ's sake. But
                 I was kind of lying on the bed with my robe
                 on propped on pillows, so it looked "bad"

BDR 529 IL: That "good" kinda bad

GatorCandie: yeah, the "good" bad.

BDR 529 IL: haha

BDR 529 IL: and then… the pillow fight?

GatorCandie: oh, we're good friends.

BDR 529 IL: I bet

GatorCandie: That was better than they time before that,
                 where we stayed in the Catskills in a motel.
                 That was funny too. The clerk totally thought
                 we were lesbians.

BDR 529 IL: haha… what motel? Was it a resort or a hotel?

GatorCandie: It was a M O T E L hideous. We were just
                 passing through. It was called the Liberty
                 Motel or something like that.

BDR 529 IL: ahh

GatorCandie: We used to go down and visit our family then
                 go drinking in NYC

BDR 529 IL: so, let me understand… I should or shouldn't expect sex on Tuesday night? I have to update my daily planner

GatorCandie: er

BDR 529 IL: hahaha

GatorCandie: I meant E.R. as in Emergency Room, actually

BDR 529 IL: wow… you must be good

GatorCandie: haha!

GatorCandie: you're making me curse you under my breath, which is silly since I'm all alone here.

BDR 529 IL: curse me? Hey… I just make Mr. Isaacs appointments. He left an hour ago

GatorCandie: Do you eat his food before he does too? Maybe I can get both of you.

BDR 529 IL: and here I thought you were a good girl

GatorCandie: oh, uh, yeah…

BDR 529 IL: ok, this is getting serious. I think i might have to order something to eat. There are never enough delivery places open late.

GatorCandie: haha, probably comes down to whoever's delivering about now.

BDR 529 IL: I might be out of luck

BDR 529 IL: See, that's what I love about room service— its at your command

BDR 529 IL: …that and the little mayonaise jars

GatorCandie: I like the little marmalade jars, even though I don't use them. All the waste, the excess, haha.

BDR 529 IL:	anything "mini" is fun... mini ketchup, mini mustard, mini jelly
BDR 529 IL:	It's the little things that make me happy ;-)
GatorCandie:	that was pretty funny actually.
GatorCandie:	I do like the mini seltzer bottles.
BDR 529 IL:	see, its universal
GatorCandie:	I'm not too high on Mini Coopers though. They corner nicely but they bog at about 45 mph.
BDR 529 IL:	A friend of mine bought one of those silly things.
GatorCandie:	do you agree with me?
BDR 529 IL:	I think I might. I only drove it once, but it's a rip off if you ask me
GatorCandie:	I kind of think they look a bit funny.
BDR 529 IL:	funny ha ha or funny queer?
GatorCandie:	funny BOTH
BDR 529 IL:	Yes, but that was a quote from Swing Blade. Moving on...
GatorCandie:	Like if you packed 10 clowns in one, you'd be all set for the Gay Circus
BDR 529 IL:	HAHAHA. Wow... I bet they never even ventured down that marketing path. You should give them a call.
GatorCandie:	Listen... I'm busy and in demand. But maybe I will.
GatorCandie:	Just in case we end up actually liking each other (presumptuous, I know) dont tell your friend I said that.

BDR 529 IL:	hahaha… presumptious? I already like you. And I'm calling him right now and telling
GatorCandie:	This conversation is becoming a tearjerker.
BDR 529 IL:	I know… I have my hankey out.
GatorCandie:	Ok. Can I listen? Make it very funny.
BDR 529 IL:	eh… he's working anyway.
BDR 529 IL:	hes a dumb cop lol
GatorCandie:	oh… cops. Did I just say that out loud? Sorry.
BDR 529 IL:	No, you typed it
BDR 529 IL:	Yeah, he's the exception to the rule…he's not cop like at all. You know, he's not a "cop" cop—with little man syndrome. He's a good guy and a rational person. All cops should be like him. The world would be a better place.
GatorCandie:	Oh, I was typing to myself while I was talking
BDR 529 IL:	quite the opposite actually
GatorCandie:	They have a mentality, generally. Or so it would seem. Stereotype, I realize.
BDR 529 IL:	yes, but he's totally not the average bear
GatorCandie:	I imagine, since he's your friend. You are not the average bear either. You're smart and funny. Most people are not smart or funny, even though I do like people as a general rule.
BDR 529 IL:	awww… What a sweet talker you are.
GatorCandie:	I know, that did sound very sincere and bucolic didn't it?
BDR 529 IL:	lol… sure it did
GatorCandie:	I have a question about drummers.
BDR 529 IL:	I believe you

BDR 529 IL:	ok, shoot.
GatorCandie:	I went on a date with a drummer and he told me that he couldn't dance because he listens to a different beat than most people. I thought I would get a second opinion so I'm asking you about this claim.
BDR 529 IL:	Well, I think he just couldn't dance, but yes, as arogant as it sounds, you do hear different parts of the music. You tend to break it down into parts. It's funny, when I hear people try to hum a song; it sounds totally different to me
GatorCandie:	It didn't actually sound arrogant. I did understand the concept, but it sounded like he wasn't trying hard enough in a way.
BDR 529 IL:	yeah… a good excuse for a bad dancer
BDR 529 IL:	I'll have to use that line one day.
GatorCandie:	We never danced; he just offered it as a reason for being a bad dancer. We only went out twice.
BDR 529 IL:	I never dance on the first date.
BDR 529 IL:	Or the second. I will on the third but forget about the fourth.
GatorCandie:	Have you ever met anyone from Match.com?
BDR 529 IL:	no, have you?
GatorCandie:	Yes. I've met two people. Not disasters, but I definitely extricated myself quickly.
BDR 529 IL:	details!!

GatorCandie:	You have to understand; firstly, I should say my profile has been viewed 17,643 times to date
GatorCandie:	I feel so... dirty
BDR 529 IL:	HAHAHAHA
BDR 529 IL:	Their hands were everywhere!
BDR 529 IL:	go on
GatorCandie:	Anyway, the first guy I met I talked on the phone with for a long time. He was pretty funny, could hold his own in a ridiculous conversation although he was a commercial photographer from Los Angeles and he kept saying everything was "crazy"
BDR 529 IL:	uuughh, yuck. Ok, so...
GatorCandie:	Anyway, I think I didn't like him because he had just moved here into his dad's house as a "stopping off point".
BDR 529 IL:	yeah, that's a bad sign
GatorCandie:	and then by the time we saw each other for the second time, he was going to stay there. ick
BDR 529 IL:	yah. I mean, I dont mean to sound elitist, but if you can't afford an apartment in Buffalo, you're doing something wrong
GatorCandie:	And the last person I met...
GatorCandie:	he's still on match.com. His screen name is ohhlovelybuffalo
GatorCandie:	You elitist bastard. Yah, it was "crazy"
BDR 529 IL:	haha. He doesn't look like he'd be your type.

GatorCandie:	Well, funny and smart is my type and ohhlovelybuffalo had potential on the phone, although the word geek kept popping into my head.
BDR 529 IL:	hmmm… I know someone perfect for you
BDR 529 IL:	;-)
GatorCandie:	:-)
BDR 529 IL:	well… you entered the text so lemme see it!
GatorCandie:	huh? How come I can't see when you enter text???
BDR 529 IL:	I'm gonna have to say… magic?

Remember earlier when I mentioned how you can set a preference within the program to see when the other person is typing? Well, this is a perfect example of when it comes in handy. When the other person types something but doesn't hit the enter key. Then you know they want to say something but they're thinking about whether or not to actually say it.

GatorCandie:	So, I'll finish ohhlovelybuffalo. Well, I already finished him, but…
GatorCandie:	So we had talked on the phone one day while I was shopping at Wegmans and maybe I was distracted but he seemed ok.
GatorCandie:	So the next day we were talking on the phone at around 6-ish and I mentioned that I had to rustle up something to eat and he said the same so I told him we should just meet and grab a bite. I hate dragging things out.
BDR 529 IL:	no no, go on
GatorCandie:	Anyway, we did the silly "where should we meet thing" and I told him that I was on

the 33 and he'd better think of something quickly because I was already close to home. And he said, "Well how about we go to my favorite place".

GatorCandie: Which turned out to be a terrible subshop that was greasy and icky. I don't want to sound elitist either, and I like subs as much as the next gal, but this place was really disgusting. And he had butter teeth. So I ate and then I left and that was it until I set my friend on him through instant messenger and she had a bunch of fun with him.

BDR 529 IL: hey… the same friend who likes me?

During one of our unrecorded conversations, she had mentioned that she showed my picture to a friend of hers and told her all about me. This "friend" kept asking Pamela to let us go on a date together—yes, odd but true. Anyway, back to the story.

GatorCandie: Yep, the very same. She's a riot. Maybe I'll show you transcripts from what they wrote to each other. She's much funnier than I am.

BDR 529 IL: haha. So, what about the other guy?

GatorCandie: what other guy? There were only two.

BDR 529 IL: Wasn't there another guy you went out with from match?

GatorCandie: Oh, "crazy" California guy and ohlovelybuffalo are two different people.

BDR 529 IL: ahh… gotcha

GatorCandie: I do have a general physical type though.

BDR 529 IL: and that is?

GatorCandie: Tallish, not fat, short brown hair. That seems to be my type although I might deviate given the chance. I'm not sure about that. Personality is key though.

BDR 529 IL: Yes, I must say that I agree. I'm so sick of beautiful girls with no brains. Who knew there were so many? You wouldn't believe some of the conversations that I've had in bars with girls.

GatorCandie: details!

BDR 529 IL: hmmm, let's see... Where to start? Well, I once told a girl that I give fake tours of the NYC to unsuspecting tourists

GatorCandie: fake tours, haha

BDR 529 IL: she got all serious and said "you know, that's not right! How long have you been getting away with it" But she said this in a serious and accusing way.

GatorCandie: haha! What the hell is a "fake" tour, anyway?

BDR 529 IL: she asked me that too. So I told her that I had a bus and would drive people around the city telling them fake information about the history of the grid system.

GatorCandie: That would actually be an awesome tour! I would sign up for that! I mean, coming up with fake names for the buildings... That would be great!

BDR 529 IL: haha. Yes, it would and you're welcome to come.

BDR 529 IL: Another time, I told a hippy girl that I work for the Craftsman company testing the effects of hammers on mice. She believed that. Yes, she actually believed that and got angry with me.

GatorCandie: HAHA

GatorCandie: I'm still laughing!

BDR 529 IL: hehe

GatorCandie: Listen, I can be gullible, so watch out for that.

BDR 529 IL: hahaha... ok

GatorCandie: I used to hang out at a bar on Avenue A a long time ago that was filled with classic New York-all types. A guy named Zab started chatting with me and then a song came on the jukebox that just threw him into rapture. He had me "listening for the riff " through the whole song

BDR 529 IL: oh no... HAHAHA

GatorCandie: "no... no... wait... here it comes..."

GatorCandie: "no, that wasn't it... here it is"

BDR 529 IL: hahahaha. I deal with those types of guys all the time "hey man, nice beat" mind if I jam with ya sometime"?

GatorCandie: I had a blind date once that took me from Long Island to China Town (I was young and foolish)...

GatorCandie: Yeah, it's all about the music.

GatorCandie: I love music very much, actually. It sounds silly, but I really do. There was a band called Morphine that was really good that did awesome things with sound.

BDR 529 IL: I love Morphine... just sax, bass and drums

GatorCandie:	No guitar, just Sax… Yep, you know them
GatorCandie:	Too bad he died of a heart attack.
BDR 529 IL:	oh really? I didnt know that
GatorCandie:	Yes, Mark Sandman died in '99. I saw what became of the band, "The Twinemen" a year ago and they were ok, but it was Sandman that made the sound.
GatorCandie:	Too serious for you? As serious as a heart attack? This occasion calls for Cinnamon Life cereal to lighten the mood.
BDR 529 IL:	oh my, I want Cinnamon Toast Crunch
GatorCandie:	We have Cinnamon Life, honey. Can I take your order?
BDR 529 IL:	More coffee, hun?
GatorCandie:	Make it snappy. I dont got all day.
BDR 529 IL:	haha… you're a natural!
GatorCandie:	Thanks, there's a future for me somewhere
BDR 529 IL:	hehe… as long as I'm around, there will always be work for you
GatorCandie:	I have never gone to a bar to meet a man.
BDR 529 IL:	Remember our deal earlier?
GatorCandie:	Oh yes, the botched boob job and prostitution gig.
BDR 529 IL:	yep
GatorCandie:	I'm having second thoughts. Getting cold feet, if you like.
BDR 529 IL:	well…you sleep on it. And while you're asleep, ill kidnap you and we can expedite this whole process

GatorCandie:	um, do you have a van?
BDR 529 IL:	No but I'll get one. With teardrop rear windows and a wolf on a mountain tire cover.
GatorCandie:	haha, ick. haha!
BDR 529 IL:	yes…it doesnt get anymore ick than that.
GatorCandie:	How about tattered curtains with little balls on them?
BDR 529 IL:	No, that's if we were going to Tiajuana
GatorCandie:	oh. I'm dissappointed.
BDR 529 IL:	well, ok… anything for you
GatorCandie:	and I realize I keep mispelling disappointed
BDR 529 IL:	Between my poor spelling and my horrible typing, I must come off like I'm not even edumacated
GatorCandie:	wolf on a mountain tire cover is classic!! How about mudflaps that say "BACK OFF" with a picture of Yosemite Sam?
BDR 529 IL:	ooohhh yes, very nice touch.
GatorCandie:	Thanks. I could do this.
BDR 529 IL:	Although this particular van should have nekked lady mudflaps I think
GatorCandie:	Betty Boop? Or is that too sophisticated and cultish?
BDR 529 IL:	yeah, no Betty… to Kitsch. How about Pam Anderson?
GatorCandie:	Betty is kitsch and Pam Anderson is not? Disparity alert!
BDR 529 IL:	ok ok… how bout just a nameless, faceless mirrored naked lady

GatorCandie:	…with a mirrored playboy bunny rabbit?
BDR 529 IL:	Yes. And playboy bunny doorlocks
GatorCandie:	That says "Playboy" in 70s script?
BDR 529 IL:	Nice touch. You're good!
GatorCandie:	You're not so bad yourself. Your trailer or mine?
BDR 529 IL:	hehe… I got me a nice doublewide—almost paid for. Only 50 more payments and she's all mine!
BDR 529 IL:	You should have seen my old trailer. I traded it for my dog and a bag of lefty sneakers.
GatorCandie:	So that's where my left shoe went.
BDR 529 IL:	Yep, gotta keep a keen eye out.
GatorCandie:	Musta lost it when I was working Penn.
GatorCandie:	Someone poked me with a pointed stick and stole my cardigan but I didnt realize that they took my shoe as well.
BDR 529 IL:	It wasnt me, I swear!
GatorCandie:	I hate to do this, but… Do you have a favorite movie?
BDR 529 IL:	Lots
GatorCandie:	One or two?
BDR 529 IL:	Hmm, Let's see… I like The Usual Suspects reference you made on your profile.
GatorCandie:	ooh, you're the first person who got that. I wanted to write the whole thing, but then I wanted to write "No more yanky my wanky, the Donger needs food"

BDR 529 IL:	Others include, but are not limited to (disclaimer) Snatch, Goodfellas, The Godfather, Rushmore, Casablanca, The Big Lebowski, Fight Club…
BDR 529 IL:	um… lot's more
GatorCandie:	Have you ever seen Ghost Dog?
BDR 529 IL:	No
GatorCandie:	I look for people who have seen it sometimes. Hearing all the movies you like, you'd like that one too.
GatorCandie:	An African American mafia hit man who models himself after the samurai of old finds himself targeted for death by the mob.
GatorCandie:	It has some funny moments and it's pretty good. Stars Forest Whitaker.
BDR 529 IL:	hmmm… sounds familiar actually. Yeah I think I saw it but I hardly remember it.
GatorCandie:	I loved it.
BDR 529 IL:	and an ice cream man. Yeah, it's all coming back to me
GatorCandie:	yes, ice cream man.
GatorCandie:	It was different, but not too different like Mullholland Drive.
GatorCandie:	I don't hate many movies, but that is at the top of my hate list.
BDR 529 IL:	that was ok.
BDR 529 IL:	ever see Man Bites Dog?
GatorCandie:	No.

BDR 529 IL:	French film. It's pretty funny if you can stand the subtitles. It's supposed to be a documentary of a film crew following around a serial killer. He eventually kills them all. It has its moments
GatorCandie:	haha. I don't mind subtitles at all. One of my favorite movies is subtitled. "Women on the Verge of a Nervous Breakdown"
BDR 529 IL:	brb… I need some water
GatorCandie:	k
BDR 529 IL:	back—oh thats good water!
GatorCandie:	Deer Park!
GatorCandie:	Little do they know…
BDR 529 IL:	Man, I can't get enough water today. I must have had 2 gallons already.
GatorCandie:	You've been out on the wata (annoying new york mother voice), so what do you expect?
BDR 529 IL:	I have these little half-size bottles of Poland Spring on the boat and I can't resist them. I could drink a case a day
BDR 529 IL:	Same for the mini ginger ales and cokes— little half size cans. Goes back to my love of minature anythings.
GatorCandie:	yes, it's the little things
GatorCandie:	I love those, although I dont drink soda. You call it soda, right?
BDR 529 IL:	oh? I would sooner give up gravity over soda
BDR 529 IL:	Soda, yes…please dont tell me you've picked up "pop"
GatorCandie:	NO NO NO NO

BDR 529 IL:	wheeew
GatorCandie:	But I do call them "subs" now.
BDR 529 IL:	well, sub, hero… that's ok
GatorCandie:	I don't order Meatball Parmigian heroes anymore. I resisted that for a long time.
GatorCandie:	But soda is soda.
BDR 529 IL:	agreed
GatorCandie:	That I don't drink, ha.
BDR 529 IL:	a bit off topic, but have you ever been to Duffs?
GatorCandie:	Is that a bar?
BDR 529 IL:	Wings
BDR 529 IL:	on Sheridan Drive—I think it's on Sheridan
GatorCandie:	Oh, yes of course. I used to work near there. Well, maybe not. I have been to Damons, not sure about Duffs
GatorCandie:	Like near NFB or closer to Transit?
BDR 529 IL:	I have no idea
GatorCandie:	k.
BDR 529 IL:	it's accross from Mattress City if that means anything to you. I can tell you that much.
BDR 529 IL:	and if you take bailey all the way down it will take you to UB South Campus.
GatorCandie:	Why for the love of God are you asking?
BDR 529 IL:	haha… no reason. They make such good wings. I am craving them right now.
BDR 529 IL:	I'm not a big fan of chicken wings but those are really good.

GatorCandie:	Oh! Well chicken wings… I could take 'em or leave 'em. Same with pizza actually.
BDR 529 IL:	listen… let's get one thing straight. There is nothing in Buffalo at all resembling pizza
GatorCandie:	I know, I'm a fan of thin, crusty crust. But you take what you can get, if you take it, which I don't very often.
BDR 529 IL:	mmm yes. Can you tell that I'm hungry?
GatorCandie:	Yes, absolutely. Is anyone still delivering, you silly boy?
BDR 529 IL:	Nope
GatorCandie:	Well, what do you have to eat?
BDR 529 IL:	Nothing. I cleaned out the fridge before I went to Vermont and I havent been shopping since
GatorCandie:	No way. What will you do? Can you call for help? haha
BDR 529 IL:	I have half & half, salad dressing and baking soda
GatorCandie:	Oh shit.
BDR 529 IL:	The baking soda has been in the fridge for months and probably has the tastes of a thousand meals locked inside. Maybe I'll mix it with some water to form a dough-like consistancy, throw it in the oven and see what hapens
GatorCandie:	hahaha. I wish there was something I could do, such as go back in time a few hours and impress on you the urgency and utterly dire need for delivery of food. I didnt realize you had NO FOOD.

BDR 529 IL:	It would have been advice ill received, as I am a man who learns from the trials of life.
GatorCandie:	over and over again, I'd imagine.
BDR 529 IL:	What does not destroy me makes me hungrier.
GatorCandie:	I could go for some Stroganoff myself.
BDR 529 IL:	Why must you teaseme, woman?
BDR 529 IL:	"teaseme"—it's French for tease me. Pronounced "te-see-may"
GatorCandie:	It is a woman's job to tease. I usually don't do it with food though.
GatorCandie:	This is new terra firma for me.
BDR 529 IL:	hahaha
BDR 529 IL:	your job to tease. Well, don't let me keep you from earning a living.
BDR 529 IL:	tease away my dear
GatorCandie:	By the way, I figured out why I can't see when you're typing.
BDR 529 IL:	it was magic, wasn't it?
GatorCandie:	grr
GatorCandie:	That'll teach ya.
BDR 529 IL:	nooooooooooo
GatorCandie:	Oh yes. Turn yours on and I will do the same.
BDR 529 IL:	ok

So this is where she finally figured out how to turn on the option to allow the other person to see when you're typing. Actually, it defaults to "On" so what she didn't know how to do was turn it off.

GatorCandie:	I appreciate these mini trials because I always learn something.
BDR 529 IL:	oh, I can't find where to turn it back on. I guess we're both flying blind.
GatorCandie:	IM preferences, Privacy and the option is in there.
BDR 529 IL:	I could be typing right now
BDR 529 IL:	or
BDR 529 IL:	now
GatorCandie:	And I wouldnt know it. I know and it drives me crazy! Not crazy like "wild with desire", mind you.
BDR 529 IL:	hahaha
BDR 529 IL:	hey! Now how did we get off teasing anyway???
GatorCandie:	You want me to name more of my favorite foods?
BDR 529 IL:	You know that I do
GatorCandie:	Homemade Peach Pie, Chicken Cacciatore
BDR 529 IL:	look… You can see when I'm typing now. I turned it back on.
GatorCandie:	oooh
BDR 529 IL:	See? Wow, now turn yours back on
GatorCandie:	haha ok. I was waiting you out, but I am not like a cat.
BDR 529 IL:	haha
BDR 529 IL:	I feel like we're both naked now
GatorCandie:	oooh I love it!

GatorCandie: As opposed to me naked and you fully clothed...

BDR 529 IL: I do my best to picture you naked as often as I can

GatorCandie: huh?

BDR 529 IL: Just jibberish. It's 1:30am and I havent eaten. Cut me some slack

GatorCandie: So how come you haven't pictured me naked? You've got TONS of slack. It would take a misstep of astronomical proportions at this point for me to dislike you.

BDR 529 IL: haha...well thank you.

BDR 529 IL: ...it's a good thing she doesnt know about my collection of doll heads with lipstick on them

BDR 529 IL: ooops... did I type that out loud?

GatorCandie: haha

GatorCandie: I mean, you're already going to do amateur surgery on me, press me into prostitution and force chicken wings and soda on me.

GatorCandie: Well it's a good thing you dont know about my collection of banister railings then.

BDR 529 IL: that would actually interest me, unfortunatly

GatorCandie: ick

GatorCandie: yes, it is unfortunate I think

BDR 529 IL: I know... it's a sad sad day

GatorCandie: haha, I'm not sure if I should chalk it all up to the deliriousness that comes with malnutrition or not

BDR 529 IL: do you get winks from 60-year-old men??

GatorCandie: ALL THE TIME

BDR 529 IL: I have 60 and 65 year old women winking at me

BDR 529 IL: dirty old birds, or courgars to use the parlance of our times.

GatorCandie: oooh send me one of their names

BDR 529 IL: ugghh… I don't know… I just deleted them

BDR 529 IL: lemme look

BDR 529 IL: heres one… nikki00112

BDR 529 IL: only 45

BDR 529 IL: bad example… she's actually kinda cute

BDR 529 IL: tlb3649

GatorCandie: frog or prince

GatorCandie: you're doing better than me

BDR 529 IL: HAHA… well that doesn't say much for ME now does it?

GatorCandie: hehehe

GatorCandie: She writes, "As friendship grows love emerges". It sounds like a bad euphemism for a guy's petie

BDR 529 IL: LMAO

BDR 529 IL: so how many condems should I bring on Tuesday? 3? I'll bring 3.

GatorCandie: HEY

BDR 529 IL: hehe… I'm just pushing your buttons

GatorCandie: I'm not that kind of girl

GatorCandie: Eventually, I could be.

BDR 529 IL: I was only kidding

GatorCandie: What size condoms would you be bringing? haha just kidding

BDR 529 IL: size? I just usually use some chewing gum

GatorCandie: how many pieces?

BDR 529 IL: haha… only one small piece of trident

BDR 529 IL: or sometimes I use cigarette wrappers. You know, the cellophane wrapper part. Whatever I can get my hands on

GatorCandie: I know, you appreciate the little things

GatorCandie: aahhhh, we bling you food, fi minutes

BDR 529 IL: haha… did you know that 80% of Asian men have cadirracs?

BDR 529 IL: the other 20% drive Rincoln Continentals

GatorCandie: haha

GatorCandie: I could actually trade sexual innuendos all day long if it didn't give people the wrong idea about me.

GatorCandie: this TLB girl is a package deal

BDR 529 IL: well… you know what they say… love goes out the door when money comes innuendo

GatorCandie: Who says that?

BDR 529 IL: Groucho Marx said that (past tense). We're way past tense, we're using bungalows now— also Groucho.

GatorCandie: Wow, I didn't know you would actually refer to someone. He was very funny. They censored most of what he said.

BDR 529 IL:	"Sir, would you like me to help you with your bags"? Groucho (standing next to two women): "No, I'll take care of the bags you just grab the luggage"
GatorCandie:	Hahaha he was great!
GatorCandie:	you should check out my friend's Match profile
BDR 529 IL:	what is her screen name?
GatorCandie:	myerunnc
BDR 529 IL:	a stolen sock monkey, aye??

When I pulled up her friend's online profile, I saw the exact same sock monkey picture that Pam e-mailed to me earlier. Thus, the sock monkey comment.

GatorCandie:	how did you think I put my hands on it so quickly?
BDR 529 IL:	was THAT some sort of innuendo??
GatorCandie:	Take it however you like it
BDR 529 IL:	I'll take it any way I can get it. Is this your sex fiend friend who likes me??
GatorCandie:	She's a lesbian, not a sex fiend.
BDR 529 IL:	Ahh, I see. It's about 2 degrees in here!
GatorCandie:	Why, is your heat off?
BDR 529 IL:	heat??? The A/C is on. I just shut it off.
GatorCandie:	Is two degrees what you like? I like the heat.
BDR 529 IL:	I like it warm, but I also like sleeping when it's cold—cuddled up in blankets
GatorCandie:	Then I'll put my feet on you if we ever get to that point. I have hot feet, or so I've been told.

BDR 529 IL:	how long do you have to be in a relationship before you can put your feet on the other person?
GatorCandie:	I think once you've had sex and begin sleeping with the person regularly. Then it's impossible to avoid.
BDR 529 IL:	Good rule of thumb (or foot)
GatorCandie:	Why did you wink at me on Match.com?
BDR 529 IL:	What do you mean? I liked your profile. I'll be honest, the picture got me first, of course, but the movie reference sealed the deal
GatorCandie:	I mean, you're not even really from Buffalo, are you?
BDR 529 IL:	well… no, but I am planning on taking one of the apartments this winter. I will be there a lot.
BDR 529 IL:	Not as a full time thing, but I will be up there quite a bit.
GatorCandie:	Ok, so since I like you I'm going to ask you what you do for a living. Maintenance man? Like Shneider from One Day at a Time? You don't roll your cigarettes into your shirtsleeve, do you?
BDR 529 IL:	yes, and I have a leather/denim vest
BDR 529 IL:	LOL. I already told you what I do.
GatorCandie:	Um, you kind of told me.
BDR 529 IL:	I own a bunch of real estate in Buffalo
GatorCandie:	Start working on your fumanchu
BDR 529 IL:	haha
GatorCandie:	Commercial? Rental units? Buy and sell?

BDR 529 IL:	Mostly buy and sell—some rental units, mostly in the Allentown area. I'm buying a few more soon and I want to make some changes, so I will be there a lot.
GatorCandie:	Buildings or houses? Am I prying and being annoying?
BDR 529 IL:	no, not at all. They are mostly single and multi-family houses. A couple of commercial buildings but not many
BDR 529 IL:	I am trying to buy a building on main street. A 6-story brick building that I want to turn into loft apartments.
GatorCandie:	Lofts are all the rage now.
BDR 529 IL:	Yep. Anyway, if that goes through I'll be there a lot.
GatorCandie:	I don't *believe* I would ever consider living in Allentown.
BDR 529 IL:	why not?
GatorCandie:	Its like NYC—a nice place to visit.
GatorCandie:	It's too city for me.
BDR 529 IL:	oh please… it's tiny! All of Buffalo is pretty small.
GatorCandie:	That's funny; the Old Pink is on Allen Street in Allentown.
GatorCandie:	I dont mean that it's big. I mean its transient; it has a feeling of temporariness.
BDR 529 IL:	I own a house right near there on College Street
GatorCandie:	The Old Pink, in all of its grunginess, is actually kind of cool.

BDR 529 IL:	I grew up in Brooklyn and NYC, so that feels comforting to me.
GatorCandie:	Well, you know I'm from Long Island so I'm a snob, ha.
GatorCandie:	I live near the Zoo, and that neighborhood feels like home.
BDR 529 IL:	That's why I'm coming on Tuesday—to that particular house on Allen. I have to check an apartment after a long-term tenant moved out and I'm having some work done to it
GatorCandie:	That sounds like a fun job. Coordinating all that stuff.
BDR 529 IL:	It is, but I'm really excited about this apartment building. It will be the biggest building I've ever owned.
GatorCandie:	or maybe not, but that's what I really enjoy doing. Project Management type stuff.
BDR 529 IL:	yeah, I've worked for a company doing that before and it's a little harder when its your money on the line. You tend to be a little stricter with the budget.
GatorCandie:	I bet. What's in your way? Anything?
BDR 529 IL:	In my way? Nothing really. I just have to meet with all the contractors to get finalized pricing, and a varience from the city and re-negotiate the price of the building. That sort of stuff.
GatorCandie:	Anybody could pull anything off with an unlimited budget.
BDR 529 IL:	exactly
GatorCandie:	Do you usually GC these yourself?

BDR 529 IL:	Well, I've never really done anything this big before, but yes.
GatorCandie:	Yes it hasnt gone unnoticed that neither of us can see when the other is typing… again :-)

At some point during the conversation, we both turned off that option that allows one to see when the other is typing.

BDR 529 IL:	I know. I said before "it looks like you got dressed", thus no longer naked which was my cute way of saying that I cannot see if you're typing any longer—a cute but cryptic way of saying it as I'm now learning.
GatorCandie:	yes
GatorCandie:	so did you
BDR 529 IL:	yes, so did I
BDR 529 IL:	I opened and designed a bar when I was 21 and ever since then I realized I like designing the space more than running the businesses
GatorCandie:	So do you ever have to go and break kneecaps or anything?
BDR 529 IL:	No, I usually just slap people with one of those yellow dishwashing gloves. That seems to do the trick
GatorCandie:	haha
BDR 529 IL:	I'm not in construction at all. I generally just own and manage property
GatorCandie:	No… I meant getting the rent.
BDR 529 IL:	oh… no, knock on wood; in Buffalo I've been very lucky with Tenants.

BDR 529 IL:	I had a house in Albany that was a pain in the ass… College kids
GatorCandie:	Albany? Wow you're all around. What made you pick Buffalo?
BDR 529 IL:	I lived in Buffalo when I was 19 for a year. I didn't go to school there, I went there with my band to play in a college town.
BDR 529 IL:	anyway…
GatorCandie:	"anyway" as in enough 20 questions?
BDR 529 IL:	no, no. I was typing.
GatorCandie:	oh, I couldnt tell.
BDR 529 IL:	Anyway…. I always liked the architecture there and the prices are very low. So, knowing this, I bought my first property there.
GatorCandie:	Would you ever get into the bar business again?
BDR 529 IL:	Yes, actually. I'm looking for a good space right now.
BDR 529 IL:	The bar I had was a wine/espresso bar. It was an art gallery, open mic poetry, exposed brick wall kind of place.
BDR 529 IL:	had a lot of character
GatorCandie:	Wow, that's cool.
BDR 529 IL:	but… the next place would be different
GatorCandie:	Such as?
BDR 529 IL:	Such as… it's sad to say, but I'm sellin' out. A "Burbon Street" type of place.
GatorCandie:	caged women dancers?
BDR 529 IL:	Please the masses

GatorCandie:	Well, you're in business to make money, not a statement.
BDR 529 IL:	exactly
GatorCandie:	I'm sure there's a place on Chippewa ready to turn over.
BDR 529 IL:	No, I want to do it here
GatorCandie:	It was kind of a joke... but I figured. The place names on Chippewa change constantly
BDR 529 IL:	oh? Why is that? Do they often fail?
GatorCandie:	Just a high turnover bar street. I guess maybe they lose their licenses and have to reopen?
BDR 529 IL:	ahh. I see.
BDR 529 IL:	I got shut down for 15 days once for serving an underage kid
GatorCandie:	Um, Im not sure they fail. It's wall-to-wall bars up and down the street, like Bourbon Street. All the barely dressed girls go there.
BDR 529 IL:	Yes, I've been down there a few times. Never in the bars but I've seen them
BDR 529 IL:	looks interesting—like theres money to be made
GatorCandie:	I climbed on a Bison in the back of the 25+ bar, Barristers there. I guess they think we're more mature.
BDR 529 IL:	ha—what do they know
GatorCandie:	Oh, I'm sure there's money there. I still go to the Crocodile once every so often. There's a silly band that plays there. 80s music. I can't resist.

BDR 529 IL:	There's a place in everyones heart for 80's music. If they deny it, they're lying
BDR 529 IL:	I just found some delicious Triscut crackers
GatorCandie:	Spread some of that dressing and imagine its parmigian
GatorCandie:	Meatball Parmigian… and yes, I will keep mispelling that word, I guess
BDR 529 IL:	That's it. I must go shopping tomorrow
GatorCandie:	I happily admit that I love 80's music. My ex, on the other hand, liked Rush.
BDR 529 IL:	If I wasnt so tired, I'd go shopping now
BDR 529 IL:	well, I'm a drummer, so I kind of had to like Rush
GatorCandie:	why oh why? zzzzzzzzzzzzzzz
BDR 529 IL:	hahaha…. it's weird… listening to Rush is almost like listening to a math equasion. So is classical music.
GatorCandie:	That's like saying that Fran Drescher had to like the singer because of his annoying nasal voice.
BDR 529 IL:	and bands like Tool or Phish
GatorCandie:	because it's so technical, you mean?
BDR 529 IL:	for me, bands like Tool, Phish, Rush, Primus, Blind Melon, etc. all kind of fall into the same category.
GatorCandie:	which is? Guitar driven?
BDR 529 IL:	Yes—kind of technical, but more… ummmmmmm "boxy" for lack of a better word

BDR 529 IL: I'm not that sure boxy is even a word at all.

GatorCandie: wow, I would love to understand what you mean.

GatorCandie: why is it "boxy"?

BDR 529 IL: It's weird. You have to train all four extremities to do different things at the same time, and some music makes all of those extremities flow in a way that seems to make sense

BDR 529 IL: I know, you must be like, "look at the ego on this moron". I'm sorry, I dont mean for it to come off that way.

GatorCandie: No, I'm very interested in understanding what you mean. I understand that the implication is that you're good in bed. I got it, you elitist, egomaniacal down-stater.

BDR 529 IL: HAHAHA

GatorCandie: So it's like a box, you mean, from one extremity to the other? Like waltzing?

GatorCandie: I love that whole "down-stater" thing by the way.

BDR 529 IL: yes, but more like a grid. And the grid is broken down into measurements, like a ruler and there are infinite combinations you could fit inbetween the measures and still stay in time

GatorCandie: So you can kind of see a picture?

BDR 529 IL: absolutly

BDR 529 IL: kind of like fractal geometry

BDR 529 IL: Do you ever listen to Tool or Blind Melon?

GatorCandie:	That's excellent. I'm sure that's why you're a good drummer. Blind Melon—errr—something about rain?
BDR 529 IL:	eh, that's their worst song—No Rain. You should download some of the more obscure Blind Melon Songs. I think they're great.
GatorCandie:	I'm getting Mouthful of Cavities right now.
BDR 529 IL:	oh that's a really good song
GatorCandie:	and Change
GatorCandie:	But not Lemonade
BDR 529 IL:	Tones of Home is good also
BDR 529 IL:	oh, and "Three is a Magic Number. I think you would like. It's a remake of the song from Rock School. Remember Rock School? It was a kid's show on PBS
GatorCandie:	I am limited to what is available online unfortunately
GatorCandie:	Which song? I'm Just a Bill?
BDR 529 IL:	no. "Three". You'll know it when you hear it.
GatorCandie:	Schoolhouse Rock?
BDR 529 IL:	hmmm… Was it Schoolhouse Rock or Rock School? I can't remember.
GatorCandie:	Schoolhouse Rock.
GatorCandie:	Do you like Pink Floyd at all?
BDR 529 IL:	I love Pink Floyd. And some Roger Waters solo stuff—like Amused to Death… GREAT album!

GatorCandie: I used to be their #1 fan. It's been awhile since I really listened though. Like I dont have anything on CD.

BDR 529 IL: Atom Heart Mother, Animals, Saucerfull of Secrets

BDR 529 IL: all good stuff

BDR 529 IL: my band used to play a ton of Floyd songs

GatorCandie: More has a great song on it though; called Green is the Colour, which is one of my favorite songs.

BDR 529 IL: yeah, More is a great album

GatorCandie: Ok, so Blind Melon is kind of folky "prog rock"

BDR 529 IL: not really. You're getting a bad example

GatorCandie: you think? I'm not saying it's bad, I'm just trying to pigeonhole it like everybody else does.

BDR 529 IL: hahaha. No, you need to hear other songs to get a real feel for them

GatorCandie: Change… harmonica hobo style

BDR 529 IL: yeah… dirty hobos

BDR 529 IL: we used to cover The Nile Song all the time

BDR 529 IL: off of More

GatorCandie: Really REALLY??? That's so cool!! I love the Nile song!

BDR 529 IL: yeah, reminds me of my early punk rock days

BDR 529 IL: hehe

GatorCandie: I'm excited!

BDR 529 IL: I've got a bike

BDR 529 IL:	you can ride it if you like
GatorCandie:	you can ride it if you like
BDR 529 IL:	it's got a basket
BDR 529 IL:	a bell that rings
BDR 529 IL:	and things to make it look good
BDR 529 IL:	:-)
GatorCandie:	haha!
GatorCandie:	Thats one crazy mofo.
BDR 529 IL:	yah
GatorCandie:	I really liked David Gilmours solo stuff.
BDR 529 IL:	Sid Barret was out there
GatorCandie:	I can dig this Blind Melon. It reminds me of when my girlfriend and I used to sit around and sing Rocky Raccoon for some reason.
BDR 529 IL:	hehe
GatorCandie:	Then you would like Mike Doughty's solo stuff. It's really paired down though. Stripped down from Soul Coughing at least.
BDR 529 IL:	yeah, I would try to download some but its taking forever tonight for some reason
GatorCandie:	do you have broadband?
BDR 529 IL:	yep

So right about here should be a dead giveaway for the timeframe in which these conversations took place—somewhere around 2001-ish. Not everyone had high-speed internet. In fact, most people used dial-up modems, and the next step up was simply a cable modem or a DSL line and that was quite costly to get. Nowadays, no one in their right mind would put up with the slow speeds of dial-up, not even on their phones.

GatorCandie: I really like all kinds of music except for country music. I even like a band that does western swing. I just can't like country though.

BDR 529 IL: yeah… i hate country also

BDR 529 IL: new country anyway

BDR 529 IL: nothing wrong with good ole Johnny Cash

GatorCandie: I like "King of the Road"

GatorCandie: and Johnny Cash. I like what Soundgarden did with Rusted Cage. That was a transformation.

GatorCandie: oh, oh and what's their name? They redid Ring of Fire

GatorCandie: Mommys Little Monster

GatorCandie: Ball and Chain

GatorCandie: Why can't I remember their name?

BDR 529 IL: I cant either

GatorCandie: um if I sit and think for a second…

BDR 529 IL: you've been standing this whole time??

GatorCandie: Social Distortion

BDR 529 IL: Social Distortion

BDR 529 IL: I never got too into them

GatorCandie: Yep, I think they're great. And Me First and the Gimmie Gimmies.

BDR 529 IL: haha. What about the Dead Kennedys?

GatorCandie: I love good covers. errr on the Dead Kennedys

GatorCandie: and the Dead Milkmen for that matter.

BDR 529 IL: "Stuart" by the Dead Milkmen is brilliant

GatorCandie: I like some Rancid

BDR 529 IL:	well listen, I should really get to bed. You're a bad influence on me… making me sleep too late in the mornings, hehe.
GatorCandie:	well listen, I think you should too.
BDR 529 IL:	are you poking fun at me?
BDR 529 IL:	'Cause if you are, forget it. I've got plenty of people dying to abuse me!
GatorCandie:	I am listening to Stuart and will give you a report the next time we talk. Poking fun? Not really. I think staying up late 'til 3am is wrong.
BDR 529 IL:	well, I'll stick around for your reaction to Stuart
GatorCandie:	It's funny so far.
GatorCandie:	"look at me! look at me! POW"
BDR 529 IL:	"HE WAS DECAPITATED"
GatorCandie:	"building landing strips for gay Martians", haha
GatorCandie:	Well, I am not one of the people lining up to abuse you, au contaire, so I hope you have sweet dreams, Jesse.
BDR 529 IL:	it was very nice talking to you again Pamela. Now, I know you're going to dream about me, but try and keep it clean, ok?
GatorCandie:	Yes, I will be thinking about your box thing.
BDR 529 IL:	and I, you.
BDR 529 IL:	lol sorry… I had to
GatorCandie:	I'll be your straight man, thats fine.
GatorCandie:	And how a little talent and an ego and an elitist attitude will get you places

BDR 529 IL:	;-)
GatorCandie:	by the way…
BDR 529 IL:	yes?
GatorCandie:	um, can we graduate to the phone maybe sometime?
GatorCandie:	or are you chicken?
BDR 529 IL:	I'll have to ask my mom. She doesn't like me using the phone too much.
GatorCandie:	Well, if you can work on her that will be great.
BDR 529 IL:	I'll see hat I can do. She says I can get my own line soon if I save my money, so, you know—fingers crossed. hehe
GatorCandie:	Consider it, is all I'm saying.
BDR 529 IL:	ok
BDR 529 IL:	goodnight cutie
GatorCandie:	sweet dreams. I like you :-)
BDR 529 IL:	I like you too

BDR 529 IL signed off at 3:26:34 AM.

What you just read was only our second conversation. We stayed up all night talking—as you can see—and by my rough count, we chatted for the better part of six hours straight. I was a little nervous when she mentioned talking on the phone. It was easy for me to be clever and charming while hiding behind my computer. Even having the once-removed feeling of being on the phone still made me a little nervous, and as you will read shortly, I tried to avoid it at all costs.

A NEW DAY & THE THIRD CONVERSATION

Looking back on these conversations makes me really wish that I had a time stamp. It can be extremely difficult to tell what day it was or how much time passed. However, I am absolutely certain that I tried to speak to her as soon as I possibly could. This was one of those she's-all-I-can-think-about situations, and I was fairly certain that she felt the same way.

BDR 529 IL:	Hello my pretty
GatorCandie:	Hello handsome.
BDR 529 IL:	How are you today?
GatorCandie:	TIRED again, but otherwise fabulous.
BDR 529 IL:	Awww, I'm sorry. Did I keep you up last night?
GatorCandie:	Just a bit. Are you washed and fed?
BDR 529 IL:	Yep, I'm as good as new
GatorCandie:	I haven't eaten yet today—soon I will. I jumped right in as soon as I got up and haven't really stopped.
BDR 529 IL:	Working from home, right?
GatorCandie:	Yep. Always do unless I'm on the road.
BDR 529 IL:	So explain to me exactly what you do
GatorCandie:	Hold on a sec. I'm having an incredibly boring conversation with someone that I must put an end.
BDR 529 IL:	Ok
GatorCandie:	Ok I'm back. I sent you a very unfunny email.
BDR 529 IL:	You sent it just now?

GatorCandie: Yes, it was the painful conversation I was just having, haha

BDR 529 IL: Ok. I'll go take a look

GatorCandie: You don't have to now. It has about 20% comedic value.

GatorCandie: brb

BDR 529 IL: Yeah, well, I don't have time to read it. I'm about to go to the gym.

BDR 529 IL: Then I have my handsome lessons at 3.

GatorCandie: what an ass.

BDR 529 IL: Haha

BDR 529 IL: Is he new?

By "is he new," I was referring to the e-mail that she sent to me, which consisted of a conversation that she had with someone else that she met on Match.

GatorCandie: This is what I NARROWED it down to, haha

BDR 529 IL: Me and him??!??!!

GatorCandie: Yeah, you both winked at me at about the same time. His match thingy is diamonds7781—ick

BDR 529 IL: I can't check it right now. I'm on my PDA and it's sooooo slow to load non-mobile websites

This was before the iPhone, before any smart phones for that matter. I had this thing and it cost a fortune and basically did nothing; however, at the time, this was the height of technology. I was on the cutting edge!

GatorCandie: Today was the first day I ever talked to him; so cut me some slack, would you?

BDR 529 IL: Slack cut, Captain.

GatorCandie: That's fine. What kind of PDA do you have? Is it integrated with cell?

BDR 529 IL: It is, but I don't have voice service activated on it. I have a seperate cell. It's a T-Mobile Sidekick. I basically just use it for email. I used to have the wireless Palm Pilot, but to be honest, this piece of junk is a little better, in my opinion.

GatorCandie: I like the Sidekick. I have a BlackBerry that has everything on it, and I'm super happy with it. Nextel.

GatorCandie: It makes me look important while I'm playing BrickBreaker.

BDR 529 IL: Yeah, I was gonna get the blackberry, but when I bought this, they only had the black and white model Blackberry. I wanted the color screen.

See my point? A color screen was a big deal during this time period. And if you think about it, it really wasn't that long ago. How far we've come—for better or worse.

GatorCandie: I have the color model. It's going to be sort of a bummer when I give it up for a flashier phone. Which I will, in Q4. So are you playing today?

BDR 529 IL: Verizon just called me and asked if I wanted to switch to DSL. I told them that I am happy with cable and that I used to have DSL and it took them 8 months to get me service. She said, "sir, we can probably do it quicker than that now".

GatorCandie: haha, I would hope so

GatorCandie: And here I was, going to send you an email to you're AT&T phone. Something about ordering some Chinese.

BDR 529 IL: No, no. I WILL be going shopping today.

GatorCandie: I have DSL and I'm happy with it. The prices are better than cable in my neighborhood, too.

BDR 529 IL: What's with the diamond and nuggets in this guy's profile?

GatorCandie: who the F knows? Who cares? We won't be speaking again, haha. I don't usually ask about stuff like that unless it comes up.

BDR 529 IL: I lost service with DSL all the time. So I lit the Verizon corporate offices on fire.

GatorCandie: Did you burn them to the ground or was it just you, a cigarette and a wastebasket?

BDR 529 IL: No, I'm not a maniac. Just a small fire in an ashtray to show them I mean business

GatorCandie: Sometimes it does the trick. And sometimes they just call the police and escort you out. It's happened for me both ways.

BDR 529 IL: And sometimes the police turn tricks. It's a crazy world we live in.

GatorCandie: And sometimes it becomes a Penthouse Forum letter and actually gets published.

BDR 529 IL: And that's when the big bucks start rollin in.

GatorCandie: You would know. You already know my game—get sold into prostitution and bad surgery for a bit of crank in return.

BDR 529 IL:	This thing cuts in and out sometimes in this area so if you lose me, ill be right back.
GatorCandie:	I'm unsure if I would know…
GatorCandie:	The thing with the Blackberry is that I cant Instant Message on it.
GatorCandie:	When I found out I was a little miffed.
BDR 529 IL:	I hardly ever use this for Instant Messaging.
GatorCandie:	You are fast with that thing though. I didnt use my last phone for IMs too much but I like the option.
BDR 529 IL:	It has a QWERTY keyboard
BDR 529 IL:	I'm terrible with phone text messages
GatorCandie:	Agile thumbs.
BDR 529 IL:	Oh yes, I've received many compliments on my thumbs
GatorCandie:	I'm really comfortable with T9 but I know what you mean.
BDR 529 IL:	I woke up to some new winks this morning also. One cute looking girl who I didn't replay to and one older lady
BDR 529 IL:	There are a lot of lonely 65 year old women out there
GatorCandie:	Why not reply to cute girl? You get more winks than I do, it seems.
BDR 529 IL:	No, this is unusual. I don't normally get that many. And besides, I'm already talking to a cute girl.
GatorCandie:	aww how sweet!

GatorCandie: Are you lookin' all shiny on match? Perhaps people are gearing up to not be lonely on Christmas. Perhaps it doesnt matter because they're 65 years old…

GatorCandie: Would you date someone over, like, 46 years old?

BDR 529 IL: Its not like I have an age limit. It depends on the person

GatorCandie: It seems like I have a fan club of the same 20 guys who send me a wink once a month.

BDR 529 IL: But 46 is a little out of my range I think.

GatorCandie: I had to put a range, but it only stems the tide a bit. There are many men that think it does not apply to them.

BDR 529 IL: Awwww, they should have a Pamela Parade every month instead.

BDR 529 IL: See… I lost ya there, didn't I

GatorCandie: The whole online dating thing is a bit bizarre if you ask me. Everyone jockeying to make themselves look better.

GatorCandie: You don't sign off when you lose me I guess, so I can't tell.

BDR 529 IL signed off at 2:25:16 PM.

BDR 529 IL signed on at 2:25:28 PM.

BDR 529 IL: what did I miss

GatorCandie: GatorCandie: The whole online dating thing is a bit bizarre if you ask me. Everyone jockeying to make themselves look better.

BDR 529 IL: ahh

BDR 529 IL: thanks

BDR 529 IL:	you're good
GatorCandie:	I guess you do sign off when you're out of coverage so I know.
BDR 529 IL:	yeah, T-Mobile is pretty good. Not too many problems, so I cant complain.
GatorCandie:	Well, you're also in one of the most heavily covered parts of the world. Its good to be in NYC.
GatorCandie:	Are you Italian?
BDR 529 IL:	yes, but there are some big mountains in the Hudson Valley that cut out service completely.
GatorCandie:	Hard to contend with hills, unless they cover the valley.
BDR 529 IL:	My mother is Italian and my father is Jewish
BDR 529 IL:	so I'm just confused
GatorCandie:	wow, trauma
BDR 529 IL:	nah, just lots of guilt
GatorCandie:	My last name was Sonessi for a long time.
BDR 529 IL:	you were married I take it?
GatorCandie:	Well you seem like a mensch to me. Yes I was.
GatorCandie:	I was tethered from 19 to 29.
BDR 529 IL:	wow
GatorCandie:	We only got married in 99 but yeah. It was a long time. Mostly good stuff though.
GatorCandie:	wow. Am I a pariah now?
BDR 529 IL:	No, you're not a pariah.
BDR 529 IL:	so what happened? What ended it?
GatorCandie:	Do you want the truth?

BDR 529 IL:	Of course, unless you don't want to talk about it
GatorCandie:	No, it's fine.
BDR 529 IL:	The truth has its qualities, when used in moderation
GatorCandie:	It may seem a bit shallow though, so be prepared.
BDR 529 IL:	hold on
BDR 529 IL:	ok... I'm prepared.
GatorCandie:	Our sex life was not good. It was pretty bad actually, and I was the one who always initiated and it started making me feel bad and bla bla bla.
BDR 529 IL:	Yes, well... That's an important part of any relationship
GatorCandie:	He's a great guy, though. But eventually it kind of permeated and tossed the boat around too much.
BDR 529 IL:	or not enough, as it would seem.
GatorCandie:	He blamed it on me for a couple of years and then he went to the doctor when it was too late and found out he had a condition.
BDR 529 IL:	what condition?
GatorCandie:	Extremely low testosterone.
GatorCandie:	It hurt a very good friendship—that whole sex thang did.
BDR 529 IL:	Was this a fact or was it a last ditch attempt to get you back—a sympathy ploy?
GatorCandie:	No, not at all. He went to the doctor when he finally woke up and found out I was gone.

BDR 529 IL:	Wow. If we ever wind up together, the pressure is on. I'm gonna have to make you cum in colors!
BDR 529 IL:	Sorry to be so crass. I've been a jerk all day
GatorCandie:	Bring on the color wheel baby, but yeah, that was a bit crass, lol.
GatorCandie:	Now, I understand that marriages today are not very strong, but mine was and I poured my heart into it.
BDR 529 IL:	You can't settle. Your life is the only one you've got
GatorCandie:	I don't have any major baggage about anything though. My sex drive is still what it always was, although now I get sex even less often than I used to, haha.
BDR 529 IL:	hahaha… damn backfiring.
GatorCandie:	"cutting off your nose" or "wise move"? YOU decide.
GatorCandie:	Now I feel like you know all this stuff about me and I dont know all this stuff about you. Its lopsided, but I can deal with it.
BDR 529 IL:	ask away… anything you wish
GatorCandie:	er, I'm not a pryer.
BDR 529 IL:	oh sure you are
GatorCandie:	OK
GatorCandie:	If you have such great thumbs, why are you single? haha
GatorCandie:	I already come in colors by the way; I just require some assistance sometimes. "Paying

attention" is the key I think. I'm fairly easy to please.

BDR 529 IL: I have been seeing this girl on and off. And to be honest, I just dont like her very much.

GatorCandie: This is current?

BDR 529 IL: she's a model and thinks she's God's gift

BDR 529 IL: She also thinks she's well read and likes to put people down who dont read her "book of the week". She's a psudeo intellectual and it drives me nuts.

BDR 529 IL: I haven't seen her in about 2 weeks

GatorCandie: Well, I can't compete with that.

BDR 529 IL: oh you cant? I think you certainly can

GatorCandie: The modelling and the book of the week? Nah

GatorCandie: I'm not a skinny mini. I'm not fat, just normal.

BDR 529 IL: she's an aspiring actress and she's terrible. She tries to make a performance out of everything.

GatorCandie: haha!

GatorCandie: What do you like about her?

BDR 529 IL: Believe me, I've seen your pictures and you are beautiful

BDR 529 IL: what DO I like about her? ummm... you know, I asked myself that very same question about 2 weeks ago

GatorCandie: Thanks. I feel like I'm in the novel, Rebecca.

GatorCandie: It's an addiction.

GatorCandie: Someone to hang with, someone who's comfortable, even if theres arguing.

BDR 529 IL:	hey... without arguing, there's no passion. I think a little arguing every now and then is healthy
BDR 529 IL:	people who dont argue at all wind up shooting each other when their in their 80's
GatorCandie:	Maybe. I think there should be a damn good reason for it though, because I don't enjoy it.
BDR 529 IL:	An argument doesnt have to be over something serious. Differing opinions in a conversation can lead to some arguing, but the good kind. The kind that you know is going to result in really good sex.
GatorCandie:	I grew up around arguing and I like peace.
GatorCandie:	Oh, debate is different. Arguments about gut wrenching problems and drama I can do without.
BDR 529 IL:	I dont mean "I cant believe you slept with Jen" arguing, I mean "Bush is a maniac" arguing
GatorCandie:	YOU SLEPT WITH JEN???
BDR 529 IL:	uhhhh, errr, no honey, I swear it!
GatorCandie:	haha
GatorCandie:	I can't believe it!
GatorCandie:	Bush IS a maniac.
BDR 529 IL:	yeah, he's almost comical. Like a cartoon character
GatorCandie:	reeeediculous.
BDR 529 IL:	you know... if I were Kerry, my incentive to win would be to NOT get murdered by Bush's henchmen after the election
BDR 529 IL:	Kerry is a moron too, though

BDR 529 IL:	We are in for a world of trouble
GatorCandie:	haha, that's an angle I hadn't considered, but that would just put Edwards in the driver's seat.
BDR 529 IL:	you just like Edwards cause he's cute
BDR 529 IL:	haha—pppffft… girls.
GatorCandie:	He sent me a wink but he's out of my range.
BDR 529 IL:	LMAO
BDR 529 IL:	That's weird… I got a wink from Kerry too!
GatorCandie:	I stick to my guns.
GatorCandie:	oooohhh nice to try to one-up me.
BDR 529 IL:	Yeah… I give America about 2 more good years before the shit really hits the fan.

Looks like I was pretty "on the money" with this call. It was just a few years later when all the problems started to happen—9/11, the real estate collapse, bank bailouts, and foreclosures.

GatorCandie:	Um, hello. The shit HAS hit the fan.
GatorCandie:	How much worse can it get? Especially if Kerry gets elected.
BDR 529 IL:	nah… wait until it becomes like Israel here and people are blowing themselves up in coffee bars
GatorCandie:	Don't open a coffee bar, whatever you do.
BDR 529 IL:	the American people won't know how to react to that. They will start "rounding up the troops" and killing every non-white person within 5 miles
GatorCandie:	Good point.

BDR 529 IL:	and before you know it, we unfreeze Hitler and we all get Volkswagens
GatorCandie:	It is the people's car.
BDR 529 IL:	da
GatorCandie:	Could you imagine Martial law?
BDR 529 IL:	Yes, martial law would be crazy. People wouldn't stand for it. I know I wouldn't.
GatorCandie:	I would go underground, start wearing black turtlenecks and berets.
BDR 529 IL:	ooohh... sounds sexy... can I come?
BDR 529 IL:	hey wait... will soup be made available?
GatorCandie:	Dunno? Has it ever been a problem for you before?
BDR 529 IL:	well... I do like soup
GatorCandie:	Sure, why not? Soup for everyone.
BDR 529 IL:	wow... what a glorious day.
BDR 529 IL:	"Born Free" playing in the background
GatorCandie:	This current one?
BDR 529 IL:	um... I don't know what you're talking about, so I'm gonna say... yes?
GatorCandie:	This current day is glorious?
BDR 529 IL:	yes... Soup for everyone and a promise of you in a black beret.
GatorCandie:	Do you really like black berets?
BDR 529 IL:	I dont rightly know. I've never owned one. I can make one out of cardboard and test 'er out for a while
GatorCandie:	Me neither. But I am a hat person.

GatorCandie:	Taker for a spin.
BDR 529 IL:	me too… I'm in my Hunter S. Thompson golf hat at the moment
GatorCandie:	haha, I'm afraid it may be loathsome.
BDR 529 IL:	somewhat
GatorCandie:	I hope you got that.
BDR 529 IL:	would I make a Hunter Tompson reference with out knowing that I would be called on it for reference?
BDR 529 IL:	I'm reading Kingdom of Fear right now. The man refers to himself as "smart" 5 times in the first two chapters
BDR 529 IL:	You've gotta love him though—that swine
GatorCandie:	Really? That's a bit over the top.
BDR 529 IL:	yes, well… so is HST
GatorCandie:	Definitely. I went through a period where I read all the radical books I could get my hands on. It's actually over now.
BDR 529 IL:	The name of my bar was Che's Rebellion… after Che Guverra. I don't know why I named it that. I guess I was going through my "rattle the cage" or "damn the man" period
BDR 529 IL:	it was a toss up between that name and "Humphry's Clock"
GatorCandie:	ha, Humphrey's Clock
BDR 529 IL:	I was young
BDR 529 IL:	;-)
GatorCandie:	Now you're going to name it T&A
GatorCandie:	How about Illuminatus?

BDR 529 IL:	nah, Free Masons I can handle, but Illuminati? No way.
GatorCandie:	You can paint the walls in paranoid, conspiratorial colors
GatorCandie:	um, I know this is going to sound stupid...
GatorCandie:	But do the illuminati exist? Do you think?
BDR 529 IL:	I don't know if they existed before the rumors, but I'm sure some people have started up sects afterwards
BDR 529 IL:	or at least tried
GatorCandie:	Makes sense. So what kind of drugs do you do on a regular basis?
BDR 529 IL:	ha... is this a trick question?
BDR 529 IL:	I smoke grass now and then... other than that, nothing
GatorCandie:	gotcha
BDR 529 IL:	you? All the good ones? Blue ones, red ones, crystal, coke, mushrooms, angel dust, crank, of course?
GatorCandie:	um, I have tried different drugs but I don't use any.
BDR 529 IL:	oh... I have tried 'em all, but I don't use any now
GatorCandie:	I have never tried crystal meth, heroine, opium, absinthe or crack.
GatorCandie:	or ecstacy.
BDR 529 IL:	I've tried ectasy, opium, heroine (smoked it once), I drank some homemade absinthe and have never tried meth or crack

GatorCandie:	I have never had a bad experience on any drug (except just once… that's a story) but they take a bad toll on the body and don't seem to be worth it, at least not very often.
GatorCandie:	Wow what is absinthe like?
BDR 529 IL:	This was home made absinthe, so it just kinda knocked me out. I didn't go blind though— what a rip off!
GatorCandie:	I guess blindness is the ultimate goal?
BDR 529 IL:	yeah… Anything worth doing, is worth doing right
GatorCandie:	Drugs are just ok to me. Nothing to get worked up about or addicted to.
BDR 529 IL:	I haven't done coke, acid or mushrooms in years and I don't think I ever will again. I might try some ectasy with the right person (you know, like Kerry…. he's so dreamy)
BDR 529 IL:	last time I did ectasy was about 5 years ago with this crazy girl and my friend Dave
GatorCandie:	I don't have any concept of how it is on Ecstacy so I don't know. But if it's like 8 hours on acid I would not be game.
BDR 529 IL:	the drugs REALLY got to her. I guess more than it did to Dave and I
BDR 529 IL:	no, no, It's only about 4 or 5 hours and it just heightens sensation. It can be quite a zesty enterprise when done with the right person
GatorCandie:	It's been 12 years since I last did acid. I remember it well.
BDR 529 IL:	arent you going to tell me your "bad experience" story?

GatorCandie:	Really? Well if it's like being buzzed on alcohol that's cool. Coke is easy; I could probably do that again if it was around. BUT, whatever on that.
BDR 529 IL:	well... we certainly wouldn't be strapped for conversation if we did some coke together
BDR 529 IL:	but... I think my coke days are long gone
GatorCandie:	Um, I was having sex with my boyfriend on acid in the dark and his hair started to look weird and I didnt like it. I had to stop the presses.
GatorCandie:	I've done coke maybe 5 or 6 times and never had a problem with it. Just a buzz, really.
BDR 529 IL:	hey... that's a good first date... how 'bout some ectasy, coke and sex all night?
GatorCandie:	haha, your idea of a good first date doesn't match mine. I dont know if I would do any kind of drug with someone I didn't know.
BDR 529 IL:	lol... I'm kidding. I just met you but I think I know you well enough to know that.
GatorCandie:	The last time I had coke in the house was about 3 years ago and it was left over from a party. It stayed in the freezer for like 3 months.
BDR 529 IL:	haha
GatorCandie:	I didn't really know how to store the stuff, so I just put it there and forgot about it.
BDR 529 IL:	ok... so just one 8 ball. I mean, it IS only our FIRST date!

GatorCandie: haha, I can't believe I'm talking so openly
                    about drugs with you. I feel like you could get
                    the wrong idea about me.

BDR 529 IL: What about you getting the wrong idea
                    about me??

GatorCandie: Men are so much more critical of women
                    than the other way around. Men are supposed
                    to be bad boys. Girls are supposed to be
                    good. Like, I actually would like to mother a
                    child eventually!

BDR 529 IL: You can be good AND honest all at the same
                    time and I won't even judge you.

GatorCandie: My girlfriend was really funny. The last time
                    we smoked pot, like a year and a half ago, she
                    was taking a hit and she said, "well, this is the
                    last time I'm smoking pot. I'm going to get
                    pregnant soon and I want to be good."

GatorCandie: She's a planner.

BDR 529 IL: haha

BDR 529 IL: it would be nice to have son or daughter…
                    but you know, once you have children with
                    someone, you're locked in for life, good or
                    bad, better or worse… for real.

GatorCandie: Oh, I know. Forever. I think it would be worth
                    it though with the right person.

BDR 529 IL: absolutly

GatorCandi: Like if my ex and I had had kids, we would be
                    fine, personality wise.

GatorCandie: But I have heard horror stories.

BDR 529 IL: So you don't think the sex, or lack thereof,
                    would have been a problem if you had kids?

GatorCandie: Oh yes, it would have been. I meant if we had kids then split up. Not that that's OK in and of itself. I just mean we would be able to raise them appropriately—Without drama. The sex would have brought us down sooner or later though. I have a pretty high drive. It was a mismatch in that respect.

BDR 529 IL: oh I'm sure you would have raised them appropriately, but it's also nice to have a mom and dad togerher.

GatorCandie: I believe it's essential.

BDR 529 IL: If you're a kid anyway. Everone I know (men anyway) that were raised by single mothers, are spoiled rotten little bastards and all the ones brought up by just men, are wild maniacs

BDR 529 IL: my typing is terrible today

GatorCandie: Really? Believe me, I think it's essentially wrong not to have a man and woman raising a child in the same house.

BDR 529 IL: all the girls from broken homes seem to be fairly well adjusted however

GatorCandie: My girlfriend is totally neurotic and had everything intact. I am not neurotic and did not. Go figure.

BDR 529 IL: Why don't you send me a picture of you with your new webcam

BDR 529 IL: and no... I don't mean a dirty picture

GatorCandie: I don't have it hooked up and I havent read the literature on it yet. I'll work on it though. Maybe tonight.

GatorCandie:	I wouldn't send you one :-) …a dirty picture that is.
BDR 529 IL:	ok. I'll see if I can dig mine out also
BDR 529 IL:	I know you wouldn't, but I didnt want you to think I was asking for one
BDR 529 IL:	even though I know you would like to send one and I would definitely like to receive it
GatorCandie:	I didn't think that. You sound like you can wait.
BDR 529 IL:	hehe
GatorCandie:	groan
GatorCandie:	not moan, but groan
BDR 529 IL:	hmmm…. is groan worse than moan?
GatorCandie:	well I guess they go together in certain instances, like "bitch and complain"
BDR 529 IL:	right
BDR 529 IL:	hey, don't blame me. Remember that sex drive thing you were talking about. Well, I might be one of few who could keep up. I think I have a higher than average sex drive.
GatorCandie:	Really? You're just teasin'
BDR 529 IL:	no
BDR 529 IL:	I'm serious
GatorCandie:	That's good.
BDR 529 IL:	In fact, I'd say it's a rare occasion when I'm not thinking about sex
GatorCandie:	haha, thinking and doing are two different things, no?

BDR 529 IL: oh yes, but there hasn't been much doing in the last few weeks

GatorCandie: I actually don't think about sex all the time except those rare days when it's ALL I can think about, but when I have sex I focus.

GatorCandie: And I never turn it down, ha. Within reason I mean, in an established relationship.

BDR 529 IL: I think it's different for women. Generally anything I think about has some sexual overtones

GatorCandie: Anything?

BDR 529 IL: yep. I'd say so

BDR 529 IL: haha

BDR 529 IL: Taxes? …yes.

GatorCandie: Well, I could be that way. Taxes??

BDR 529 IL: Driving? …yes.

GatorCandie: Driving, definitely.

GatorCandie: I love watching a good-looking guy drive a stick shift for some reason, haha. That's my little secret.

BDR 529 IL: *Note to self* on next trip to Buffalo, rent a car with a manual transmission

GatorCandie: haha

GatorCandie: Do they rent those??

BDR 529 IL: I don't think so

GatorCandie: And it used to be all you could get in Costa Rica.

BDR 529 IL: heh… tell me about it

BDR 529 IL: LOL

GatorCandie: ha, I'm remembering the convo I had with Diamonds

BDR 529 IL: I was laughing at my little joke

BDR 529 IL: even while typing I laugh at my own jokes… how pathetic

GatorCandie: haha! I do the same thing.

GatorCandie: I'm thinking, "This is SO funny"

GatorCandie: I am SO witty.

BDR 529 IL: and it's hard to get the emphasis on the right words

BDR 529 IL: you want to make sure the other party got the full, unbridled power of your joke

GatorCandie: The sheer muscularity. I know.

BDR 529 IL: haha

GatorCandie: Are you fearless? Do you think it will be weird when we meet?

BDR 529 IL: it's quite hard to convey sarcasm sucessfully while chatting online… quite the challenge

BDR 529 IL: when we meet? hmmm…. I don't know

GatorCandie: I think you do allright. I think someone who isn't on the same page makes it difficult to convey anything, much less subtle sarcasm.

BDR 529 IL: this whole internet thing is bizzare… I mean, you know the person before you meet them

GatorCandie: Though your sarcasm isn't alway subtle…

BDR 529 IL: its not?

GatorCandie: I know. That's why I don't like to linger online. It doesn't seem "real".

BDR 529 IL: but it is definitely interesting

GatorCandie:	Just Kidding. Most of the time it is subtle until it gets to sex.
GatorCandie:	Then, no subtlety
BDR 529 IL:	I know… without my piercing eyes in front of you, it's hard to make my blunt sexual references work
GatorCandie:	I can imagine.
BDR 529 IL:	its a curse, I know, but… one I can deal with
GatorCandie:	I think you're being truthful, and that's ok actually. I like men who exude sexuality as long as they don't overdo it and become inappropriate.
BDR 529 IL:	theres a bit of truth in all jokes, but for the most part, I am a very respectful guy
GatorCandie:	I like pressure applied.
BDR 529 IL:	when in the right places, sure.
GatorCandie:	I think it's a talent—one that might not make you any money—or at least not a lot of money, but a good talent.
GatorCandie:	I think that's partially what I meant when I said in my profile that I like people who have a good understanding of people.
BDR 529 IL:	it's hard to find someone who understands you as well as you understand them, and I don't mean that to sound insensitive
BDR 529 IL:	but most people really just "dont get it"
GatorCandie:	What do you mean?
GatorCandie:	haha … Get it?
BDR 529 IL:	yes, got it lol.

BDR 529 IL: everyone seems to bob around in their own little world, never trying to understand what other people are thinking

GatorCandie: I know. The talent to pay attention and understand is what makes someone a good lover. Sorry to always make it about sex.

BDR 529 IL: when it comes to sex, despite my bluntness, I am not the jump in the sack kinf of guy. I'd much prefer a long night of playing

GatorCandie: wow. How's that for peace, love and understanding?

BDR 529 IL: haha

GatorCandie: Are you ready to talk to me? Because I have to run to the post office and I'd love to talk to you for a minute or two while I go. Then we can go right back to IM if you like. Have I sold it?

BDR 529 IL: I dont know… to me, Id rather play in bed all night than have straight sex with someone for 45 minutes

GatorCandie: Straight sex? um, is there any Gay sex in your past?

BDR 529 IL: haha… no…. you know what I mean

GatorCandie: yes of course I do.

BDR 529 IL: hehehe…. sure…. do you want me to call you? I will try but I dont know what kind of cell service I will have here

BDR 529 IL: wow, I have to go to the post office too. I didnt realize it was so late.

GatorCandie: ok, you can try 716.699.6299 I'm running.

BDR 529 IL: ok…im going too. I'll be back in about 15 minutes. I'll try and call on my way to the PO

BDR 529 IL is away at 4:20:56 PM.

BDR 529 IL: hey…. are you back yet?

Auto response from GatorCandie: …gurgle….

BDR 529 IL returned at 4:44:45 PM.

BDR 529 IL: I tried to call you back, but I got your voicemail

BDR 529 IL: I left a message

BDR 529 IL: did I scare you off??

BDR 529 IL: hehe

BDR 529 IL: uh oh…. maybe I did

BDR 529 IL: hmmmm… guess I did

Auto response from GatorCandie: …gurgle….

BDR 529 IL: look, this just isn't working out. I think we should start seeing other people.

She didn't respond for a few minutes.

BDR 529 IL: she returns

GatorCandie: You're already seeing someone else!!

BDR 529 IL: I had to move on!!

GatorCandie: WTF

BDR 529 IL: hehe

GatorCandie: I got to hear your New York accent for 1 minute then you were gone.

During our one-minute phone conversation, she asked me about my band and if I liked the songs that we recorded.

BDR 529 IL:	Just to expand on what I was saying earlier. It's not that I dont like the music, it's just that I would make a lot of changes on the album
BDR 529 IL:	is my acent that bad?
GatorCandie:	You would want more creative control.
BDR 529 IL:	I have all that I want. But the album is already mixed. And I would spend the money to remix it, but the other guys in my band are all cheapskates
GatorCandie:	Your accent is a bit strong, but you have to understand that I dont hear them every day. Mine would come back after talking to you for an hour or so though.
BDR 529 IL:	they all (except one) live with their parents and only one of em works
GatorCandie:	yikes
GatorCandie:	zoinks, raggy
BDR 529 IL:	yeah, so, it's like…we go out to the diner and they're all looking over the bill to see if they owe $5.26 or $5.27
GatorCandie:	haha I hate that. Just split it.
BDR 529 IL:	yeah… so I'll be damned if I'm going to support their childish "gimme gimme" attitudes
GatorCandie:	Sounds like you've thought about this alot.
BDR 529 IL:	ha… could ya tell?
GatorCandie:	maybe a little ;-)
GatorCandie:	So, there is something that you could have done to make it more to your liking but you decided it wasn't worth it.

BDR 529 IL: yeah. I still might do it. I dunno.

BDR 529 IL: after you hear it, I'll tell you my thoughts

GatorCandie: k. is there any particular "riff" I should be listening for?

BDR 529 IL: LOL

GatorCandie: haha

BDR 529 IL: "liiiiiiisten for it"

GatorCandie: its like that cheese commercial... "wait for it..."

BDR 529 IL: hehe

GatorCandie: I'm sure the raw material will be good, with all those good influences you've had.

BDR 529 IL: and as for those cell phone headsets, I prefer the good old days when the people talking to themselves could be safely branded as crazy

I'm referring to Bluetooth headsets. Remember way back when everyone had a Bluetooth plugged into their ear, which in turn, made it seem like everyone was talking to themselves.

GatorCandie: I listened to "Cross Town Traffic" today.

BDR 529 IL: I get to sit in cross-town traffic tomorrow

GatorCandie: Oh, then I will probably get on your nerves a bit. I have a wireless headset always on.

BDR 529 IL: hehe, well... you're the exception, 'cause I already know you're crazy.

GatorCandie: It sounded good. I don't listen to Hendrix very much so... Oh! And I listened to "She's like a Rainbow" the other day. That was fun.

GatorCandie: ha, good point

BDR 529 IL:	my cell phone has a radio in it
GatorCandie:	But since its wireless, sometimes you cant even tell I'm wearing it.
GatorCandie:	It does?
BDR 529 IL:	I didn't discover this until the third or fourth week that I had it.
GatorCandie:	Is it any good? I would like a cellphone with an mp3 player in it.
BDR 529 IL:	It's pretty good. I rarely use it because you need the headset to hear it
GatorCandie:	therein lies your problem
BDR 529 IL:	yes… a catch 22
GatorCandie:	I miss New York talk radio
BDR 529 IL:	There are a lot of Pink Floyd influences in our music, I think
GatorCandie:	I used to listen to Joy Bahar all the time. I think Floyd is good, but I wore them out in my youth and sometimes I have trouble going back to it.
BDR 529 IL:	I listen to a lot of internet talk radio. The Lou Gentile show… paranormal stuff
GatorCandie:	Do you believe in the paranormal?
GatorCandie:	Damnit my maid left again without leaving me food!!
BDR 529 IL:	do I believe? Well, I've seen some weird stuff, but nothing solid enough to call proof, so mainly it's for the entertainment value
GatorCandie:	Entertainment. Yes I could see how it could be funny.

BDR 529 IL:	do you?
GatorCandie:	Believe in paranormal?
BDR 529 IL:	yes
GatorCandie:	Absolutely not.
BDR 529 IL:	not even in the slightest?
GatorCandie:	I don't believe in astrology either, ha, although my girlfriend tells me Scorpio's and Gemini's are compatible.
GatorCandie:	No, and I guess I'll just get out of the way that I don't believe in God either.
BDR 529 IL:	I don't believe in astrology at all, but… what's your sign?
GatorCandie:	You are a Scorpio right?
GatorCandie:	She noticed that I think.
BDR 529 IL:	No, Cancer.
GatorCandie:	oh, wrong person? Who knows? She told me that Scorpio's and Gemini's were compatible. I thought when I reported back to her.
BDR 529 IL:	Growing up with both Jewish and Catholic families, I learned that God is a pretty good businessman, probably nothing more
GatorCandie:	I don't follow any of that though. I hate to say it, but I am a classic Gemini
BDR 529 IL:	you reported back already??
GatorCandie:	yeah, Jesus a carpenter.
BDR 529 IL:	all the Jews are loaded and we know the Catholic Church is taking out any payday loans in the near future

GatorCandie: Of course. After I told her that you winked at me she started planning our wedding. She thinks we were meant to be because your match thingy is the only funny one she's seen. She is about right, unfortunately.

GatorCandie: The Jews secretly rule everything.

BDR 529 IL: unfortunately??? Am I not good enough??

GatorCandie: haha! Absolutely you are.

BDR 529 IL: hey…whataya think of Bjork

GatorCandie: She's ok. I don't follow her though. Or do you mean her looks?

BDR 529 IL: no her music. I love her

GatorCandie: I never came down on it either way. I wouldn't shut it off but I don't think she rocked my world when she had the opportunity.

BDR 529 IL: yeah. Some of her stuff is pretty bad, but the good stuff is solid gold

GatorCandie: I am a big fan of the band Innocence Mission.

BDR 529 IL: so you said you sent me a very witty email once. Do you happen to have a copy of it?

BDR 529 IL: never heard of them. What type of music?

GatorCandie: No, is the new me boring you?

BDR 529 IL: you boring me??

GatorCandie: kinda folky, but not hippy, the singer Kate Peris has a very clean high-end voice that I love. It sounds like you'd fall in love with her just to know her.

GatorCandie: I hear her music and my heart breaks sometimes. I get chills.

BDR 529 IL:	I know what you mean. I get that from Radiohead sometimes
GatorCandie:	I already looked for the email.
GatorCandie:	It sounds like we could teach each other a lot; because there's another band I never got into. I hear how great they are, but never really bothered with it.
BDR 529 IL:	no luck aye? I just thought it would be funny to see what you wrote, not knowing me
BDR 529 IL:	oh you should bother, immediately!!!!
GatorCandie:	The only problem is…
GatorCandie:	except for Mazzy Star, I don't like depressing music.
BDR 529 IL:	She's great
BDR 529 IL:	its not depressing, at least I dont think so
GatorCandie:	I know. What isn't depressing?
BDR 529 IL:	true
GatorCandie:	no! I mean, what are you referring to?
BDR 529 IL:	any music that can fill you with emotion is doing its job, whatever that emotion may be
GatorCandie:	Most things aren't depressing!!
GatorCandie:	haha
BDR 529 IL:	I dont find Radiohead OR Mazzy Star depressing, unless you allow them to be
GatorCandie:	Don't tell me you get depressed easily.
BDR 529 IL:	No. I think that if you are easily depressed, then I could see how that music would affect you that way

GatorCandie: Well, when I listen to music I like, I try to
                  understand the lyrics and feel it. Mazzy Star
                  is all about relationships gone or going wrong.

BDR 529 IL: see, with her, I rarely listen to the words, I just
                  kind of let her voice blend in to the whole
                  melody

BDR 529 IL: if you concentrate too much on lyrics, you
                  can lose the feel for the song as a whole

GatorCandie: I like sexual, like Morphine or stupid and
                  bouncy like Soul Coughing or uplifting like
                  Innocence Mission.

BDR 529 IL: Radiohead is GREAT sex music

GatorCandie: You think so? I believe if I understand the
                  lyrics the music makes more sense to me.

GatorCandie: k. I will get some Radiohead. What shall
                  I get?

BDR 529 IL: You should download 10 or so various
                  Radiohead songs and try 'em all out

BDR 529 IL: it depends of the piece of music. Some music
                  is lyric driven and some is music driven. It's
                  different for each person's ear.

GatorCandie: I wish good restaurants delivered

BDR 529 IL: you know I agree with you there

GatorCandie: Theres a bar/restaurant called Fat Bobs that
                  has the best food but sometimes its a hassle
                  to stop what youre doing and go.

GatorCandie: Obviously, I've heard Creep. That jumped out
                  at me.

BDR 529 IL:	definitely download Myxomatosis, I Might be Wrong, There There, Optimistic, Paranoid Andriod
GatorCandie:	I am listening to High and Dry
GatorCandie:	I could listen to this for a long time.
BDR 529 IL:	yeah, that's a good one but not very indicitive of the rest of their music
GatorCandie:	really? What about Fake Plastic Tree?
BDR 529 IL:	kind of... Songs like the ones I listed above are more electronic based, but not in a bad way
BDR 529 IL:	what else do they have?
GatorCandie:	I'm about to listen to Paranoid Android
BDR 529 IL:	that's a great one
GatorCandie:	ack, its just that you can't tell until you try to download, and there's a lot of live rif-raf
BDR 529 IL:	yeah
BDR 529 IL:	Rabbit in The Headlights is probably my favorite
GatorCandie:	his voice sometimes reminds me of Rufus Wainwright's.
GatorCandie:	I like Fake Plastic Tree.
GatorCandie:	Cant get Rabbit.
BDR 529 IL:	Rabbit in Your Headlights most acuratly describes them I think
BDR 529 IL:	you didnt like Paranoid Andriod?
GatorCandie:	Not as much as High and Dry and Fake Plastic, but yes.

BDR 529 IL:	I use Bearshare and ever since I downloaded Microsoft Service Pack 2, it hasn't worked properly
GatorCandie:	k, got DJ Shadow version of Rabbit. I'm waiting
GatorCandie:	well atleast you know the problem. It would be a pain to get it to work properly. See Bearshare probably knew about the pack but didn't update. They may know the HKey workaround though.
BDR 529 IL:	the "Reverse Light Massive Attack Remix"… lol… or just DJ Shadow?
GatorCandie:	JUST DJ Shadow, haha
BDR 529 IL:	good
GatorCandie:	I am wary of Massive bla bla remixes
BDR 529 IL:	actually… Massive Attack is a really good band, but I agree with you on all the remixes
GatorCandie:	There is a Magic Carpet Ride remix by Rednex that kicks ass though.
BDR 529 IL:	;-)
GatorCandie:	interesting drum work in this song
BDR 529 IL:	how far into Rabbit are you?
GatorCandie:	"washed down the toilet"
BDR 529 IL:	hehehe you're the coolest…. most people would have said 1:42 minutes
GatorCandie:	ok, it's a remix so I can tell its weird
GatorCandie:	There is something sinister about this song
BDR 529 IL:	yeah, under the right circumstances, rainy night, candle light, it can bring you to tears

BDR 529 IL:	Blow Out is cool too
GatorCandie:	Is that angst I hear?
BDR 529 IL:	hehe… might be some angst… kids these days
GatorCandie:	haha, brb I have to wash my hands
BDR 529 IL:	ok
GatorCandie:	Well, all I can say is, "what kind of sex are you having" haha
BDR 529 IL:	um… what kind of sex do YOU think im having??
BDR 529 IL:	none at the moment
GatorCandie:	none, for the last little while, haha
BDR 529 IL:	correct! Give the girl a prize
GatorCandie:	what shall it be?
BDR 529 IL:	what would you like?
GatorCandie:	ha
GatorCandie:	stalemate I guess
BDR 529 IL:	I was waiting for your prize request
GatorCandie:	A six-pack of Gatorade? I love Gatorade.
BDR 529 IL:	cherry or orange??
GatorCandie:	It never matters what the flavor is. I am a connoiseur.
GatorCandie:	But I fear I mispelled that.
BDR 529 IL:	I'm trying to find a song from an old band I was in. I'll see if I can mail it to you. I like it… kind of upbeat
GatorCandie:	Connoisseur
GatorCandie:	It wasn't that bad, actually

BDR 529 IL:	off by one s.... I've seen worse
GatorCandie:	I would love that
GatorCandie:	I love Gatorade.
GatorCandie:	Did I say that?
BDR 529 IL:	I think you did
GatorCandie:	One of the sweetest gifts I ever got was a case of Gatorade. :-)
BDR 529 IL:	get the girl what she likes!
GatorCandie:	exactly!
BDR 529 IL:	so I guess diamond man isnt impressing you at all
GatorCandie:	what does he have?
GatorCandie:	bullshit?
BDR 529 IL:	diamonds?
GatorCandie:	No, I adore gemstones but diamonds are kind of boring.
GatorCandie:	I would like to get a kunzite next, actually.
GatorCandie:	I used to work for a jewelry manufacturer so I saw alot of stuff.
BDR 529 IL:	I really like diamonds
GatorCandie:	really? eh
GatorCandie:	No color.
BDR 529 IL:	I dont wear them or anything, I just love to look at em
BDR 529 IL:	quite the opposite... there are thousands of colors in a diamond
GatorCandie:	I used to have a really nice one; I know they can be beautiful. But I love color.

BDR 529 IL:	I was never much into jewelry
GatorCandie:	Guys really shouldnt be. My opinion of course. They should be into cars and stuff.
BDR 529 IL:	old fassioned?
GatorCandie:	Me? Just a bit. I like men who are men I guess.
GatorCandie:	I think channel set wedding rings are nice as long as they dont get silly.
BDR 529 IL:	I agree… except for the liking men part
GatorCandie:	And I usually don't go for Italian, gold chain wearing types.
BDR 529 IL:	you mean I shouldn't' wear my gold horsehead necklace??
BDR 529 IL:	heheh
GatorCandie:	Or the Italian horn?
GatorCandie:	Its up to you.
BDR 529 IL:	lol
GatorCandie:	Do you have a pinkie ring?
BDR 529 IL:	I dont wear any jewelry
GatorCandie:	That's good …and its a relief.
BDR 529 IL:	you thought I was serious about the horsehead??
BDR 529 IL:	ok, the song is on its way to you
BDR 529 IL:	it's from an old band that I dont play with anymore. The CD I sent you is totally different
GatorCandie:	k, Im excited
GatorCandie:	nothin yet
BDR 529 IL:	its still sending
BDR 529 IL:	oh…it just sent

GatorCandie:	Are you at your home computer?
BDR 529 IL:	my laptop
GatorCandie:	Check out Innocence Mission…
GatorCandie:	…or not if you cant
BDR 529 IL:	I tried before, but Bearshare isn't letting me do anything
GatorCandie:	Limewire, baby
BDR 529 IL:	oh yeah? I'll check it out
BDR 529 IL:	did the email make it to you ok?
BDR 529 IL:	I hate sending them out alone… so young and unattended
GatorCandie:	like tender peas
GatorCandie:	It's receiving now.
BDR 529 IL:	coolio
BDR 529 IL:	brb
BDR 529 IL:	i have returned
GatorCandie:	hello!
BDR 529 IL:	why hello
BDR 529 IL:	I sent you one other
GatorCandie:	The computer wouldnt automatically open it. I had to fenagle, but I got it and I like it.
BDR 529 IL:	cool…thanks
BDR 529 IL:	like I said, the CD I sent is totally different
GatorCandie:	I don't know if I ever told anyone that I would chew my own arm off for them.
BDR 529 IL:	hehe
GatorCandie:	Nice brass

BDR 529 IL: just like being in Mexico

BDR 529 IL: or at least a Mexican restaurant

GatorCandie: haha, yeah a tableside serenade, eardrums in pieces in the arroz con pollo

BDR 529 IL: HAHAHA

GatorCandie: You're easy to laugh with and I appreciate that.

BDR 529 IL: yah… you can't take yourself too seriously

GatorCandie: A message was sent to you that was returned to the sender (bounced) because it would have caused your mailbox quota to be exceeded.

BDR 529 IL: oh… sorry

GatorCandie: wtf? I will check into this

BDR 529 IL: delete the other song

BDR 529 IL: that should leave enough room

GatorCandie: No, I use outlook, so there shouldn't be a problem

BDR 529 IL: hmmm

GatorCandie: It auto deletes stuff in my inbox on delivery

BDR 529 IL: same with me

BDR 529 IL: see… isn't this weird? I feel like we've been on our first and second date already

BDR 529 IL: yet we havent even met

GatorCandie: we haven't even really talked on the phone!

BDR 529 IL: I know

BDR 529 IL: I'm listening to Morphine "You Look Like Rain" and a baby in a neighboring apartment is crying in the background. It really works well with the song.

GatorCandie:	So I'm in a holding pattern. Tell me
GatorCandie:	Oh I love "You Look Like Rain"—not so much with the crying children
BDR 529 IL:	picture one low crying child over the sax
BDR 529 IL:	hehe… it works
GatorCandie:	oh yeah, it would work. I like it. Its like Pink Floyd with the dogs but you'd have child protective services all over your ass.
GatorCandie:	would you kindly send it again? It stopped auto deleting my emails for some reason.
BDR 529 IL:	I already re-sent it
GatorCandie:	smartie
BDR 529 IL:	8-)
GatorCandie:	haha, I've never seen that smilie
GatorCandie:	O:-)
BDR 529 IL:	:-!
GatorCandie:	ick
BDR 529 IL:	:'(
BDR 529 IL:	as a whole, I am against all smileys
GatorCandie:	you use em
BDR 529 IL:	I know… this is a new development for me.
GatorCandie:	I resist until the person I'm talking to uses them, then I'm like, "ok they dont think it's cheesy, so fine"
BDR 529 IL:	haha… I was against them for so long, but I guess, I became numb to them
BDR 529 IL:	desensitized if you will (even if you won't)

BDR 529 IL:	like seeing that video of the woman getting hit by the train. It used to make me physicaly ill to watch, but now, I throw people in front of trains all the time
GatorCandie:	I am not desensitized, I'm aware of them but I realize people use them in place of sweet sentiments so I think its ok.
GatorCandie:	haha
GatorCandie:	HAHA
GatorCandie:	I love this song
BDR 529 IL:	really, cool
GatorCandie:	its right up my alley
GatorCandie:	a dark alley, to be sure
GatorCandie:	Reminds me kind of Black 47
BDR 529 IL:	ha… I can see that
BDR 529 IL:	I like the banjo… it was added later
GatorCandie:	its fun
GatorCandie:	I like fun music.
BDR 529 IL:	yeah… I like all music really
GatorCandie:	ok, fine. So do I but I REALLY like fun music
BDR 529 IL:	I can tell that your mood is easily influenced by your surroundings
GatorCandie:	yes, I usually go with it, but I can make the mood too.
GatorCandie:	and I do. Sometimes I light up a room.
BDR 529 IL:	sometimes? You seem like you would light up a mortuary

GatorCandie: Thanks! Well, sometimes I go with the existing mood, if I'm unsure of myself until I get my footing. But that's my secret.

BDR 529 IL: notanymoreitsnot…I'mtellingEVERYONE!

GatorCandie: damn it!

BDR 529 IL: yep

GatorCandie: Consuela will console me

BDR 529 IL: hey, I have an imaginary friend named Consuela

GatorCandie: You can't have her, she's mine!!

BDR 529 IL: at least she keeps telling me she's imaginary

GatorCandie: haha

GatorCandie: What does YOUR Consuela look like?

GatorCandie: haha, I'm loving this

BDR 529 IL: like Carmen Electra

BDR 529 IL: and she has these weird bodyguards that think she really IS Carmen Electra

BDR 529 IL: and the cops and the Judge seem to believe her also

BDR 529 IL: but I know whats really going on!

BDR 529 IL: ole Consuela can't fool me

GatorCandie: HAHA

GatorCandie: My Consuela sort of looks like that but shes also my completely inept maid so she wears a short black skirt

BDR 529 IL: you just keep her around for the sex?

GatorCandie: haha, I dont know WHY I keep her around anymore.

GatorCandie:	She has a large chest that I can cry into.
BDR 529 IL:	I had a maid for a while, but she refused to bathe me, so out the door she went
GatorCandie:	haha
GatorCandie:	You've never been able to find one, huh?
GatorCandie:	Did you get my email?
BDR 529 IL:	no… lemme go look
BDR 529 IL:	"OE removed access to the following unsafe attachments in your mail: Train to Chicao Mike Doughty.mp3"
GatorCandie:	WHAT?
GatorCandie:	It is NOT unsafe.
BDR 529 IL:	im sure it's not
GatorCandie:	It's as safe as me!
GatorCandie:	O:-)
BDR 529 IL:	Outlook Express is under the Microsoft Nazi regime
GatorCandie:	You would love that song too.
GatorCandie:	heil
BDR 529 IL:	does Consuela live in or out?
GatorCandie:	in, of course
BDR 529 IL:	hmm… so you have a sexy Spanish live-in maid?
BDR 529 IL:	she any good in bed?
GatorCandie:	I'm not that easy to pry into, haha
GatorCandie:	what's your email address?
BDR 529 IL:	?? You just emailed me

BDR 529 IL:	FMDC@optonline.net
GatorCandie:	I know, but my window won't let me see for the moment
BDR 529 IL:	do you own your house?
GatorCandie:	Any more questions?
BDR 529 IL:	hehe… just wondering
GatorCandie:	Those messages crossed.
GatorCandie:	No, I don't. I moved in here when I moved out.
GatorCandie:	I kind of like it here and it's easy.
BDR 529 IL:	yeah…Kathleen Moreland is a nice woman
BDR 529 IL:	:-)
GatorCandie:	Who's that? My landlady?
BDR 529 IL:	hehe… just a guess… am I wrong?
GatorCandie:	it's kind of weird how you keep doing that.
BDR 529 IL:	it's a real estate program I have… gives me all the information… but so far, it's all been wrong with you!
GatorCandie:	'splain lucy
BDR 529 IL:	except for that your house is assessed at $129,900, it was built in 1920 and the lot is approx 70 x 140
GatorCandie:	is that all? That's surprisingly low.
GatorCandie:	I would guess at about 200k actually.
BDR 529 IL:	well… I have a house in Buffalo that was assessed at $88,900 and I sold it for $225,000, so go figure.
GatorCandie:	oh, that's right. I forgot about that.
BDR 529 IL:	I never told you that

GatorCandie:	Do you have all the extraneous private dicking for me in you worked out?
GatorCandie:	Oh, I know, but I knew that and just forgot about it.
GatorCandie:	I worked for a homebuilder.
BDR 529 IL:	lol… it wasn't premeditated. I was working on something else and your address was on the pad in front of me, so I couldnt resist
GatorCandie:	I understand. I always actually wanted to do Private Investigations.
GatorCandie:	But it's like misfortune. Its funny when its not you.
BDR 529 IL:	I once tried to place an ad in the local paper that simply read "detective wanted"
BDR 529 IL:	but they wouldn't let me print it without a phone number
GatorCandie:	haha
GatorCandie:	I like it
BDR 529 IL:	yeah, it's good. I've always wanted to use it
BDR 529 IL:	Saint Mark's Church on Woodward looks like a nice building
GatorCandie:	FREAK!!
GatorCandie:	I hear the bells all the time.
BDR 529 IL:	hey… nice pants!
GatorCandie:	HAHAHA
BDR 529 IL:	I'm sorry. Am I really freaking you out? I keep forgeting that you don't really kno me
GatorCandie:	I love this neighborhood. See how close I am to the zoo?

BDR 529 IL:	yep… right on parkside
GatorCandie:	uh, it's a little weird because you don't.
BDR 529 IL:	ok, I'm sorry. I'll stop
GatorCandie:	I have the ordinary tools—you have special tools. I'm adjusting though.
BDR 529 IL:	I'm harmless
BDR 529 IL:	unless you're a mesquito, then it's lights out sucka!
GatorCandie:	That's good. I see the giraffes on my way home all the time. It's neat.
BDR 529 IL:	I haven't been to a zoo in years
BDR 529 IL:	unless you count Staten Island
GatorCandie:	Really? I think they're great.
GatorCandie:	More like the Bronx
BDR 529 IL:	at least there are some redeaming qualities to the Bronx
BDR 529 IL:	NONE for Staten Island
BDR 529 IL:	unless you like the smell of garbage
BDR 529 IL:	then its oooooooo-tay
GatorCandie:	Yeah the dump is no prize
GatorCandie:	When I was a teenager I worked at a strip mall in Oceanside, kind of near a landfill. Everybody who worked there called it the 'rat mall'
BDR 529 IL:	ha… yes, it's pretty gross
BDR 529 IL:	wow… did you get any work done today, or have I been talking your ear off all day

GatorCandie:	Oh, I've been getting some work done, making some calls. I did alot this morning.
BDR 529 IL:	that's good. I feel like I've been keeping you up all night and keeping you from your work all day.
GatorCandie:	well, you have been keeping me up at night, but not from my work. It has to get done, because if it doesnt... Pamela has to shop at KMart
BDR 529 IL:	and Consuela has to take the next donkey back to Madrid
BDR 529 IL:	is she from Spain?
GatorCandie:	Yeah, or wherever the hell she's from
GatorCandie:	haha
GatorCandie:	Jesse?
BDR 529 IL:	yes Pamela?
GatorCandie:	tell me a secret
BDR 529 IL:	ok
GatorCandie:	I sent you another email. See if that works.
GatorCandie:	So what's your story pretzel man?
GatorCandie:	I've always wanted to quote that.
BDR 529 IL:	ha
BDR 529 IL:	a secret?
GatorCandie:	yes, a secret.
GatorCandie:	The more I look at that word, the funnier it seems.
BDR 529 IL:	I've never wanted to talk to anyone as much as I was looking forward to talking to you today

GatorCandie:	Really?
GatorCandie:	I wonder why. I mean…
BDR 529 IL:	yes… and I'm not just giving you a line… You were on my mond all night last night
BDR 529 IL:	my mind
BDR 529 IL:	and my mond
BDR 529 IL:	I know this is probably future relationship suicide, but it's a secret, so I told you
GatorCandie:	Suicide? How could it be used against you in a court of law later?
GatorCandie:	I guess I'm ordering Chinese.
BDR 529 IL:	I'm not sure, but I know one of the rules is not to disclose how much you really like the other person in the beginning of the relationship.
BDR 529 IL:	hehe
GatorCandie:	Rules? haha, I've told you all KINDS of bad things about me.
BDR 529 IL:	and dont let the other person know exactly what you're feeling until you know what they are feeling
BDR 529 IL:	but I figure rules are out the window at this point
GatorCandie:	Well, I said "I like you"
GatorCandie:	that's a pretty strong statement, actually.
BDR 529 IL:	is it?
GatorCandie:	yes, it is.
BDR 529 IL:	:-)
GatorCandie:	If you could hear me say it, you would know.

GatorCandie: Did I tell you I sent an email?

BDR 529 IL: yes… I didn't get it yet

BDR 529 IL: oh… here it comes

GatorCandie: Sorry, I forgot.

GatorCandie: I have a secret.

BDR 529 IL: ok

GatorCandie: I truly wonder if I would live up to your expectations, being all 9 car ownin' model datin' ex-bar owner guy. I am after all, just myself, and I'm all that but I'm not ALL that.

GatorCandie: and I'm not fishing, I'm just telling you my secret.

GatorCandie: Lo Mein and Garlic Beef?

BDR 529 IL: I wonder if you have built me up too much in your head. I'm not Brad Pitt and not exactly Bill Gates. I am just me. I think I have a lot to offer, but I'm not the collar out, gold chain wearing player driving around in a Porsche—not that that's what you want, nor is it something to aspire to be. Lol, I mean, I'm doing okay and I'm fairly decent looking, but I'm not ALL that either.

BDR 529 IL: ever try chow fun??

GatorCandie: I LOVE chow fun. I order it ALL the time!!

GatorCandie: wide, frat noodles

BDR 529 IL: those noodles started their own Fraternity?

GatorCandie: I havent built you at all… haha

BDR 529 IL: wow… what a wonderful age we live in

BDR 529 IL: you havent built me up, but you just took bits of information and formed a character that I don't think I am

GatorCandie: no, not at all. These are components of what makes you you, actually.

GatorCandie: Just like being smart and pretty makes me, me.

BDR 529 IL: I'm sure there is a lot more to you than just being smart and pretty

GatorCandie: It's not as if I havent listened to everything you've told me.

BDR 529 IL: what do you mean?

GatorCandie: I mean, to me, you are the whole person I've met. Of course I havent met all of you, but I could list a bunch of your good qualities if my feet were pressed to burning coals. Or even if they weren't.

GatorCandie: There's a Chinese restaurant in Chinatown that I love, called Wo Hop. At least it used to be there.

BDR 529 IL: well, all I know is I love talking to you and when I look at that picture of you with those big blue eyes, I just melt

GatorCandie: Well, I know you're exciting and funny and when I look at that picture of you with the cigar in your mouth, I think, "that doesnt seem like the person I'm talking to"

GatorCandie: but of course it can be

BDR 529 IL: hahaha… that was more of a goof picture than anything else

GatorCandie: all "playerd"

GatorCandie:	I love the picture of you with your buddy's arm around you.
GatorCandie:	You look so handsome.
BDR 529 IL:	why thank you
GatorCandie:	sure. Its true.
GatorCandie:	anyway, Consuela is not here to mop my tears with her bosom, so stop it.
BDR 529 IL:	:-[
GatorCandie:	why red faced?
BDR 529 IL:	I'm blushing for all the compliments
GatorCandie:	oh, you can handle it. I'm like that, so you'll have to, haha
GatorCandie:	You sealed it. I will order my usual, shrimp chow fun wif baby cohn
BDR 529 IL:	mmm…sounds good
GatorCandie:	it is. They know it's me right away, even though they don't come out and say it.
BDR 529 IL:	haha… same here
BDR 529 IL:	yet they always ask for my pome numba
GatorCandie:	They're shy over there at China Star. I'm sure you can find its proximity to where I live PRETTY EASILY
GatorCandie:	haha
BDR 529 IL:	ha
BDR 529 IL:	uh oh…. that wasnt you was it?
GatorCandie:	doing what?
BDR 529 IL:	someone IM'ed me and was asking weird questions

GatorCandie: who was it?

BDR 529 IL: so I answered thinking it was you screwing
                    with me

BDR 529 IL: it was a girl from match

GatorCandie: nah, I only have one screen name

BDR 529 IL: well... she must think I'm nuts now

BDR 529 IL: lol

BDR 529 IL: oh well

GatorCandie: I wouldn't mess with you like that.

GatorCandie: did you get the email?

BDR 529 IL: it just seemed weird cause I dont ever get
                    random IM's really

BDR 529 IL: yes, it still won't let me play it. After it
                    unzipped, it said the same nonsense as before

GatorCandie: Well, it wasnt random... you sent the same
                    letter to her that you sent to me!!

GatorCandie: oh well, sorry

BDR 529 IL: ??

GatorCandie: sorry you couldnt open it, because it's a
                    good song.

BDR 529 IL: no, the same letter stuff

GatorCandie: oh, haha the match email. "so we winked..."

BDR 529 IL: I must have put my screen name in it

GatorCandie: yes, you did, but the email got booted.

BDR 529 IL: what do you mean?

GatorCandie: the match elves erased your email address

BDR 529 IL: I'm lost

BDR 529 IL:	'splain
GatorCandie:	ok, I will do better than that… give me a sec
BDR 529 IL:	yes, but I don't send my screen name to many people
BDR 529 IL:	so it was sort of a surprise when I got the IM
GatorCandie:	did you get my email
BDR 529 IL:	yes

She sent me a copy of the email that I sent to her when I first reached out to her on Match. For some reason, when sending emails through the Match interface, they remove any email addresses from the body of the text. For example, if you write something like "Hi. I'm Jesse and my email is jesse@mail.com," they erase the email. I suppose that they do it to prevent spam. I thought that bit needed a little more explanation for you, reader. So, there ya go.

GatorCandie:	Do you see how your email address is gone?
GatorCandie:	Did it say anything good? Could she be a Consuela?
BDR 529 IL:	oh… That is weird… that means they completely screened the message and rewrote it
GatorCandie:	nah, it just takes out email addresses.
BDR 529 IL:	oh…. yes…I see…. I was reading it wrong
GatorCandie:	You have to write them out, not do the blabla@blabbityblab.com
BDR 529 IL:	yes
GatorCandie:	Funny how they do that, huh?
BDR 529 IL:	bastards
GatorCandie:	Sons of Bitches! Lets burn them down!

BDR 529 IL: let's do it. I'll pick you up at 8

BDR 529 IL: do you have a ninja outfit... or an evildoer outfit of any sort?

GatorCandie: I can wear all black... no num chucks though

GatorCandie: sure, of course. Evildoer I am

BDR 529 IL: wait. So... NO num chucks???

BDR 529 IL: forget it. I'm out.

GatorCandie: haha, you're so wishy washy

GatorCandie: ok, the latest wink Ive gotten: iamnotsoeviljohnnym

GatorCandie: why oh why? See, this is what I do for entertainment. Look at my winks.

BDR 529 IL: lemme go look

BDR 529 IL: HAHAHAHAHAHAHAHAHAHA

BDR 529 IL: paintball pictures ALWAYS gets the liz-adies

BDR 529 IL: is that a paintball helmet or does he just wear it for general safety

GatorCandie: oh my god, I only read his blurb and didn't look at the rest. It's horrible! haha, THIS, right here is my misfortune, and you're laughing at it!!

BDR 529 IL: it's only YOUR misfortune for a few seconds... its this guys poor misfortune forever

GatorCandie: those are atv helmets actually

GatorCandie: haha

GatorCandie: ok, look at this one. This is a stereotypical match profile:

She sent me the link to the profile.

GatorCandie:	He's one of my regulars.
BDR 529 IL:	I enjoy fine dining, cocktailing, a little wildness
GatorCandie:	who calls it "cocktailing"? Is that anything like "tailgaiting?"
GatorCandie:	He could never make me laugh.
BDR 529 IL:	you've spoken to him before?
GatorCandie:	of course not
GatorCandie:	I just know, silly
BDR 529 IL:	oh come on… I'm already laughing
BDR 529 IL:	ahhh… he seems like a nice guy
BDR 529 IL:	but cocktailing?
BDR 529 IL:	thats bad
GatorCandie:	look at this guy: oh by the way, is this annoying? I think its funny but I could see how you might get annoyed.
BDR 529 IL:	no no
GatorCandie:	"i think i am a fun person to be around. i like to be spontanious. i am very straight forward and honest. i know what i want and work hard to get it. i am looking for an honest person who will like me for me. honesty is very important."
BDR 529 IL:	why would I get annoyed?
GatorCandie:	I hate that stuff about honesty. I could go on for about 5 minutes about "honesty"
GatorCandie:	Oh, I dont know… just trying to be aware of you.

BDR 529 IL:	yeah… no one ever says, "I'm really looking for a liar. Someone who bullshits me all the time and sleeps with all my friends"
BDR 529 IL:	I think Honesty is implied
GatorCandie:	that's dannyaqqua69
BDR 529 IL:	69….. yeeeeaaaaahhhhh
BDR 529 IL:	LMAO
BDR 529 IL:	poor danny
GatorCandie:	OH, YOU KNOW IT BABY
GatorCandie:	ugh!
BDR 529 IL:	WOAH… danny is somethin else
GatorCandie:	I know, a real firecracker.
BDR 529 IL:	I love the people who list "skinny dipping" as their turn offs
BDR 529 IL:	like it's an unavoidable charastic in a person
BDR 529 IL:	no…not him….he's a "skinny dipper"
BDR 529 IL:	what would mother think
GatorCandie:	haha
GatorCandie:	did he say skinny-dipping was a turnoff?
BDR 529 IL:	no…not him, but I've seen that a lot
GatorCandie:	have you really?
BDR 529 IL:	you know… you check off the things you like and don't like, and skinny-dipping is an option, but I wouldnt exactly call it a "torn on" or a "turn off"
GatorCandie:	I have never seen that, but Ive been looking at men mostly.
GatorCandie:	I wonder what mine says?

BDR 529 IL:	like "Animals I dont like: Fleas"
GatorCandie:	I know, but I like when someone writes "I have: fleas". That's funny
GatorCandie:	Yep, there it is. Skinny Dipping.
GatorCandie:	Who wouldn't like that?
GatorCandie:	All naked in water? It happens every day!
BDR 529 IL:	skinny dipping, flirting, thrills, and erotica...... hmmmm....
BDR 529 IL:	ya think we could fit all that into one date?
GatorCandie:	haha
BDR 529 IL:	hehe
GatorCandie:	depends on where we were I guess
BDR 529 IL:	and we'd still have to fit soup and sandwiches in there somewhere
GatorCandie:	Bring your laminated porn magazine to the hottub and...
GatorCandie:	say boo then be all flirty
GatorCandie:	thrilling
BDR 529 IL:	I was thinking we could fight crime naked in swimming pools
GatorCandie:	Ooh baby, but where does the erotica come in? Just asking.
BDR 529 IL:	you'll have the laminated porn magazines
GatorCandie:	There was a magazine I got until it went out of print and online.
BDR 529 IL:	what was it called?
GatorCandie:	I dont do the online porn thing.
GatorCandie:	Libido. www.libidomag.com

GatorCandie:	I cruise over every so often but it's not the same.
BDR 529 IL:	pretty good... I could see how the actual magazine was better
GatorCandie:	I still have my copies. It was really an awesome magazine. I used to buy it at Border's. I always got looks, haha.
GatorCandie:	So then I became a subscriber and my ex was not pleased.
BDR 529 IL:	you know... your turning me on!
GatorCandie:	Sorry :-)
BDR 529 IL:	sorry???
GatorCandie:	well, I didnt mean it.
GatorCandie:	I hate getting all turned on then not being able to do much about it.
BDR 529 IL:	yes, I agree... but I have decided that I definitely like talking about sex with you
GatorCandie:	k! So what else about sex should we talk about?
GatorCandie:	It is my favorite subject.
BDR 529 IL:	haha... anything you like
GatorCandie:	what turns you on?
BDR 529 IL:	you for starters
BDR 529 IL:	I like subtle gestures
BDR 529 IL:	but there are certain things that I like that probably most guys dont
BDR 529 IL:	for one, I like pale skin on girls
GatorCandie:	details!
GatorCandie:	pale skin?

BDR 529 IL:	I've been told Im crazy, but yes
BDR 529 IL:	I don't like women with dark tans
GatorCandie:	Like very white, with no Italian or Greek in them or just not tanned?
BDR 529 IL:	well… just not tan
BDR 529 IL:	a girl's neck and shoulders are very sexy I think—or at least they can be.
BDR 529 IL:	and, once I know the person well eonugh, I like to play games in bed
GatorCandie:	games? Like what?
BDR 529 IL:	maybe one day you'll see
BDR 529 IL:	O:-)
GatorCandie:	oh pleeeease tell me
GatorCandie:	a hint maybe?
BDR 529 IL:	hmm…well, I could dress you up in all different outfits
GatorCandie:	yes, ok go on.
BDR 529 IL:	hey, enough about me. I'm giving it all away
BDR 529 IL:	hold on
BDR 529 IL:	brb
GatorCandie:	I can't believe you put me on hold at such a critical moment!
BDR 529 IL:	lol… I'm sorry
GatorCandie:	haha
BDR 529 IL:	continue please
GatorCandie:	You can't just say something like that and stop!
BDR 529 IL:	sure I can

GatorCandie:	what kind of outfits?
GatorCandie:	is there a pout-y smiley?
BDR 529 IL:	hehe… and by the way, a pouty face is also a turn on
GatorCandie:	Why?
BDR 529 IL:	well it can be
GatorCandie:	if…?
BDR 529 IL:	on the right person
GatorCandie:	no info.
GatorCandie:	nothin'

There was a short pause on my end. I explain this short pause below.

BDR 529 IL:	lol—sorry, a friend of mine came over and I didn't think it would be appropriate for him to see what we were talking about
BDR 529 IL:	so I closed the window for a second
BDR 529 IL:	he just came by to pick up his keys—he forgot them here earlier.
GatorCandie:	gotcha
GatorCandie:	thanks for your discretion.
BDR 529 IL:	oh I dont kiss and tell
BDR 529 IL:	even though we havent kissed
BDR 529 IL:	I'm still not tellin
GatorCandie:	you're sweet
GatorCandie:	that was not sarcasm
BDR 529 IL:	so, I told you mine. What are your turn ons?

GatorCandie: Um, Im trying to think of something very tame to tell you.

BDR 529 IL: tame???

GatorCandie: yes, vague, like yours were

BDR 529 IL: well, I can get less vague as the night progresses

GatorCandie: I like kisses on my neck.

BDR 529 IL: that's all I get?

GatorCandie: um, Im trying to think of things that normal people would say, haha

BDR 529 IL: haha... I think we both know that neither of us are very normal

GatorCandie: do we?

BDR 529 IL: so fire away. It would be hard to shock me at this point.

GatorCandie: I cant!

BDR 529 IL: why not?

GatorCandie: because if your abnormalitites don't fit mine, it would be a bummer. Even worse, you're totally vanilla and I get disappointed!

BDR 529 IL: listen, I promise you that I am not toally vanilla

GatorCandie: I like whatever feels good. satisfied? haha

BDR 529 IL: ok, you tell me one sexual abnormality and I'll follow up with one

GatorCandie: no you first!

BDR 529 IL: no no... This is your game, sista

GatorCandie: I sometimes like aggressive sex.

BDR 529 IL:	do you like hands around your neck?
BDR 529 IL:	hair being pulled?
GatorCandie:	maybe
BDR 529 IL:	you like to get raped, but willingly
GatorCandie:	well, I still like all the fuzzy stuff during actually
BDR 529 IL:	you can fuck or you can make love—it's the combining of the two that makes for a perfect relationship
BDR 529 IL:	sexually anyway
GatorCandie:	I am totally jumping out of my skin right now yikes
BDR 529 IL:	I'm sorry; it was the easiest way to say it
GatorCandie:	what, the "fucking" thing? It was the throat and hair thing that got me jumping actually.
BDR 529 IL:	hehe
BDR 529 IL:	vanilla… sheesh
GatorCandie:	I am so uncomfortable right now.
BDR 529 IL:	oh no… why?
GatorCandie:	well, in a good, smiley sort of way but still…
BDR 529 IL:	I'm sorry… The last thing I wanted to do was to make you feel uncomfortable
GatorCandie:	you didnt, really.
GatorCandie:	It's part of the charm of my kink I think.
BDR 529 IL:	ha
BDR 529 IL:	the uncomfortable feeling of a helpless little girl in the hands of a man who could do whatever he wants to her?

GatorCandie:	You've been here before, I think.
BDR 529 IL:	what else do you like?
GatorCandie:	I'm having a hard time concentrating on the question.
BDR 529 IL:	you shouldn't have to think
GatorCandie:	haha, I can't believe I'm speechless! This, like, never happens!
GatorCandie:	What else do I like? um, everything else spins off that wheel I think.
BDR 529 IL:	yeah, well… I think we are pretty much on the same page there
GatorCandie:	Though Im a big fan of my gspot.
GatorCandie:	Which could have nothing to do with any of that other stuff.
BDR 529 IL:	you'll have to introduce us one day
BDR 529 IL:	hehe
GatorCandie:	yikes
GatorCandie:	hello internet dating
BDR 529 IL:	am I still a faceless internet dater to you?
GatorCandie:	of course not!
GatorCandie:	we have a date, I think.
GatorCandie:	In your hotel room—omg
BDR 529 IL:	still not sure, aye?
BDR 529 IL:	is that bad?
BDR 529 IL:	it's not a room…. its a big suite
BDR 529 IL:	theres a water park in the room
BDR 529 IL:	and a carosel

GatorCandie: haha

GatorCandie: hey, I'm on your page kimosabe. I'm just still stunned.

GatorCandie: It takes alot to get me to this point, where I can't think of anything to say and I start sounding brainless

BDR 529 IL: you know…we could knock out two fantasys at once!

BDR 529 IL: lol…just kidding

GatorCandie: why, are you renting a van?

BDR 529 IL: well…. not entirely kidding, but if it will prevent me from getting slaped, then I'm kidding

BDR 529 IL: a van? Well, can you just be walking into YOUR hotel room and someone is in the dark waiting for you??

GatorCandie: nah, it doesnt fit, but if… well it really couldn't fit

GatorCandie: because

BDR 529 IL: wait no… lemme hear "if"

GatorCandie: I like the talking parts

BDR 529 IL: you mean the luring you into the van part?

GatorCandie: but wait!!! stop the presses! this is crazy, we've never met and I couldn't really do it!!

BDR 529 IL: I know… were just talking

GatorCandie: My head is clear again I think.

BDR 529 IL: and "stop the presses"? Do you know how long that takes??

GatorCandie: haha!

GatorCandie:	actually, I really didn't, but it would be for me!
GatorCandie:	I'm worth it, haha
BDR 529 IL:	I know you are
BDR 529 IL:	so, why wouldnt it work?
GatorCandie:	because you want no talking.
GatorCandie:	and I like that sort of thing
BDR 529 IL:	no no…When I say no talking, I mean no "hi, how are you—get to know you stuff"
GatorCandie:	oh, then theoretically it could work if you said the right things
BDR 529 IL:	what are the right things?
GatorCandie:	my heart is racing
BDR 529 IL:	hehe
GatorCandie:	Sorry, I cant tell you them. Catch 22 there.
GatorCandie:	sorry…brb
BDR 529 IL:	aggh…you can't leave me now!!
BDR 529 IL:	haha
GatorCandie:	my mom's on the phone and she never calls…
GatorCandie:	sorry! Hopefully it wont be too long
BDR 529 IL:	no… Take your time hun
BDR 529 IL:	I just wrote out a magnifcently naughty scenario…. remind me to tell you later
GatorCandie:	aaaackkk!
GatorCandie:	you are such a tease!!
BDR 529 IL:	hehe… go talk to mom
BDR 529 IL:	this is getting good
GatorCandie:	grr

BDR 529 IL:	still on the Phone?
GatorCandie:	I just got off.
BDR 529 IL:	Are we still talking about your phone call or...
GatorCandie:	I haven't talked to my mom in like 2 months
BDR 529 IL:	oh? How is she? Do you two not get along?
GatorCandie:	Oh, yeah we get along fine! I have a 12 year old brother that keeps her busy.
BDR 529 IL:	oh
BDR 529 IL:	any other siblings?
GatorCandie:	She's not very good about keeping in touch.
GatorCandie:	Yes, I have a 27 year old sister who works in Manhattan.
BDR 529 IL:	do you talk to her often?
GatorCandie:	She works for a company called UE Media. Yes we talk every other week or so.
BDR 529 IL:	give me one second... I just need some water
GatorCandie:	Your googling her, I know it...
BDR 529 IL:	no... haha
BDR 529 IL:	so... do you want to hear another secret?
GatorCandie:	Absolutely
BDR 529 IL:	I turned down a boat ride around Manhattan, a BBQ and sex with an ex-girlfriend to talk to you today
BDR 529 IL:	not that I would have gone to the ex's house anyway
GatorCandie:	wow, should I feel special?
BDR 529 IL:	so you dont really get credit for that one

BDR 529 IL:	you should... I really enjoyed talking to you today
BDR 529 IL:	I had no desire to do any of the other things
GatorCandie:	ok, then I do. Was it worth it?
BDR 529 IL:	of course it was
BDR 529 IL:	it still is
GatorCandie:	good, I'm glad.

A few minutes passed with no typing from her. Thus, the following tumbleweed question.

BDR 529 IL:	was that a tumbleweed that just went by?
GatorCandie:	haha, sorry. I'm processing information.
BDR 529 IL:	oh yeah? Like what?
GatorCandie:	you, pulling my hair
BDR 529 IL:	oh... you didn't even get to hear Operation "Two fantasies with One Stone" scenario
GatorCandie:	Please, I would love to!
BDR 529 IL:	you walk into your hotel room. You flip on a light, put your things down on the coffee table and start unbuttoning your blouse while you walk towards the dark bedroom. As you get about halfway into the room you see me sitting in a chair. You're very close to me and you freeze. Just as you are about to turn and run away I grab you. I turn you around, put my hand over your mouth and rip open your blouse. I throw you on the bed and yell at you to get on the floor. You look at me and I can see the fear in your eyes. You are frozen. I yell at you "GET ON THE FLOOR, NOW!" You climb off the bed and onto the floor. "Get

on your knees and face the wall". You can't see me but you know that I'm getting closer to you. You feel my hands gather your hair and pull it towards me so it arches your back. You feel my other hand slowly come up from your waistline, over your breast and up towards your neck. With one hand on your neck and one still holding your hair, I turn your head around and kiss your tear soaked cheek...

BDR 529 IL:	I could go on and on
GatorCandie:	wow
GatorCandie:	its perfect except the tears
BDR 529 IL:	it's a work in progress
GatorCandie:	minor detail though. I've never done that before.
BDR 529 IL:	neither have I
GatorCandie:	really??
GatorCandie:	must be something like it.
BDR 529 IL:	what have you never done?
BDR 529 IL:	maybe I'm misunderstanding you
GatorCandie:	knees and wall
BDR 529 IL:	no... I've never done that
GatorCandie:	have you ever been with a girl like me?
BDR 529 IL:	yes... I have but I've never gone to that level with it
GatorCandie:	I think I'd be game for that
BDR 529 IL:	so would I
GatorCandie:	eventually, I mean
GatorCandie:	You can thank Martin Klein for this.

GatorCandie: He was my first ever boyfriend.

BDR 529 IL: and that's what got you into it?

GatorCandie: yes. Sounds weird but true. And I'm so grateful, because no one I ever dated from that moment on ever had a proclivity for it right out of the gate.

BDR 529 IL: until…

GatorCandie: I've had a few confused boyfriends in my day

GatorCandie: So it would take like 6 months or more.

BDR 529 IL: 6 months??? Were you dating boyscouts?

GatorCandie: Well, I went slowly with the "different" stuff.

BDR 529 IL: so he was the most sexual guy you've ever been with?

GatorCandie: No, not sexual, just aggressive. Aggression doesnt actually come naturally to most guys. And it takes a lot of brains to pull that stuff off.

BDR 529 IL: who was the most sexual and why?

GatorCandie: Well, maybe Mark Lopez. He really got into it eventually and didn't really have a problem throwing me around and being really forward in public. We just experimented with alot of things I guess. We did something, actually, that I'd never do again. I actually found a limit.

BDR 529 IL: now I need details!!!

GatorCandie: Like what the something was?

BDR 529 IL: yes

GatorCandie: I'm warning you… it's off the deep end.

BDR 529 IL:	I consider myself officially warned
GatorCandie:	He cut me and sucked my blood out of the cut. It was cool, and ok but I decided I didn't really like it.
BDR 529 IL:	that's not so bad. Childish and silly, but not bad.
GatorCandie:	really.
GatorCandie:	what would be then?? haha
BDR 529 IL:	what did you mean by "forward in public"
GatorCandie:	I'm not sure.
GatorCandie:	I can't say.
GatorCandie:	I plead the 5th.
BDR 529 IL:	no dice
BDR 529 IL:	you must
GatorCandie:	why? Look, Ive spilled all these beans, and you want me to spill more?
BDR 529 IL:	you're at the point of no return
GatorCandie:	um, I guess he used to just turn me on in public, which I love, with things he said and such.
BDR 529 IL:	I get the feeling you're holding back on me
GatorCandie:	I mean, said whispering in my ear.
GatorCandie:	What might I be hiding?
BDR 529 IL:	you plead the 5th on ear whispering?
GatorCandie:	well, it was almost paralyzing for me.
BDR 529 IL:	oh... I could think of some things to whisper to you
BDR 529 IL:	O:-)

GatorCandie:	I wonder why there is no devil smiley
BDR 529 IL:	I know... but the angel works well for both situations
GatorCandie:	yes, as sarcastic irony
BDR 529 IL:	remember how we were talking about being turned on and no way to properly handle it?
GatorCandie:	...haha yeah
GatorCandie:	I guess there's lots of stuff I could tell you, but it almost seems unnatural to tell you like this.
BDR 529 IL:	try... tell me
GatorCandie:	I'm sorry to say this but my girlfriend is going to be on her high horse about how I should listen to her until the end of time when I give the quick report.
GatorCandie:	she knows all about me.
GatorCandie:	I told her about how I mentioned the van thing and she went on and on about what you should do. It was funny.
BDR 529 IL:	oh really? Did she have any good suggestions?
GatorCandie:	oh, I can't remember exactly.
GatorCandie:	ok, I have a sort of funny thing to tell.
BDR 529 IL:	ok good
GatorCandie:	...off topic
GatorCandie:	like I told you, you and diamonds winked at me at about the same time, but I responded to you first and you sent me an email first. Anyway, it turns out that amazingly enough you are both named Jesse. Weird huh? So Kris started referring to you as HER Jesse, because she was against this other guy. I

	haven't spoken with her today though so she doesnt know what a jerk he is. I will NEVER live it down. Ever.
GatorCandie:	Ever
BDR 529 IL:	haha... that is funny. And how dare he parade my name around with such illregard for its reputation
GatorCandie:	exactly. It's not like your name is Mike, right?
BDR 529 IL:	I know
BDR 529 IL:	that bastard
BDR 529 IL:	so do you realize that we have been talking since about 1:00
GatorCandie:	Yes, on and off.
GatorCandie:	As for the other stuff I've done, it's your turn to spill the beans.
BDR 529 IL:	MY TURN? All of those "beans" were in your bucket but I tipped them over
GatorCandie:	have you ever done anything outrageous?
BDR 529 IL:	hmmm... well, outside of what we already talked about, in varying degrees, I've done some other interesting stuff
BDR 529 IL:	I had sex in an elevator once
GatorCandie:	details!
BDR 529 IL:	I've been with 2 girls on 3 seperate occasions
GatorCandie:	lucky you
BDR 529 IL:	but dont get the wrong idea—I'm not a man-whore or anything
BDR 529 IL:	they were 3 very isolated incidents
GatorCandie:	I understand. I've been there.

BDR 529 IL: the elevator… It was in high school. The girl I was dating had a broken leg the year before, so they gave her the key to the elevator

GatorCandie: so you had plenty of time

BDR 529 IL: yes… it was great… you had to use the key to operate the thing, so once the doors were closed, we were pretty much safe all day because no one ever used the elevator

BDR 529 IL: in fact, I'm not exactly sure why we had it at all

BDR 529 IL: I suppose the elevator was installed so the school could be considered wheelchair compliant, but I never saw any handicapped people use it

GatorCandie: I had sex in a Victoria's Secret dressing room.

BDR 529 IL: oooohhhh…. did you end up buying what you were trying on??

GatorCandie: haha, I can't remember!

BDR 529 IL: I had a girlfriend for a while that used to like to pretend that she was a little girl. She would really get into the whole role-playing thing.

GatorCandie: Such as?

BDR 529 IL: this is a little off the deep end

BDR 529 IL: I dont know if you're ready

GatorCandie: ok, I don't have to like it. Diapers right?

BDR 529 IL: no!!!!

GatorCandie: k. go on.

BDR 529 IL: she would pretend she was a little girl. I would lie on the bed and she would jump on as if she were playing. She would drop her toy on my lap and ask "whats that" when she went to grab it. She would ask me things like "can I see it"? "Whats it for" "can I touch it"? "can I lick it"

BDR 529 IL: you get the picture

GatorCandie: Wow, you'll have no problems with me, haha

BDR 529 IL: reeeeally

GatorCandie: That's definitely in the deep end of the pool for me.

BDR 529 IL: yeah… she was out there, but she was pretty good at it

GatorCandie: I pretty much like to remain an adult during all of sex.

BDR 529 IL: haha… yeah, same here. I'd be lying if I didn't admit that it creaped me out a bit.

BDR 529 IL: that's the part that was a little weird

GatorCandie: Well, if you can maintain an erection during that, you're doing ok, haha. I'm not making fun of you by the way. Men are such good people.

BDR 529 IL: well, its not like she WAS a child. I mean… lol… she was in cute little lingerie and touching me… so… it was pretty easy to put the other stuff aside

GatorCandie: Well, dont ever do anything you don't absolutely love doing with me, because I like lots of stuff.

BDR 529 IL: I have a feeling that we would not have to ask each other what we like or dont like

GatorCandie: There's nothing I really have to have except occasional aggression and some Os

GatorCandie: But there's lots of other stuff I enjoy doing and I'm sure there's tons Ive never done.

BDR 529 IL: like what? What interests you?

GatorCandie: that I havent done?

BDR 529 IL: or that you have?

GatorCandie: a lot of it centers around words, I think

GatorCandie: words and the mood

BDR 529 IL: yeah

BDR 529 IL: or the location

GatorCandie: I like sweet, aggressive talk. I like being a good girl, a naughty girl, and a bad girl. I like being encouraged to come. I like being discouraged to come sometimes in the right context.

BDR 529 IL: mmm… I like the way you think

GatorCandie: really.

BDR 529 IL: so the first time we meet, I'll be sitting accross from you, having a drink, knowing full well what we would like to be doing to each other

BDR 529 IL: how badly you want me to pull your hair back

GatorCandie: er, you're bad.

GatorCandie: um, there is another taboo that I enjoy that you probably already guessed at, but I wont tell unless you hit it.

BDR 529 IL: I was just about to go into such naughty detail

BDR 529 IL: good thing you stopped me

GatorCandie: no, dont stop! haha

BDR 529 IL: is the other taboo something physical?

GatorCandie:	yes.
BDR 529 IL:	anal sex?
GatorCandie:	well, sure but that's not really taboo anymore is it?
GatorCandie:	wow, I sound awful!
BDR 529 IL:	no you dont
BDR 529 IL:	I'm drawing a blank… tell me!
GatorCandie:	no, I cant and I wont.
BDR 529 IL:	you must and will!
GatorCandie:	sorry, I cant.
BDR 529 IL:	do you like to be hit?
BDR 529 IL:	like… light slaps in the face?
BDR 529 IL:	the same "role playing" girlfriend used to like that
GatorCandie:	wow, it's been a long time since I've done that, but yes. I was thinking of something tamer, which is kind of funny.
BDR 529 IL:	oh you're killing me…. you MUT tell me
BDR 529 IL:	MUST
BDR 529 IL:	not you MUT
BDR 529 IL:	lol
GatorCandie:	oh, it's along the same lines
GatorCandie:	haha
GatorCandie:	but I can't tell you still.
BDR 529 IL:	why cant you?
GatorCandie:	I just cant, I guess. Sorry to be difficult but the words wont get typed and they wont get said.

BDR 529 IL:	do you like to be pee'd on?
BDR 529 IL:	kicked?
GatorCandie:	omg NO
BDR 529 IL:	thrown off bridges?
GatorCandie:	NO NO NO
GatorCandie:	haha
GatorCandie:	in front of trains, yes
BDR 529 IL:	haha
BDR 529 IL:	hot wax??
BDR 529 IL:	dripped on your nipples?
BDR 529 IL:	bitten?
GatorCandie:	uh, maybe… never tried that
GatorCandie:	bitten, sure
BDR 529 IL:	but thats not it?
GatorCandie:	right
GatorCandie:	theres a whole subgroup of people who do it!! it's so simple and thats why you havent thought of it
BDR 529 IL:	are you just trying to het me to say every dark and perverted thing I can think of?
GatorCandie:	haha, no!
BDR 529 IL:	dominatrix?
GatorCandie:	no, silly
GatorCandie:	what do you mean by that anyway?
BDR 529 IL:	you know… dress up in leather and torture or get tortured

GatorCandie:	like serious physical pain? No, not by a long shot.
BDR 529 IL:	I was never int the whole leather thing
GatorCandie:	it seems a bit contrived actually
BDR 529 IL:	yes, exactly
BDR 529 IL:	I have so many vivid dirty thoughts going through my head right now
BDR 529 IL:	if you could see what going on inside my head right now??? Wheeew
BDR 529 IL:	I just can't think of it
BDR 529 IL:	its prob staring me right in the face
BDR 529 IL:	give me some clues
GatorCandie:	well, if you're patient youll get a big one in a few.
BDR 529 IL:	hahaha
BDR 529 IL:	I should have known
GatorCandie:	maybe, I guess

She had a friend of hers send me an instant message telling me what she was talking about, which you will find out momentarily. And for the record, I don't find it to be particularly off the "deep end" as she would put it. Especially if you consider all of the crazy things that people are into these days.

GatorCandie:	haha
GatorCandie:	Is that off the deep end?
BDR 529 IL:	it was obvious… you were right. I was thinking too hard
BDR 529 IL:	No. I don't think so

GatorCandie:	are you still on the trolley so far? Anything weird? Do you like to be pee'd on?
BDR 529 IL:	hahahha… no, but you said taboo and I wouldn't consider spanking taboo

Clearly by now you know that she was talking about spanking; however, in the event that you didn't catch on, it's *spanking*—or more specifically, being spanked.

GatorCandie:	really? haha
BDR 529 IL:	oh… I'm ON the trolly
GatorCandie:	haha
BDR 529 IL:	so… have you been telling your girlfriend the whole twisted tale?
GatorCandie:	no not at all. Actually, it's kind of funny.
GatorCandie:	GatorCandie: BDR 529 IL
GatorCandie:	could you just IM him and tell him spanking for me?
OdddGirrrl71:	spanking for you??"
GatorCandie:	well, just say "spanking"
BDR 529 IL:	HAHAHAHA
GatorCandie:	OdddGirrrl71: you just want me to tell him "spanking"—one word!? haha
GatorCandie:	yep, thats it
GatorCandie:	then I will leave you alone my sweet
OdddGirrrl71:	done
BDR 529 IL:	That is too funny
GatorCandie:	GatorCandie: thank you :-)
OdddGirrrl71:	told ya he was Italian

GatorCandie:	yeah
GatorCandie:	Sorry I bothered you with that
OdddGirrrl71:	it's ok, I'm bleeding profusely too, which explains all
OdddGirrrl71:	no meds
GatorCandie:	period?
OdddGirrrl71:	no, single shot to the head
OdddGirrrl71:	period
BDR 529 IL:	haha
GatorCandie:	She's good.
BDR 529 IL:	I'm sorry. I'm still stuck with dirty thoughts in my head
GatorCandie:	I know the feeling. But it's still good to laugh, I guess. At the end of the day I am me.
BDR 529 IL:	you know what I never did today?
GatorCandie:	Went shopping. But you told me you don't listen so I never said anything.
BDR 529 IL:	you were right
BDR 529 IL:	so was I for that matter
GatorCandie:	See? I figured the reference to Chinese would spur you.
BDR 529 IL:	it should have
BDR 529 IL:	what a fool I've been
GatorCandie:	There was nothing else I could do, sweetie!
GatorCandie:	Are there any pizza places open in Nanuet still? Is Nanuet where you are?
BDR 529 IL:	hehehe… now you're spying on me!! Nanuet is a few towns over

GatorCandie:	No, actually I was NOT spying on you! I told you I wanted to send a text message to your phone... But I didn't know the carrier, so I reversed it and the "town" comes up, too.
BDR 529 IL:	oh... yes... there are some places open but it would have to be some sort of fast food and I really dont want that right now
GatorCandie:	what will you do?
BDR 529 IL:	well... I know what I won't do
BDR 529 IL:	eat something!
GatorCandie:	no, you must! At least order a pizza and you'll have it if you want it.
BDR 529 IL:	all the pizza places are closed
GatorCandie:	oh. bubble burst.
BDR 529 IL:	yes
BDR 529 IL:	I could go to the supermarket
BDR 529 IL:	but that sounds like a lot of work
GatorCandie:	yes, the supermarket. You have to eat.
BDR 529 IL:	I don't think I'll starve to death in my sleep, but maybe I'll go
GatorCandie:	you should go, but call me
BDR 529 IL:	and I should shave too
BDR 529 IL:	maybe I'll shave in the supermarket
GatorCandie:	perfect. You won't have to clean your sink
BDR 529 IL:	send Consuela over to clean my sink
GatorCandie:	Right away.
GatorCandie:	I would share her with you.
BDR 529 IL:	ugghh... I'm insulted

GatorCandie:	why?
BDR 529 IL:	Oh… I thought you wrote you wouldn't share her with me
GatorCandie:	No, I would!
BDR 529 IL:	perfect
GatorCandie:	imagine my surprise when you said you were insulted
BDR 529 IL:	i know, I'm sorry
GatorCandie:	Do you want to know how I learned how to masturbate? It's kinda funny.
BDR 529 IL:	yes, I do
GatorCandie:	My mom had a book about the female body, written for women, which I read when I was nine. One part of the book had very dry but explicit intructions on how to masturbate. That is how I learned, haha.
BDR 529 IL:	did it work at age 9?
GatorCandie:	of course
BDR 529 IL:	you had an orgasm at 9???
GatorCandie:	well, its not like I had SEX!
BDR 529 IL:	I know, I just didn't think you COULD have an orgasm at 9 years of age.
GatorCandie:	you didnt?
BDR 529 IL:	I don't think so?
BDR 529 IL:	hmmm… maybe I did
GatorCandie:	maybe I was 10 but no older than that, because that's when my mom gave me a preliminary talk.

BDR 529 IL:	you know, I can't remember when the first time I masturbated was
GatorCandie:	nocturnal thingies
BDR 529 IL:	oh I'm sure, but I mean full-blown masturbation
GatorCandie:	I guess maybe it seems wrong that I did, but I was reading pretty much anything I could get my hands on. That was just one of the many things I read.
BDR 529 IL:	hey, its very usefull information
GatorCandie:	Yeah, my first time having sex was kind of a cute debacle though.
BDR 529 IL:	do tell
GatorCandie:	Well, Mark wouldnt "fit"! So we went and asked his brother for advice. So when I lost my virginity, it was with me on top after careful planning, haha.
BDR 529 IL:	Hahaha—Good for Mark!
GatorCandie:	consensus
GatorCandie:	He said it would "provide me with more control"
BDR 529 IL:	its good you could come to some agreement
BDR 529 IL:	and I assume it worked out well for you
GatorCandie:	And I was already on birth control, because my mom told me that I should tell her if I thought I might start having sex, so I did. So we went to the family GP and he gave me a script.
GatorCandie:	Yeah, it worked out fine. I think I did it sort of right.

BDR 529 IL:	my frist girlfriend was also on birth control, even though she was a virgin
GatorCandie:	See, that's smart I think.
BDR 529 IL:	oh believe me, I thought it was great!!
BDR 529 IL:	once you get used to sex without condoms, it's hard to go back
GatorCandie:	Well nowadays it's different.
GatorCandie:	At least that's what I hear.
BDR 529 IL:	yes, I agree. I only meant if you're in a relationship
BDR 529 IL:	I was with my first girlfriend for 4 years, so I was used to not using a condom. The next girlfriend I had wasnt on the pill so condoms joined us in the bedroom, and it just wasn't the same. Would that be considered a threesome? Me, her and a condom?
GatorCandie:	No, not technically a threesome—it was a twosome, which is much better than a onesome. I can't take birth control any more though.
BDR 529 IL:	but you know, you adjust
BDR 529 IL:	oh no? Why not?
GatorCandie:	well, it messes too much with my hormones so at some point my ex and I just started using condoms and I was a much happier girl.
BDR 529 IL:	yeah. That's what I've heard from a lot of girls. That the birth control drives them crazy
GatorCandie:	I would get these non-characteristic mood swings

GatorCandie: Like I would cry for no reason. It was wrong, and my ex would just look at me and not know what to do. It was awful!

GatorCandie: So I finally said forget it after a year of trying different pills and whatnot, it just wasn't worth it.

GatorCandie: the tumbleweed is in your court

There were a few moments of silence, which were rare during our conversations. Because of this, everythime there was a little silence or a short break. One of us would question the other as to why, or, at least, make mention of it.

BDR 529 IL: sorry... my brother just called

BDR 529 IL: not at all. I wouldn't sacrifice my sanity

GatorCandie: hey, I like you. You're pretty cool.

GatorCandie: How's your brother? Older or younger?

BDR 529 IL: haha. Where did that come from?

BDR 529 IL: younger

BDR 529 IL: hes 25

Which made me about twenty-nine or thirty at the time that these conversations took place.

GatorCandie: I was just thinking about you while the tumbleweeds were blowing.

BDR 529 IL: aww

GatorCandie: Wow, if my sister didn't like guys your age...

BDR 529 IL: is she as cute as you?

GatorCandie: yes and no

BDR 529 IL: how so?

GatorCandie:	well, the bridge of her nose is slightly wider than mine but essentially she is very pretty. We had different dads but alot of it came from my mom.
GatorCandie:	Personality wise though, she's still a bit of a brat.
GatorCandie:	she actually has Italian genes, whereas I do not.
BDR 529 IL:	ahh... well... you are high on the cute scale, so its hard to compete. Italian genes? I have German slacks.
GatorCandie:	She and I never competed with each other for anything, which is kind of funny. We have gone out drinking with each other in the past couple of years and she's a riot.
GatorCandie:	thank you for the compliment ;-)
BDR 529 IL:	its good that you have fun together
GatorCandie:	Oh yeah, we don't see each other very often so its easy.
BDR 529 IL:	ok, should I go to this stupid supermarket? I'm feeling very lazy.
GatorCandie:	YES YES YES!!
GatorCandie:	My sis used to think I was such a "geek"— nose in the book and all
GatorCandie:	I love that word!
BDR 529 IL:	hehe
BDR 529 IL:	ok, but while I go, you have to get your webcam set up
BDR 529 IL:	is it a deal?
GatorCandie:	nope

BDR 529 IL:	hmm… you drive a hard bargain
GatorCandie:	that will not be happening tonight, kimosabe. It requires thought and stuff, and I'm way too high and tired to do that right now.
BDR 529 IL:	understood
BDR 529 IL:	:-(
GatorCandie:	going to the supermarket sounds much easier
BDR 529 IL:	ok, I'm gonna do it
GatorCandie:	do it!
BDR 529 IL:	you want me to do it?
BDR 529 IL:	is that what you want?
GatorCandie:	I want you to
GatorCandie:	that is what I want
BDR 529 IL:	haha, ok. Will you be here when I get back?
GatorCandie:	I might. How long will you be gone?
BDR 529 IL:	About 20 minutes or so. I'm just gonna get a salad or something
GatorCandie:	did you take your profile down?
BDR 529 IL:	no
GatorCandie:	well it is
GatorCandie:	down I mean
BDR 529 IL:	hmm… lemme look
GatorCandie:	and your wink is gone
BDR 529 IL:	Really???
GatorCandie:	I would not kid ya, handsome.
BDR 529 IL:	I'm looking at it now
GatorCandie:	oh well, supermarket!

BDR 529 IL:	You know something funny?? Ever since you appeared on my wink list, your mutual wink icon was askew—it was stuck off to the side
BDR 529 IL:	strange, huh?
GatorCandie:	maybe because you're askew?
BDR 529 IL:	possibly
GatorCandie:	yeah, your profile is gone, darlin
BDR 529 IL:	no. What screenname did you use?
BDR 529 IL:	search for it
BDR 529 IL:	7474505B
GatorCandie:	anyway, I'm going to… yep, that's it. it's still in my email list, but not my wink list
BDR 529 IL:	that's so weird
BDR 529 IL:	why??
BDR 529 IL:	I need answers!
GatorCandie:	rest my eyes for a minute. If Im not up, call me and wish me sweet dreams.
GatorCandie:	haha, yes, I agree.
BDR 529 IL:	ok. I'll be back

Upon my return from the supermarket, Pamela's autoresponder was on. She had fallen asleep, which is understandable, considering it was the middle of the night. I didn't get to talk to her until the next evening.

Auto response from GatorCandie:	If you're seeing this it means that I fell asleep. Call me if you want. Otherwise I'll talk to you tomorrow. Goodnight darlin'

THE FOURTH CONVERSATION

BDR 529 IL signed on at 8:20:59 PM.

GatorCandie:	hullo?
BDR 529 IL:	Uhhh… haaallo??
GatorCandie:	hey Tito where you been at?
BDR 529 IL:	You know… If I were a black dude, and I had a kid, I would name him Entre
BDR 529 IL:	Whataya think?
GatorCandie:	Yeah, and hopefully your wife would be named Chamaka Nice
BDR 529 IL:	Hardy Har. So how was your day?
BDR 529 IL:	Busy?
GatorCandie:	runnin' around
BDR 529 IL:	Give me a sec, I have to dissconnect from this T-Mobile thing and get on my laptop
GatorCandie:	be right back

BDR 529 IL signed off at 9:09:42 PM.

BDR 529 IL signed on at 9:11:04 PM.

BDR 529 IL:	ok. I'm back
BDR 529 IL:	you be front
GatorCandie:	brb again

A few minutes passed before she returned.

BDR 529 IL:	are–you–choking?

GatorCandie:	obviously you can't read the sign! You're supposed to perform some kind of German maneuver on me arent you?
BDR 529 IL:	I was trying, but I couldn't find you
BDR 529 IL:	I looked all over the apartment
BDR 529 IL:	but no choking Pamela to Heimlicht! I know that's not the right way to spell it but that's how I'd like to pronounce it.
GatorCandie:	sorry I was on the phone with one of my clients
BDR 529 IL:	oh I'm sorry
BDR 529 IL:	I didn't mean to bug you
GatorCandie:	I didn't expect it to take that long
BDR 529 IL:	no problem
GatorCandie:	ok, do you want to read something really funny?
BDR 529 IL:	why yes I do
BDR 529 IL:	was that it?
GatorCandie:	no, I just sent you an email that Kris just sent me. She's a nut.
BDR 529 IL:	ok… I'll go take a look

She sent me a Match profile that her girlfriend wanted to post, but for some reason, Match wouldn't allow it.

BDR 529 IL:	haha
GatorCandie:	I can't imagine why Match wouldn't let her post it
BDR 529 IL:	That's it? As-is? They wouldn't post that??
GatorCandie:	no

BDR 529 IL: no to what? Was it not as-is?

GatorCandie: It was as-is and no they wouldn't post it.

BDR 529 IL: hmmm... that's really weird

GatorCandie: I know, its MATCH that's weird, not us.

BDR 529 IL: yes, very odd indeed

BDR 529 IL: did she inquire as to why they wouldn't allow it?

GatorCandie: um, are you serious? It had nothing to do with her!!

GatorCandie: it was funny, especially the part about smashing someone in the head with it, but...

BDR 529 IL: I don't get it. What do you mean it had nothing to do with her?

GatorCandie: I mean, it's just a monologue.

BDR 529 IL: why would they not allow that?

GatorCandie: um, not sure I guess. Maybe the "smashing heads" part.

GatorCandie: But then again, they posted yours and there's nothing true in there either, as far as I know.

BDR 529 IL: I doubt it. I get to post about arranging lap dances for poor children on my profile

BDR 529 IL: it's a wacky world we live in, sista

GatorCandie: you don't seem like yourself today.

BDR 529 IL: I dont? What seems different about me?

BDR 529 IL: there has to be more to it. There's nothing there that is the least bit offensive.

GatorCandie: OdddGirrrl71: and why won't match publish that???? I wrote them back saying "you people are so annoying, what's the big freaking deal

	here????", but no response. I want answers!! ha
GatorCandie:	maybe the head smashing part
OdddGirrrl71:	??? I've seen worse on match
OdddGirrrl71:	it's not like I'm saying, "whoever I date from match will get their skull smashed by me" I hate censorship, ha
BDR 529 IL:	she should just try and re-post it. Another screener will get their hands on it and probably allow it.
GatorCandie:	Unsure. Maybe it's me. I just ended a pretty tense conversation and perhaps I'm the one who's "off".
BDR 529 IL:	tense? Good or bad?
GatorCandie:	OddGirl73: oh and under "favorite things" I wrote —- finding new ways to torture and bloody Julie Andrews... big deal
GatorCandie:	there it is
BDR 529 IL:	that was it... The word "torture" I bet. It probably threw up a red flag.
GatorCandie:	she's wacked, ha
BDR 529 IL:	haha
GatorCandie:	we wrote a bible when we were in high school
GatorCandie:	haha, I can't remember what we called it, but we referred to ourselves as quasi deities
BDR 529 IL:	so did I!
GatorCandie:	really??
BDR 529 IL:	Mine was more of a manifesto—"The church of the Gooey Death and Discount House of

Worship"—a religion that my friends and I made up.

BDR 529 IL: It was pretty long, but I remember that abortion proceedures were manditory for both men and women once a month

GatorCandie: yikes.

GatorCandie: our bible was just a bunch of rules & regulations and a few theories here and there.

GatorCandie: it was pretty long, though

BDR 529 IL: yeah, I started it when our highschool decided they were going to censor (rewrite all articles in our school paper) that dealt with obscene topics—or at least their idea of obscene.

GatorCandie: "Discount House"? No tythe?

BDR 529 IL: their idea of obscene was pretty twisted

BDR 529 IL: nope... all the salvation you want for $9.95

GatorCandie: pay one price. Cool, but I believe in a sliding scale.

BDR 529 IL: nah... we are all equally worthless

GatorCandie: yes, that is true. Calvinism rocks!

GatorCandie: I mean, if you have to be saved, it should cost you something

GatorCandie: I was the editor of our Lit Mag

BDR 529 IL: True anarchy... lol. I remember all the little punk rock kids that would wear anarchy patches on their jackets. They would be the first ones huddled up in their mother's arms if true anarchy existed in our society—although we could no longer really call it a society.

GatorCandie: I know. Crushed.

BDR 529 IL:	editor... that's cool! Was it fun?
GatorCandie:	Um, it was ok, but I wrote somewhat gorey fiction and I was the only one. There was alot of poetry to wade through and then I had to correct some pretty bad grammar.
GatorCandie:	I'm not a fan of poetry as a rule.
BDR 529 IL:	I've really been turned off to poetry, mostly because of the poets themselves.
BDR 529 IL:	everyone is a poet these days
BDR 529 IL:	every little highschool girl has her "poem" as their away message on whatever trendy device that they're currently using.
BDR 529 IL:	soooo "deep"
BDR 529 IL:	they must be sooo complex
BDR 529 IL:	NO ONE understands them
GatorCandie:	Exactly. I could write poetry too! But we need another poet like we need little needles pushed into our closed, sleeping eyes
BDR 529 IL:	wow
BDR 529 IL:	haha
GatorCandie:	what's wow?
BDR 529 IL:	"needles in closed sleeping eyes"—even worse than in open eyes! You never see it coming.
BDR 529 IL:	that's serious
GatorCandie:	I know, you would keep trying to open them but you'd have to take the needles out first
GatorCandie:	sorry for the graphics
BDR 529 IL:	Don't be.
GatorCandie:	I guess it was kinda gross

BDR 529 IL:	yeah, but in a good way
GatorCandie:	I could write a poem about that actually
GatorCandie:	I would entitle it "Poetry Needles"
BDR 529 IL:	hehehe
BDR 529 IL:	do it!
BDR 529 IL:	thats one thing I never got over… I can't stand to see real gore on TV. It makes me so sick
GatorCandie:	Me too. I really don't like horror movies
BDR 529 IL:	man… what's his name… oh, Bukowski… That was one poet I could deal with.
BDR 529 IL:	horror movies I can take. It's gore that I can't stand. Like, real gore (or Al Gore). Fake movie gore is what it is and doesn't bother me but…
BDR 529 IL:	but real actual gore
BDR 529 IL:	yuck
BDR 529 IL:	I'll never understand how people watch movies like Faces of Death
BDR 529 IL:	I wouldn't make it through 5 minutes of one of those movies
BDR 529 IL:	as for Bukowski, I like him 'cause he wasnt really a poet. He was just an angry, drunk, horney pervert who happened to have a way with words.
GatorCandie:	Oh, gotcha. Yeah, I know. I watched a movie when I was a kid, I'll never forget it. By kid I mean like 15 years old. Der Todisking or something

GatorCandie: I don't know Bukowski. Obviously I've heard of him and probably read something somewhere, but I'm pretty much anti-poem

BDR 529 IL: yes. I totally agree

GatorCandie: It had a rotting corpse timelapsed every so often, just in different places in the movie

BDR 529 IL: you're a girl. At least you never had to sit through countless hours of listening to you girlfriend's poetry. And in highschool, EVERY girl had tons of poems to share

BDR 529 IL: Your "needles in the eyes" bit is more appealing than listening to some of this so-called poetry.

GatorCandie: Really? My friend and I wrote tons of stuff, but never really poetry. Aimless rambles really.

BDR 529 IL: so do YOU want to hear a rather strange story??

GatorCandie: absolutely!

BDR 529 IL: ok

BDR 529 IL: its long but at least it's pointless so stop me when you've had enough

BDR 529 IL: a have a friend named Andrew

BDR 529 IL: I've known him since I was about 12 and he is still one of my closest friends

BDR 529 IL: we have always been in bands together—hung out pretty much every night with our other friends…

BDR 529 IL: you know, as close as friends can get pretty much.

BDR 529 IL: Andrew has always been a little off, but that's what I like about him

BDR 529 IL:	so anyway
BDR 529 IL:	a few years ago, he moved to Colorado with a bunch of other guys that I know and he lived out there for a while
BDR 529 IL:	and decided that he was going to come out of the closet and tell everyone that he was gay
GatorCandie:	k
BDR 529 IL:	we all kind of knew it—but he told us officially
BDR 529 IL:	so cool… Andrews' gay
BDR 529 IL:	no problem
GatorCandie:	right
BDR 529 IL:	another year or so went by
BDR 529 IL:	and he started acting strange
BDR 529 IL:	I don't think that he ever told his family by the way
GatorCandie:	uh oh
BDR 529 IL:	just his close friends
BDR 529 IL:	he was getting depressed all the time
BDR 529 IL:	on and off Zoloft and whatever other psychology drugs they were putting him on
BDR 529 IL:	geting worse and worse until he was totally manic
GatorCandie:	right
BDR 529 IL:	he was a completely different person—this is about 3 months ago
BDR 529 IL:	he started doing crazy things
GatorCandie:	such as

BDR 529 IL:	he bought two brand new cars in the same day
BDR 529 IL:	two of the EXACT same car if I remember correctly
GatorCandie:	wow
BDR 529 IL:	the next day he bought another car—a brand new Honda
BDR 529 IL:	no job
BDR 529 IL:	no money
BDR 529 IL:	just credit
GatorCandie:	good credit I guess
BDR 529 IL:	yes, excellent credit
BDR 529 IL:	he took out a $20,000 personal loan and started buying all this crap
BDR 529 IL:	he had 2 cell phones
GatorCandie:	oh no
BDR 529 IL:	anyway, you get the picture
BDR 529 IL:	so…
BDR 529 IL:	he's now totally off the deep end
BDR 529 IL:	this is about 2 weeks ago
GatorCandie:	right
BDR 529 IL:	he took an apartment
BDR 529 IL:	decided to sell two of the cars and get a job
BDR 529 IL:	I thought… ok, back to normal
GatorCandie:	good
BDR 529 IL:	so…
BDR 529 IL:	a week ago, he drove his car to the airort

BDR 529 IL:	drove up to departing flights terminal
BDR 529 IL:	LEFT his car running right outside the door to JFK
BDR 529 IL:	walked in
BDR 529 IL:	bought a first class ticket to Denver.
BDR 529 IL:	so now he's in Denver
BDR 529 IL:	they impounded the car of course
GatorCandie:	wow
BDR 529 IL:	one of the other cars is in an airport parking lot in Boston for some reason
BDR 529 IL:	and the third car is somewhere in NYC. Whereabouts unknown.
GatorCandie:	how do you know this?
BDR 529 IL:	he told me this on the phone the other day
BDR 529 IL:	when I was in Vermont, he called me from Denver
BDR 529 IL:	I didn't know about the car at the door to JFK though.
BDR 529 IL:	so… remember my cop friend that I was telling you about the other day?
GatorCandie:	yes
BDR 529 IL:	he is really good friends with Andrew also
BDR 529 IL:	he got a call from a doctor and a detecive in Denver
BDR 529 IL:	Andrew started following some girl around the street
GatorCandie:	oh no

BDR 529 IL:	yelling "OK dad, is this what you want?? I'm gonna fuck this girl". This is the information that I got from my cop friend but to me, it totally sounds nothing like Andrew.
BDR 529 IL:	so of course, she calls the cops
GatorCandie:	shit
BDR 529 IL:	they arrestd him and sent him to a mental hospital to be held for 90 days
BDR 529 IL:	that's the story
GatorCandie:	good, maybe they'll find out what's really wrong and fix him up
BDR 529 IL:	crazy... this guy was TOTALLY normal and then POW... off the deep end.
GatorCandie:	I'm sorry.
BDR 529 IL:	so am I. I'm actually amazed
BDR 529 IL:	I wouldnt have believed it if I didn't see it first hand. It's really sad and I wish I could help him. This is one of the best people on earth. Andrew is so smart, quick-witted—a genuinely a nice guy. He just snapped.
GatorCandie:	well, there's obviously something very wrong
BDR 529 IL:	ya think??
GatorCandie:	yeah, but I mean like neurological or something
BDR 529 IL:	yes... I think it was the mixing of "psychology drugs", alcohol and whatever else he was putting in his body for months and months had something to do with it.
GatorCandie:	oh, yeah drugs can complicate things
GatorCandie:	what a bummer

GatorCandie:	Can he accept visitors?
BDR 529 IL:	you want therapy? Buy a puppy, but stay AWAY from all that Zoloft, Paxil, Prosak, blah blah blah
BDR 529 IL:	nope... no visitors except family
BDR 529 IL:	and to be honest, I wouldn't know what to say or do even if I could see him. And he's way the hell in Denver.
GatorCandie:	really?
BDR 529 IL:	there is a lot of other stuff I'm leaving out
BDR 529 IL:	just weird shit that went on for months
GatorCandie:	oh, personal type stuff?
BDR 529 IL:	no, just stuf I wouldn't bore you with
GatorCandie:	3am phone calls?
BDR 529 IL:	tons... showing up crying at my door countless times—which I can deal with. I mean, he's my best friend and that's what I'm here for but...
BDR 529 IL:	lying about stuff. Lying about what other people said. Totally uncharacteristic for him. He may be nuts but he's never been a liar.
GatorCandie:	got it
GatorCandie:	wow, I could see why his hospitalization might be a relief
BDR 529 IL:	90 days in the klink under a doctor's supervision is the best thing for him now, I think. I hope.
BDR 529 IL:	yes... he would talk to strangers... he asked a mother wheeling her baby in a cariage if he could take pictures of them and use them in

	his book, but in a very weird, hyped up, "I'm crazy" kind of way
GatorCandie:	You didn't sleep with him, did you? haha
BDR 529 IL:	hahahahaha
BDR 529 IL:	what do you think?
GatorCandie:	sorry, it seemed funny at the time
GatorCandie:	am I SO NOT FUNNY right now??
BDR 529 IL:	nah. Believe me, I have a sense of humor about it at this point. And the normal Andrew would have a sense of humor about it as well. He's not himself; he's someone else.
BDR 529 IL:	at least I know he's not going to get himself killed while he's in the hospital
BDR 529 IL:	which was a real threat for a while. Andrew is not exactly a fighter. Hes 6'4 and about 150 lbs soaking wet
GatorCandie:	that sucks though. I can't imagine the pain of seeing your friend spiralling then finally being so fed up with it that you don't even want to see him
GatorCandie:	wow
BDR 529 IL:	I mean, I do want to see him, but he is not Andrew right now. He is a completely different person and I don't know how to help him.
BDR 529 IL:	anyway, wasn't that a delightful story??
GatorCandie:	He probably is in a chemical way
GatorCandie:	Not a delightful one, but one that would be on MY mind pretty often if it were close to me.

BDR 529 IL:	I wouldn't tell just anyone this. In fact, I've been extremely quiet about it
GatorCandie:	I can imagine.
GatorCandie:	I would probably just carry it around with me, too
BDR 529 IL:	oh well… moving on
GatorCandie:	on up? to the east side?
GatorCandie:	To a deeeluxe apartment in the sky?
BDR 529 IL:	hahha…. we cover that song
GatorCandie:	cool!
GatorCandie:	Click this link to see a cool item for sale on eBay.
GatorCandie:	Good for a quick chuckle.
BDR 529 IL:	haha
BDR 529 IL:	"WORDS CAN'T DESCRIBE THE LEVEL OF AWESOMENESS THIS ITEM ENTAILS"
BDR 529 IL:	lol
GatorCandie:	haha, it's pretty good
GatorCandie:	stupid but good
GatorCandie:	I "sold" spam jelly on eBay as a lark once. I said you could "use it to shine your shoes"
BDR 529 IL:	haha
GatorCandie:	Quality, Grade AA–2 cups!
BDR 529 IL:	mmm mmm good
GatorCandie:	It had a variety of uses. Such as "disguise your underarm odors"
BDR 529 IL:	do you use eBay a lot?

GatorCandie:	Yes, I do.
GatorCandie:	Buy 'n Sell
BDR 529 IL:	anything special?
BDR 529 IL:	let's see what you've got for sale… maybe I'll buy something
GatorCandie:	I ended up with an extra Blackberry from Nextel so I swapped the broken one out for a new one and sold it within 4 hours for $329.00
GatorCandie:	I didn't need it because I have extra phones lying around everywhere already
BDR 529 IL:	do you have anything for sale now?
GatorCandie:	no
GatorCandie:	I mostly buy now
BDR 529 IL:	what are you bidding on now?
GatorCandie:	nothing at the moment, but I bought a DVD version of the movie "Clue" recently
BDR 529 IL:	⅄
BDR 529 IL:	Elaine: "fake, fake, fake, fake"
BDR 529 IL:	hehe… Seinfeld reference
GatorCandie:	I've been using my friend's to assist in feedback but you could probably see my ME page. I used to sell to make money a couple of years ago. It's so easy and people will buy anything. I'm not an accumulator.
BDR 529 IL:	send me a link
GatorCandie:	I haven't looked at it or used it in a long time
BDR 529 IL:	do you watch Seinfeld?
GatorCandie:	never :-\

BDR 529 IL: really???

GatorCandie: I don't watch TV

BDR 529 IL: Seinfeld and The Simpsons—gotta have it

BDR 529 IL: like a drug

GatorCandie: really? I don't even really have a TV

BDR 529 IL: "even really"?

BDR 529 IL: I ask everyone who tells me that they don't watch TV if I can have theirs.

GatorCandie: Well my ex kept pretty much everything. I figured I'd "clean slate" it.

BDR 529 IL: ahh, good move. Makes sense.

GatorCandie: You can have it. It's the TV my mom bought me for my 16th birthday that I never watch because I don't get channels at my place and I never bothered getting a dish here.

GatorCandie: But dont worry, my life is full.

GatorCandie: I just told him to keep everything.

BDR 529 IL: easiest way

GatorCandie: Yeah, and I felt bad that I disrupted his life so completely.

GatorCandie: He was very distraught for a while.

BDR 529 IL: time heals all wounds

BDR 529 IL: except decapitation… time won't heal that

GatorCandie: Thats true. There's some permanency there.

BDR 529 IL: I need some water

BDR 529 IL: brb

BDR 529 IL: ok

BDR 529 IL: much better

GatorCandie:	feeling more hydrated?
BDR 529 IL:	not yet… but soon. It takes a few minutes to kick in
GatorCandie:	I just was thinking about onions
GatorCandie:	because with me, it's always about the onions
BDR 529 IL:	yes, yes it is.
GatorCandie:	this time they were dehydrated
BDR 529 IL:	were you kind enough to re-hydrate them?
BDR 529 IL:	do you re-hydrate?
BDR 529 IL:	or just hydrate?
GatorCandie:	I guess, re-hydrate? Symantics?
BDR 529 IL:	yes please
GatorCandie:	coffee, tea or symantics?
GatorCandie:	Can I take yer order hun?
BDR 529 IL:	french toast, coffee light no suger and hold the symantics
GatorCandie:	haha, it's your dime
GatorCandie:	I take my coffee light, no sugar too.
BDR 529 IL:	you know, I just might order that tomorrow
BDR 529 IL:	light with half & half?
GatorCandie:	no, milk if I can get it. Otherwise half & half
BDR 529 IL:	I like half & half 'cause you can use less so your coffee stays hotter longer
BDR 529 IL:	so there
GatorCandie:	half & half is really big up here and I don't remember it being that way downstate

BDR 529 IL:	haha... big "up here". I'm fairly certain that half & half has made its way to refridgerators throughout the Nation.
BDR 529 IL:	everyone loves half & half. It's an Anerican institution.
GatorCandie:	k, I just remember those little milk pitchers in the diners. They don't really have them like that here.
BDR 529 IL:	So you're telling me that diners in Buffalo don't have little milk pitchers on the tables? You do get those little single serving half & half things though, right?
GatorCandie:	yes, exactly. I have to ask for milk and it comes in an orange juice glass.
GatorCandie:	I don't request it very much anymore; because of the way I like my eggs.
BDR 529 IL:	ummm... okaaaaay.
GatorCandie:	The eggs are enough for anyone to take and I choose my battles carefully
BDR 529 IL:	I'm out in space today
GatorCandie:	Yeah, everything okey dokey?
BDR 529 IL:	yes, all is well. Thank you for asking. Please elaborate on the eggs.
GatorCandie:	I'm so particular about my eggs that I developed a reputation a very long time ago. Once, Kris and I and some guys (her pre-lesbian days) went to a diner...
GatorCandie:	we all ordered. When our food came she got all dramatic and said, "OH MY GOD..."

GatorCandie:	"I can't believe it!!" (wringing her hands, fingers to the temples)
GatorCandie:	and we're all like, "what's wrong??"
GatorCandie:	and she says, "My Eggs…"
GatorCandie:	"THEY'RE PERFECT!!"
BDR 529 IL:	hahahaa
GatorCandie:	of course, I did not laugh.
GatorCandie:	I cant believe we're still friends, dammit
BDR 529 IL:	All of my friends are old friends too
GatorCandie:	I used to have this long pink trench coat in High School. She said that my personality changed whenever I wore it and she started calling it "the pink possession"
GatorCandie:	I just said it made me look hot and she was jealous
BDR 529 IL:	haha. I'm sure you looked lovely in it.
GatorCandie:	So I bought one last season and told her
BDR 529 IL:	I had a trench coat that I wore everyday too. Not pink however. Mine was black with little bronze safety pins that I put around the bottom and the collar
BDR 529 IL:	Trying to be a little punk rocker
GatorCandie:	Were you?
BDR 529 IL:	yep, or at least as punk rock as a middle-class suburban high school kid can get. Me and about 5 other people in our school were the only ones into punk rock. In those days, it was all about Bon Jovi, big hair, bands like Poison… it made me ill.

BDR 529 IL: My friends and I had a terrible but fun punk rock band called "The Condemned"

GatorCandie: I was always odd out because I was "different" but got along with almost everyone. I was in AP classes with all the geeks and normal classes with everyone else.

GatorCandie: haha The Condemned is a good name

BDR 529 IL: yeah, lol. We thought so… we were just god-awful but we put on a damn good show. Smashing guitars whenever possible. Since we were just a bunch of broke kids, we had this one crappy guitar that we would smash over and over. We would losen the screws that attached the neck to the body so it could be easily smashed, re-assembled and smashed again at a later date.

GatorCandie: HAHA. That's too funny. I only kept a few true friends. I wasn't a "joiner"

BDR 529 IL: wanna see a picture of Dave; my long time, once punk rock friend who now lives completely off the grid on 40 acres in Vermont.

GatorCandie: haha, yeah

BDR 529 IL wants to directly connect.

BDR 529 IL is now directly connected.

I sent the picture of Dave. Dave was, and still is, quite a character. He's probably one of the smartest people that I know. Dave along with Andrew, my other long-time friend that I mentioned earlier. Dave has a Ph.D and all kinds of other degrees, he has been published several times yet barely works. He lives up in the woods with his family in Vermont. They bought the proprerty outright so he only has to pay property taxes. They generate their own electricity, pump their own water—they are truly off the grid. I've spent a few weekends up there with him, and it's rough to live that way, especially if you're not used to it. One quickly realizes how much we take for granted when thrown into a situation where a simple glass of clean water is a chore to produce.

GatorCandie: We had bunches of cliques in high school

GatorCandie: wow, what can I say about this elixer?

BDR 529 IL: you wouldn't believe it by looking at him, but he has a Ph.D

GatorCandie: He looks like he would be handsome under different circumstances

BDR 529 IL: yeah, he's a good lookin' guy I guess

BDR 529 IL: when he's not filthy

GatorCandie: right, I'm sure theres a story. I hope there's a story

BDR 529 IL: oh tons. Dave and I got into more trouble than anyone should

BDR 529 IL: but those stories are for another time

BDR 529 IL: I've told too many stories today already

GatorCandie: tired?

BDR 529 IL: a little, but no big deal

BDR 529 IL: I couldn't fall asleep now anyway

GatorCandie: Me at 16, haha

She sent me a picture of her from her early high school days. She was simply beautiful, and as much as I wanted to hold back and say nothing, the words slipped out of my mouth, down my arms, onto my finders and typed the words,

BDR 529 IL:	wow, you're beautiful
GatorCandie:	haha, thanks. I never knew where I got all those teeth
BDR 529 IL:	so pretty. I could just eat you up!
GatorCandie:	I'm sure I had bite marks all over my arms actually, haha
BDR 529 IL:	at 16? Tsk, tsk
GatorCandie:	Oh well, I was all sunshine and light anyway.
BDR 529 IL:	↲
BDR 529 IL:	Here's a picture of my brother and I

I sent her a picture of my brother and I all decked out in a big beautiful suite in Atlantic City. Back in those days, I was making a really good living and I would pay for these ridiculous suites, limo rides back and forth to Atlantic City, a couple of thousand bucks each for my brother and I. In retrospect, had I saved or invested even a fraction of the money that I threw away on stuff like that, I wouldn't be as broke as I am today. Then I think about all the stories that came along with those fun times, all of the crazy things that we did. Sometimes, I start to tell someone one of the crazy stories from back in the day and I stop myself. I stop myself because it sounds like I'm lying, like I'm making it up. So rather than to potentially look like a liar, I just don't tell the stories.

GatorCandie:	Wow there's a lot of gold in that picture, with two black t-shirts
BDR 529 IL:	It's a suite in Atlantic City. What's a casino without gaudy gold furniture?
GatorCandie:	very true. I have a secret though…
GatorCandie:	I have never been in a casino, ever.
BDR 529 IL:	oh my, really?

GatorCandie:	When I went to the Montreal F1 race, I walked through the casino, to get to the other side—kind of like a chicken.
BDR 529 IL:	hardy-har. But seriously, you've never been to a casino?
GatorCandie:	yep, no casinos. I've just never gone to one I guess.
BDR 529 IL:	It's not the gambling I like, it's the ridiculous suites, overdone buffets, and the general excess that is purely American
GatorCandie:	It's funny how I can know so much about such a variety of things but when it comes to simple stuff like Seinfeld and Casinos, no dice
BDR 529 IL:	we should have it on our flag
GatorCandie:	purely Italian
BDR 529 IL:	Italian??? Obviously you haven't been to a casino
BDR 529 IL:	Its mostly Asian businessmen and Korean women
GatorCandie:	The gaudiness, I mean
GatorCandie:	Don't get me wrong; my great grandma had plastic covering everything
BDR 529 IL:	actually, that particular casino is The Borgata. Its one of the really nice ones, despite the gold

I sent her some more pictures of the room and such.

GatorCandie:	I can see how it would be a hoot
BDR 529 IL:	me, 3am, big bathroom, bigger whirlpool.

SEVENTY THOUSAND WORDS BETWEEN STRANGERS

GatorCandie: wow you're cute

BDR 529 IL: awww thanks

GatorCandie: I love nice hotel rooms.

BDR 529 IL: me too. I don't know why

GatorCandie: Because you get to mess 'em up!!

BDR 529 IL: did I show you the pictures of The W Hotel from last weekend?

GatorCandie: nope

BDR 529 IL: I think I told you about it

GatorCandie: uh, I dont think so

BDR 529 IL: My friend Sal and I rented a suite at The W

BDR 529 IL: he slept in my bed!

GatorCandie: with you?

BDR 529 IL: haha, yes. I went to sleep first and when I woke up, I found a big, drunken Sal passed out at the other end of the bed

I sent some more pictures to her from The W hotel.

BDR 529 IL: this size room is a big deal for NYC

GatorCandie: wow, great pillows

BDR 529 IL: Sal in my bed—after my initial shock, I decided to take a picture.

GatorCandie: ack

GatorCandie: that's alot of plaid to wake up to

Sal was wearing his plaid pajama bottoms in the picture.

BDR 529 IL: Here's another picture of Sal, when he's not half naked in my bed, haha.

GatorCandie:	the other part of the picture! And a big gold neck chain!
GatorCandie:	great picture
BDR 529 IL:	hehehe. That's my Sally boy!!
GatorCandie:	looks like a good guy
BDR 529 IL:	oh he is. He's like a brother to me.
BDR 529 IL:	yes, Sal is the best
BDR 529 IL:	one of my best friends
BDR 529 IL:	the type of guy that would do anything for you
GatorCandie:	somehow, he looks it
GatorCandie:	he's got nice eyes
BDR 529 IL:	you want em? 10 bucks and they're yours.
BDR 529 IL:	per eye of course
GatorCandie:	haha, I was wondering about that, with his coloring and all
BDR 529 IL:	no that was a joke. They're natural. I was just kidding
GatorCandie:	I thought you were going back into surgery for a minute
GatorCandie:	because I do have my own
BDR 529 IL:	ok, I've got a great Sal story
GatorCandie:	do tell
BDR 529 IL:	as you can see, Sal is very …well, stereotypical Italian "ay… ova here… forgetaboudit" type of guy
BDR 529 IL:	so, one day, we are out on my boat…
BDR 529 IL:	a bunch of us and Sal

BDR 529 IL: Sal decides that he wants to jump off the boat and go swimming

BDR 529 IL: so he does. Meanwhile, we slowly start to drift away from him, but I know he's a good swimmer and I have my eye on him the whole time.

BDR 529 IL: he's fine and we are now about 1,000 feet away from him

BDR 529 IL: this is the middle of the Hudson River mind you—a major waterway

BDR 529 IL: so anyway…

BDR 529 IL: Sal's bobbing around in the water—gold chain, sunglasses and all

BDR 529 IL: and another boat pulls up

BDR 529 IL: they get close and ask, "Are you ok"?

BDR 529 IL: Sal replies, "its ok, Mo. I'm waitin' for someone. Thanks though"

GatorCandie: haha

BDR 529 IL: haha—"waiting for someone"… like he was standing on a street corner

BDR 529 IL: meanwhile, to anyone else, it looks like he's stranded, lost, or in some kind of trouble

GatorCandie: I love people like that—everything's fine

BDR 529 IL: hehe

BDR 529 IL: he might as well have been smoking a cigarette. In fact, there's a good chance that he was smoking a cigarette.

GatorCandie: I find that I really calm down when everybody else is all flustered.

GatorCandie:	otherwise, I'm normal
BDR 529 IL:	I typically don't get too flustered, regardless of the situation.
BDR 529 IL:	I usually remain fairly collected
GatorCandie:	Like when someone spills something all over the place. I get calm
BDR 529 IL:	wow, there were the exact same number of characters in those last two sentences
GatorCandie:	how would you know that??
BDR 529 IL:	the way hey line up
GatorCandie:	oh, let's test
BDR 529 IL:	I already counted
GatorCandie:	FINE
BDR 529 IL:	hehehe
GatorCandie:	and I was going to throw it in word
BDR 529 IL:	there are 14 steps to my apartment
BDR 529 IL:	it's 28 steps to my parent's front door
BDR 529 IL:	I count. I think most drummers do
BDR 529 IL:	It's weird, when someone knocks on the door, I dont hear "knock, knock, knock, knock, knock"
BDR 529 IL:	I see the number 5
GatorCandie:	wow. I'm speechless again
GatorCandie:	well, I can see that actually because I do that with telephone rings
BDR 529 IL:	and I'm preeeetttyy sure it's not OCD
GatorCandie:	yeah, you can be sure all you want

BDR 529 IL: brb, I have to wash my hands again. I wash them every 17 minutes

BDR 529 IL: hehe—just kidding

GatorCandie: that's a relief…

GatorCandie: A friend of mine has OCD, diagnosis and all. Her thing is cleaning.

GatorCandie: So we can be throwing back Jagermeister shots until 3am and suddenly she'll get up and start spraying down the counters

BDR 529 IL: oh really? Send her over

GatorCandie: I already tried that; it's only HER house, not other peoples

BDR 529 IL: hmmmm, there has got to be a way around that

GatorCandie: yeah, pregnancy

GatorCandie: it fixed her right up

GatorCandie: now she's just neurotic about other stuff

BDR 529 IL: is the kid's skin all red from the scrubbing?

GatorCandie: she's still pregnant. We shall see.

GatorCandie: She finally settled on a normal name too, thankfully

BDR 529 IL: what name?

GatorCandie: Kaitlin Rebecca

BDR 529 IL: pretty

GatorCandie: Yes and I'm grateful.

BDR 529 IL: hey, did you set up your webcam as promissed?

GatorCandie: no, I did not

BDR 529 IL: bad girl

BDR 529 IL: no TV for a week!

BDR 529 IL: which shouldn't be hard for you

GatorCandie: exactly, it's too easy

GatorCandie: but the good part is, I totally avoided the Olympics

BDR 529 IL: thank God

GatorCandie: not on NPR though, and the Republican Convention is coming, ugh

BDR 529 IL: yes I know. The City will be a mess

GatorCandie: I know, my sister is freaking

GatorCandie: she has no interest in the political process either, which makes it harder for her I think.

BDR 529 IL: a few days and it will all be over

GatorCandie: Well, its not like one would ever turn up in Buffalo, so I can't comment too much, but I think it would excite me either way.

BDR 529 IL: a Republican Convention would excite you?

GatorCandie: Democrats or Republicans, I mean

GatorCandie: Well sure, I could find them in the bars and chat 'em up, then make fun of them.

GatorCandie: Democrats, too. I think there's something about people who "rally" like that, that's um… a little off

BDR 529 IL: yeah, people who know where they stand before they hear the issue. Sillyness

BDR 529 IL: "I'm Consertive". "I'm a liberal". Jesus, just be a person with an opinion. How can someone be so blindly partisan and NEVER go against their party? It just doesn't make sense.

GatorCandie:	why aren't we talking about sex?
BDR 529 IL:	haha. We're not???
GatorCandie:	I know, it drives me crazy that my sister has NO opinions.
BDR 529 IL:	at least she's honest about not being interested
GatorCandie:	She would be one of those beautiful girls with "no brains" in a way. I love her though.
GatorCandie:	Don't get me wrong; she's smart in her own way.
BDR 529 IL:	be right back
BDR 529 IL:	back
GatorCandie:	front
BDR 529 IL:	side-to-side
GatorCandie:	I've got these two songs in my head, jockeying.
BDR 529 IL:	and they are?
GatorCandie:	I wish they would just go away
GatorCandie:	"This or That" by Black Sheep and "Scenario" by A Tribe Called Quest
BDR 529 IL:	hahaha
GatorCandie:	and when I wrote "front" they came barreling back into the foreground
BDR 529 IL:	I was listening to the Black Sheep the other day
GatorCandie:	Strobelight Honey
BDR 529 IL:	"wanna good time, only give em what they want"
BDR 529 IL:	"can I hear a hey"
GatorCandie:	"can I hear a hey"

BDR 529 IL:	"hey"
GatorCandie:	"can I get a yo"
BDR 529 IL:	"yo"
GatorCandie:	this darlin' is creative
BDR 529 IL:	Black Sheep something… errr "native"?
GatorCandie:	"can't be violated or even desepticated"
BDR 529 IL:	"can't be violated or even dece
BDR 529 IL:	damn
BDR 529 IL:	too quick
GatorCandie:	"I got brothers in the jungle"
GatorCandie:	cousins on a quest
BDR 529 IL:	cousins on a quest
GatorCandie:	haha
BDR 529 IL:	damn, that's 2 for you
GatorCandie:	sorry
BDR 529 IL:	you win
GatorCandie:	you can HAVE the next line
BDR 529 IL:	I don't need your pity
GatorCandie:	nah, I just never knew the words to the next line
BDR 529 IL:	AHH HAAAA!
GatorCandie:	sumpin sumpin sumpin in the forest may they rest
BDR 529 IL:	ha. "Mr. Long—the 9 point 5'er"
GatorCandie:	"Dres Black Sheep slam now"

BDR 529 IL:	"cause he's the suger dick. The suger dick daddy, Mr. long, of the Black Sheep here to point out whats wrong"
BDR 529 IL:	"with MC's, like these—poppin that buuuulllshit, please."
GatorCandie:	you go my brotha
BDR 529 IL:	haha, great. Thanks a lot. Misery wants company, ay?
BDR 529 IL:	now we BOTH have it stuck in our heads
GatorCandie:	"then of course, the choice is yours"
GatorCandie:	"engine engine numba nine"
GatorCandie:	"on the NY transit line"
BDR 529 IL:	well I'm not having it. Nothing a little Perry Como's "Magic Moments" won't cure
GatorCandie:	haha
GatorCandie:	or tiny bubbles
GatorCandie:	or worse yet
BDR 529 IL:	⌧ whisteling… "maaaaa-gic, mooooo-ments"
GatorCandie:	"Free Bird"
GatorCandie:	Scenario is even worse!
BDR 529 IL:	I know
GatorCandie:	"bust a nut inside ya eye to show you where I come from. I'm vexed fumin I've had it up to here"
BDR 529 IL:	"how dat sound? Oooooooohhh"
GatorCandie:	"head for the border go get a taco"
GatorCandie:	"sit back relax and let yourself go, don't sweat what ya heard but act like ya know"

GatorCandie:	haha
GatorCandie:	"I gotta go, I gotta go, I gotta go"
BDR 529 IL:	"powerful impact—boooom from the canon"
BDR 529 IL:	I don't know too many lyrics off hand to this one
GatorCandie:	haha!
BDR 529 IL:	"the real cock diesel"
GatorCandie:	"try to read my mind, just imagine"
GatorCandie:	"chocolatey choco the chocolate chicken"
GatorCandie:	"the chicks they were kickin"
BDR 529 IL:	"New York, North Kacalaca and Compton"
GatorCandie:	"checka checka check it out"
BDR 529 IL:	ok, wan't it out of your head? How 'bout some Third Base
BDR 529 IL:	The Cactus
GatorCandie:	all that she wants?
BDR 529 IL:	oooh I've got a good song on
BDR 529 IL:	Pixies "Where is My Mind"
GatorCandie:	what?
GatorCandie:	that's over my head
BDR 529 IL:	don't know it???
GatorCandie:	I don't think so
BDR 529 IL:	did you see Fight Club?
GatorCandie:	yes, I did see Fight Club
BDR 529 IL:	it's the song in the last scene when all the buildings blow up and tumble to the ground as they watch from the window.

BDR 529 IL:	not that you would remember
GatorCandie:	well, "the rhythm is in sync, the rhymes are on time"
BDR 529 IL:	I can't think of other lyrics with this playing
BDR 529 IL:	wow, weird lag in my typing
GatorCandie:	:-X
BDR 529 IL:	it's taking a second or two for it to actually show what im typing
BDR 529 IL:	sllooooooow moooootion
GatorCandie:	damn cable modems
BDR 529 IL:	no no, my actual typing. I type the characters on the keyboard and a milisecond later they show up on the screen
GatorCandie:	oh, that's hard to contend with
GatorCandie:	Do you have a lot of windows open? I wonder if you're getting a virus.
BDR 529 IL:	no. Just you, kid-o
BDR 529 IL:	and my music folder
BDR 529 IL:	I think I have a heat problem
GatorCandie:	When I get a virus, everything slows way down for just a minute and then goes back to "normal". Heat could do it
GatorCandie:	oh yeah, laptop.
BDR 529 IL:	I have this tray that my laptop sits on. It has USB powered fans to cool the computer. I have never seen a laptop that could actually function at full capicity on someones lap
GatorCandie:	really? cool.
GatorCandie:	I know it. They're much better on a desktop.

BDR 529 IL:	when I was younger, a friend and I built a water-cooled computer
BDR 529 IL:	it was cool. It was a dual processor PII
GatorCandie:	wow cool
BDR 529 IL:	which was a big deal at the time
BDR 529 IL:	yeah, but eventually it had condensation problems and died entirely
GatorCandie:	haha, you could almost see that coming a mile away
BDR 529 IL:	yeah, we couldn't get our hands on freon, so water had to do
BDR 529 IL:	I looked forever for a tiny condensor and evaporator but couldnt find one small enough to be practical
GatorCandie:	how small do they come?
BDR 529 IL:	the smalest I could find at the time was about 1 foot square
GatorCandie:	Oh no, that put "The Harder They Come" into my head. What is going on??
GatorCandie:	That's a bit impractical.
GatorCandie:	one and all
BDR 529 IL:	hey, why AREN'T we talking about sex???
GatorCandie:	we aren't?
BDR 529 IL:	hmmm
GatorCandie:	"let's talk about sex, baby, lets talk about you and me"
BDR 529 IL:	"let's talk about all the good things and the bad things, that may be"

BDR 529 IL:	I once tried to make a mini water-cooled system for my penis
GatorCandie:	haha
GatorCandie:	I think they talked mostly about the bad things in that song
BDR 529 IL:	you didn't hear the extended version where they all go to Walt Disney World
GatorCandie:	"like a dumb son of a gun oops, he forgot the condoms"
GatorCandie:	I have a thing for lyrics. They follow me around.
BDR 529 IL:	call the cops
GatorCandie:	Lock 'em up
BDR 529 IL:	wow, I just had one of those great, full 3-second back cracks
GatorCandie:	I have a song that is trying to get into my head but I can't remember the words.
BDR 529 IL:	you don't get too many of those
BDR 529 IL:	hahaha... it's trying
GatorCandie:	Oh I know, they're special.
GatorCandie:	Rudy something
BDR 529 IL:	oh... I know. Uummm... hold on
BDR 529 IL:	The Clash...
GatorCandie:	yes, The Clash
BDR 529 IL:	it's on the tip of my tongue
GatorCandie:	Rudy Cant Fail
GatorCandie:	but that's not the one

GatorCandie: the other one is by Desmond Dekker I think. The one that's trying to get in

GatorCandie: Rudy Cant Fail is a great song.

GatorCandie: Sing, Michael, Sing

BDR 529 IL: The Specials... A Message to Rudy

GatorCandie: Yes... The Specials. Exactly

BDR 529 IL: "this is ... a message to you Ru-dy"

GatorCandie: How could I think Desmond Dekker???

GatorCandie: Great song though

GatorCandie: Now I have a non-stop Ska torrent

BDR 529 IL: this Service Pack 2 shit is messin' with Bearshare. This is NOT acceptable.

BDR 529 IL: rude girl

GatorCandie: Limewire baby

BDR 529 IL: did you download Service Pack 2 yet?

GatorCandie: Is that "Rudi"?

GatorCandie: Nope

BDR 529 IL: don't

GatorCandie: ok

BDR 529 IL: no, rude girl... like a rude boy

BDR 529 IL: that's what they used to call the ska boys

GatorCandie: I know... I got it

BDR 529 IL: sory. Over explaining

GatorCandie: I know the WHOLE history, my friend

BDR 529 IL: ok, ok. Just don't hit me again—please!

GatorCandie: haha, I didn't

BDR 529 IL: ok, I got it. If anyone asks, I fell

GatorCandie:	sorry for the aggression
GatorCandie:	it's hard to hear my joking, "I got it, I got it" tone
BDR 529 IL:	that's what they all say
GatorCandie:	no, they don't ALL say that
BDR 529 IL:	well, not alll of 'em
BDR 529 IL:	but a few of dose dudes said SOME shit
GatorCandie:	speaking of, I broke a guy's ribs once, haha
BDR 529 IL:	that's horrible. He should have been old enough to cut his own food
GatorCandie:	I know. Beefsteak Charlie's
BDR 529 IL:	that bastard
BDR 529 IL:	why did you break his ribs? Acident, or??
BDR 529 IL:	for fun?
GatorCandie:	Kind of an accident
GatorCandie:	When I was in Tae Kwon Do, there was a "cocktailing establishment" that all the bank people my ex worked with went to…
GatorCandie:	and he used to call me to come down, so sometimes I did
GatorCandie:	anyway, a couple of guys thought it was funny that I had a green belt and one of them wanted me to take a swing at him
BDR 529 IL:	uh oh
GatorCandie:	and he pestered me for like 2 hours
GatorCandie:	so, I drink super light most of the night. I was almost completely sober, and he wasn't

GatorCandie: I didn't want to make a fool out of him by cracking him on the chin or doubling him over by hitting him in the tummy, so I went for the area near his heart, where most people have some flesh and muscle.

GatorCandie: well, my ex called me at work the next day telling me that I broke three of his ribs. I felt really bad.

GatorCandie: It was all kind of joking in a way.

BDR 529 IL: kind of? Lol—I bet he never asked you to hit him again

GatorCandie: He was just standing there, saying "hit me, hit me". So I said ok.

BDR 529 IL: can't say he didn't ask for it

GatorCandie: There was a bunch of people watching because he was going around telling everyone that I wouldn't hit him for some reason.

BDR 529 IL: some reason? He was probably loaded

GatorCandie: I guess, but that was his problem. I never really imagined that I would seriously hurt him.

BDR 529 IL: a few broken ribs never killed anyone

BDR 529 IL: well, this century anyway

GatorCandie: I guess. That was the only "bar fight" I've ever been in

BDR 529 IL: admit it; you go from bar to bar shaking down people for money, don't you?

GatorCandie: nah, I don't like bars very much. Now, cocktailing is a different story

BDR 529 IL: ummm. Oh yes… "Cocktailing" …suuuure.

GatorCandie:	It was always novel to everyone when I came down so it was almost like I was a celebrity.
BDR 529 IL:	did you get a red carpet rolled out for you?
GatorCandie:	No, but everyone was always like "it's Carl's wife!!" like it was some big thing. I suppose because it was always all the people who worked at the bank. The same people all day long.
BDR 529 IL:	I really can't stand bars for very long these days
GatorCandie:	Yeah, the music has to be very good.
BDR 529 IL:	or maybe they just all liked you as much as I do and enjoyed your company
GatorCandie:	well, yes they did but it was probably just because I didn't work with them all day and I had a fresh perspective, you know?
BDR 529 IL:	yeah
GatorCandie:	Of course it was the same for me—all these people were happy to see me, so it was cool. They used to ask me questions all the time, as if they were never let out of the bank and allowed to talk to other non-bank people.
BDR 529 IL:	a bank is sort of like a people aquarium
BDR 529 IL:	I feel like feeding those tellers over the glass—pinch some fish flakes in there
GatorCandie:	yes, I've never worked in a super huge place like a bank. HSBC headquarters. I've worked for large companies, but small branches
GatorCandie:	Here, teller, teller, teller
BDR 529 IL:	haha

BDR 529 IL:	so, you're in sexy, silk lingerie, right?
GatorCandie:	pull my hair please.
BDR 529 IL:	hahaha
GatorCandie:	I knew there was a reason why I liked you
BDR 529 IL:	what's my motivation?
BDR 529 IL:	have you been bad again??
GatorCandie:	the sharp intake of breath
GatorCandie:	um, because I like it?
BDR 529 IL:	that's good enough for me
GatorCandie:	I am unfortunately wearing pink capris and a ribbed white tank top.
BDR 529 IL:	see, tonight I'm more in a "press you up against the wall, pull your hair back and glide my hand slowly up your thigh" mood
GatorCandie:	wow, ok
GatorCandie:	I believe I could provide you with the kind of feedback you would expect from that
BDR 529 IL:	ya think so?
GatorCandie:	I think I could definitely get into "slow and accurate" tonight
BDR 529 IL:	pressed up against the wall, your back to me, I wishper in your ear "do you want me to make you cum now?
GatorCandie:	I would say, "Yes please"
BDR 529 IL:	I'm sorry. I was… thinking
GatorCandie:	that's ok
GatorCandie:	I'm unsure about cyber sex, haha, but I think you turn me on

BDR 529 IL:	I'm unsure about it myself, you know… because it's so… silly!
BDR 529 IL:	but you definitely turn me on
GatorCandie:	so I have an off topic question.
BDR 529 IL:	ok, good!
GatorCandie:	what's your thing about the phone?
BDR 529 IL:	I don't really have a thing about the phone…. it just seems easier to express yourself this way. The words seem to flow smoothly. Probably because I have time to think before I speak, though you'd never know it
BDR 529 IL:	plus, zero uncomfortable silence
GatorCandie:	silence doesn't have to be uncomfortable
BDR 529 IL:	no, it doesn't, I agree
BDR 529 IL:	but it sometimes is
GatorCandie:	I like your voice.
GatorCandie:	It's a good voice.
BDR 529 IL:	why thank you…
BDR 529 IL:	you know, when you left me that "headache" message, I actually chuckled out loud
BDR 529 IL:	it was so cute
GatorCandie:	ha, I thought you would like it. It was actually true.
BDR 529 IL:	awwww… I gave you a headache
GatorCandie:	don't worry, headaches don't really slow me down, but I felt like a had a bit of a hangover
GatorCandie:	Please god, that's not "love hangover" trying to get in, is it???

Hearing, or rather reading those words made my heart sink. Not in a bad way, mind you, it was in a good yet scary way. Here's this amazing person that I think I'm falling in love with. Now she's telling me that she is falling in love with me. All this, and we never met or even talked on the phone for more than one minute. I truly didn't know how to reply, so I simply laughed it off which, in retrospect, was most likely the wrong thing to do.

BDR 529 IL: hahaha

GatorCandie: I hear you knocking, but you can't come in.

BDR 529 IL: its competeing with the songs

GatorCandie: "open the door and let them in, yeah"

BDR 529 IL: I can't come in????

GatorCandie: Where's MY motivation?

BDR 529 IL: "because I like it"

GatorCandie: ;-)

GatorCandie: I'm totally grinning

BDR 529 IL: so am I. I am rarely at a loss for words, however, it seems to happen quite a bit with you

GatorCandie: haha, you're fun.

BDR 529 IL: see, if you hustled today, I could be looking at your pretty face on your webcam right now, but nooooo... you had to stay up late last night talking to some jerk you met on match.com. A witty and clever jerk I must admit, but a jerk nonetheless.

GatorCandie: yeah, some jerk

BDR 529 IL: I'll give you this; he's a handsome devil

GatorCandie: yes he is

GatorCandie: incoming funny…

GatorCandie: after not hearing from Kris for like 2.5 hours, she sends me this:

For the life of me, I can't remember what she e-mailed to me. Even reading further through the string, I still cannot figure out what it was. Suffice to say, it must have been something funny or having to do with complimenting yourself. Maybe you'll be able to figure it out because I surely cannot.

BDR 529 IL: I do and it drives my brother nuts… whenever he's around and he see's me looking in a mirror, I say "hellllooooo handsome"

GatorCandie: Like, "hellllooooball" from the honeymooners?

BDR 529 IL: yep

GatorCandie: OdddGirrrl71: she came with a purse, that had a wallet wtih a ISA card in it, a hairbrush, and she had a bionic ear

OdddGirrrl71:   sorry, wrong box, haha

GatorCandie: wtf? haha

BDR 529 IL: yeah… if I had a nickle for everytime I heard someone say that…

BDR 529 IL: …I'd be homeless.

GatorCandie: exactly!!

BDR 529 IL: so I got an email from a girl from match who's nickname was deeeznutz. She was one of those white hip-hop girls

GatorCandie: was that her match screen name?

BDR 529 IL: no, it was similar though. There were some __ or — in there, somewhere

BDR 529 IL: and a number

BDR 529 IL:	like deeez_nutz37 or whatever
GatorCandie:	k
BDR 529 IL:	"let's kick it, yo"—Her words, not mine.
GatorCandie:	wow, yeah, kick this!
BDR 529 IL:	"Yo baby, I love you more than you know, but you did me wrong. Give one dude a BJ shame on you; give two dudes a BJ, shame on me".
BDR 529 IL:	"Love Always",
BDR 529 IL:	"Spoony"
GatorCandie:	huh?
BDR 529 IL:	ah… you never heard Spoony Luv, from up above?
GatorCandie:	no

BDR 529 IL wants to send file Crank Yankers—Spoonie Luv Orders Roses.mp3.

BDR 529 IL:	it's actually pretty stupid, but then again, so am I… so it all works out
BDR 529 IL:	it just goes downhill from here
BDR 529 IL:	I dunno… sometimes, silly things make me laugh
GatorCandie:	I'm trying to find it…
BDR 529 IL:	that's a pretty bad one… I have some much funnier ones
BDR 529 IL:	well… forget that. I'll send a different one. It's much better
GatorCandie:	k
BDR 529 IL:	I'll send it to your email
GatorCandie:	k

BDR 529 IL:	sending
BDR 529 IL:	…sending …sending …sending …sending
GatorCandie:	give it to me baby
BDR 529 IL:	you want it, don't you?
GatorCandie:	you're pretty fly for a white guy
BDR 529 IL:	"fly" haha. I think I'm gonna try and bring "fly" back into everyday conversation.
GatorCandie:	pimp of the year
BDR 529 IL:	"how high, real high, 'cause we just so fly"
GatorCandie:	mac daddy
GatorCandie:	"the daddy mac will make ya"
BDR 529 IL:	"A caddy for ma' daddy, somethin new for moms too. A coat for Mr. Long and some hookers for the crew". Lyrical genius!
GatorCandie:	haha
GatorCandie:	My favorite Black Sheep line:
GatorCandie:	"clockin from the corna while ya eatin a knish"
GatorCandie:	ok, here's something funny
BDR 529 IL:	where?
GatorCandie:	It's supposed to read "fun gal 4u 2000"
GatorCandie:	but to me, all I can see is "fungal 4u12000"
BDR 529 IL:	hahaha
GatorCandie:	That's how I read it and I wondered why someone would put that down as a name, ha
BDR 529 IL:	subconciously, thousands of men are being turned off to/by her
GatorCandie:	well if you saw her face it wouldn't be a stretch

GatorCandie:	that was cruel and I take it back
BDR 529 IL:	too late, you already said you
GatorCandie:	I really should be punished
BDR 529 IL:	you're a judgemental freak
BDR 529 IL:	later toots
GatorCandie:	wha??
GatorCandie:	No, I'm really not!
GatorCandie:	but...
BDR 529 IL:	I know you're not. I was kidding
GatorCandie:	ugly people are um... ugly
BDR 529 IL:	sad but true
GatorCandie:	I don't mean that in a really bad way.
BDR 529 IL:	I mean, I'm not exactly Mel Gibson but it must be hard to be really ugly

This was before everyone started to hate Mel Gibson. If this conversation took place today, I might have said George Clooney.

GatorCandie:	OdddGirrrl71: so then I blew her fucking head off with my gun, and to this day no one knows the real story. Let's keep it that way.
OdddGirrrl71:	sorry, wrong box
OdddGirrrl71:	just kidding
GatorCandie:	haha
OdddGirrrl71:	question before i get off of here
OdddGirrrl71:	what time are you waking up tomorrow?
GatorCandie:	haha, 8
GatorCandie:	And this is my best friend.
BDR 529 IL:	hahahaha

BDR 529 IL:	did you get the email??
GatorCandie:	lemme check again
GatorCandie:	haha
GatorCandie:	That's too funny, yet idiotic all at the same time.
BDR 529 IL:	haha
GatorCandie:	"shizzy with the nizzy"
GatorCandie:	ha
BDR 529 IL:	"Sin-ciz-erly, Spoony"
GatorCandie:	"long walks on the beach, nights by the fireplace and sushi, badonkadonk".
GatorCandie:	"must have back, don't steal my stuff"
BDR 529 IL:	hahahaha… that's my favorite line "don't steal my stuff"
GatorCandie:	that was funny but now I must wash
BDR 529 IL:	haha
BDR 529 IL:	it's Spoony, baby. Gotta keep it real than a mofo

Clearly, this would have been much funnier to you, reader, if you were familiar with Tracy Morgan's Crank Yankers material. If you're not and you have a decent sense of humor, I strongly recommend listening to it.

GatorCandie:	oh yeah, thas what im talkin 'bout
GatorCandie:	foshizzle
BDR 529 IL:	so are you going to let me keep you up all night again?
GatorCandie:	no, but you were going to call me and wish me sweet dreams so I could have some.

If you remember, we were supposed to say good night hours ago, but, as always, we just kept on talking and talking and the hours kept on passing and passing. She really wanted me to call her and I was avoiding it at all cost. I'm not exactly sure why I was so afraid to talk to her on the phone. I suppose that I was nervous because I liked her so much and I was fearful that I might lose my charm through a bad phone call or by not having enough time to come up with a witty and appropriate retort. As you'll read later on, I made excuse after excuse as to why I couldn't call. It became ridiculous at a point. Anyway, this silly attempt at saying good night doesn't work for another few hours until we finally say the words for real at four in the morning... read on.

BDR 529 IL:	ok. Give me a few minutes to get my cell out da glovie, ya heard?

I let a few minutes pass and pretended to go down to the car to get my phone out of the glove compartment, but the truth was, the phone was sitting right next to me on the desk. I was just stalling for time. Time to come up with the courage to actually call her.

BDR 529 IL:	ok, goodnight sweetie
BDR 529 IL:	or, good-niz-ight as Spoony would say
GatorCandie:	k good night
BDR 529 IL:	all that time and all i get is "k good night"?
BDR 529 IL:	I guess the songs I sent beat the love headache out of you!
GatorCandie:	er, Consuela and I are unsure of what to say
BDR 529 IL:	take your time to consult with her
GatorCandie:	You've got a real type of thing going down, gettin' down—There's a whole lot of rhythm going round

BDR 529 IL:	geez, I hope you don't pay consuela by the hour
GatorCandie:	That's what we came up with. Haha, I might be a bit delirious
BDR 529 IL:	she's either brilliant or a fool
BDR 529 IL:	one or the other
GatorCandie:	she's just an underpriveleged housekeeper with a nice butt
BDR 529 IL:	I know where she's comin' from.
GatorCandie:	where? Same place as you?
BDR 529 IL:	no. East Third and Main. I see her on my way to work in the morning
GatorCandie:	haha!!
GatorCandie:	LMAO
BDR 529 IL:	I need a guy to follow me with a snare drum and cymbal
GatorCandie:	you really do!
GatorCandie:	or just have one of those buzzy things that will play on demand or something
BDR 529 IL:	I tried to get that homeless guy to do it, but he wore too many sweaters and it scared me
GatorCandie:	You know, he was wearing all those sweaters so it wouldn't hurt when you poked him with that stick of yours
BDR 529 IL:	he had the sweaters before he ever met me
GatorCandie:	I gave him those sweaters! Well... Consuela did
BDR 529 IL:	foiled again
GatorCandie:	She does all my dirty work. I got it like 'dat

BDR 529 IL:	nice
BDR 529 IL:	are you consulting with Consuela again?
GatorCandie:	Oh, uh sorry. Yes.
BDR 529 IL:	you know, as her fake attorney, I'm entitled to 10% of her wages
GatorCandie:	llámeme por favor
GatorCandie:	how would you like them? Have you discussed it with her?
BDR 529 IL:	um… over easy with a side of home fries
GatorCandie:	I just spill beans onto her dresser
GatorCandie:	I really love home fries.
GatorCandie:	with onions of course
BDR 529 IL:	tell her I said that no self respecting Spaniard world work for a swine like Pamela
GatorCandie:	can I tell her in German?
BDR 529 IL:	kein Selbst, der Spaniard respektiert, würde für ein Schwein wie Pamela arbeiten
GatorCandie:	kein Selbst, der Spaniardweltarbeit für ein Schwein respektiert, mögen Pamela
GatorCandie:	you're alwaya a 1/4 step ahead of me
BDR 529 IL:	no no, that's 2 for you 1 for me
GatorCandie:	(I was counting the beats)
BDR 529 IL:	I was counting the beats too. Three in a can these days. Back in my day you could get 8 beets for a nickle
GatorCandie:	I grow beets in my garden though. (SO WHAT?? you must be wondering)
BDR 529 IL:	haha

GatorCandie:	a tree grows in Brooklyn, a garden in my strip of city grass
BDR 529 IL:	hardly a Tree Grows in Brooklyn. According to my information, you have the second largest piece of land on the block
BDR 529 IL:	and the grass is always greener (much greener) across the street and two doors down, isn't it?
GatorCandie:	have you made sure that no tree is growing?
BDR 529 IL:	I have salted the earth
GatorCandie:	Jesse the Barbarian
GatorCandie:	gone forth and multiplied?
GatorCandie:	or divided?
BDR 529 IL:	a little from column A, a little from column B
BDR 529 IL:	we pretty much broke even
BDR 529 IL:	come on, I thought that was pretty funny. I'm cracking myself up here
GatorCandie:	it was funny!!
BDR 529 IL:	see, I knew it!
GatorCandie:	It just added to my general feeling of comfort and contentedness in talking to you on this computer for hours and hours on end
GatorCandie:	no sarcasm there, by the way
BDR 529 IL:	I know. It was too sweet to reply to
GatorCandie:	so for sweetness, I get silence. Ok, I see how it is
BDR 529 IL:	you get silent adoration
BDR 529 IL:	should I come tuck you in or are you gonna come tuck me in?

GatorCandie: are you in bed already, Mr. Laptop guy?

Laptops, or notebooks as they were commonly called, were very expensive and not nearly as widespread as they are today. That explains her "Mr. Laptop guy" comment. Back then, it was quite a big deal to have a laptop.

BDR 529 IL: kind of. I haven't gone through my usual routine of wraping up power cords and putting them away, but I think everything is going to find it's way to the floor tonight

GatorCandie: cheater

BDR 529 IL: yeah. Laptop... pffft. They should call it the "hot as lava machine"

BDR 529 IL: whos battery lasts about three and a half seconds

GatorCandie: It's about all the heat you're going to get tonight though

BDR 529 IL: you stopping by?

BDR 529 IL: bringing Consuela?

GatorCandie: I was calling you!

GatorCandie: Consuela went to bed.

BDR 529 IL: oh. I told you, my cell is in da glovie, yo

GatorCandie: glovie? Meaning what?

BDR 529 IL: man, you're not up on your lingo

BDR 529 IL: glovie = glove box

BDR 529 IL: in the whip (whip = car)

GatorCandie: Oh, I thought that meant a leather case

GatorCandie: I'm so white

BDR 529 IL: hahah

BDR 529 IL:	word. And lest anyone think that I wear one of those God-awful leather belt cases for my cell phone!
GatorCandie:	oh well, I guess it's fine.
GatorCandie:	I left you a goofy message
BDR 529 IL:	there's a young black kid who lives next door…
BDR 529 IL:	he's about 17 or so
GatorCandie:	yes
BDR 529 IL:	he's a good kid. He stops by sometimes to say hello. We became friendly.
BDR 529 IL:	I call him Rochester
GatorCandie:	ha
BDR 529 IL:	Oh Rochester, get me a glass of water, would you?
BDR 529 IL:	He replies, "why yes sir, Mr. Jesse sir"
BDR 529 IL:	he plays right into it. It's hilarious
GatorCandie:	ha, that's pretty good
GatorCandie:	Missa Jesse
BDR 529 IL:	yeah, but now I owe the kid 40 acres and a mule
BDR 529 IL:	can you believe it??
GatorCandie:	well, maybe he could just ride a donkey as far as it will go
BDR 529 IL:	leave me a message on my phone
GatorCandie:	I did. It was a silly message
BDR 529 IL:	you should leave me a diferent kind of message

There was a moment of silence between us.

BDR 529 IL: is this that silent adoration??

GatorCandie: sort of…

BDR 529 IL: if Consuela is holding a gun to your head, say, "I believe Georgia is the Pelican State"

Another few minutes went by without her typing anything.

BDR 529 IL: hello??

BDR 529 IL: helloooooo

BDR 529 IL: was it something I said?

GatorCandie: no, sorry. I was just leaving you a message. But it didn't end up being what I wanted it to be. So I sang a song, haha

GatorCandie: Actually I don't think it's a song; it's just some words I heard in a song.

GatorCandie: uh oh you're all upset with me

BDR 529 IL: hmmmm

GatorCandie: call your vm

There must have been some lag going on in the internet, because I didn't see what she had typed until a few minutes later. That's why I responded to her as I did.

BDR 529 IL: ok, well, I suppose you fell asleep

BDR 529 IL: or

BDR 529 IL: consuela has taken you hostage

BDR 529 IL: OR consuela has fallen asleep and you took her hostage

GatorCandie: meaning what?

GatorCandie: why do you say that?

BDR 529 IL:	bacause you haven't said anything in 10 minutes
BDR 529 IL:	I usually assume the worst and Consuela was an obvious suspect
GatorCandie:	It's easy to take an underpriveleged home-worker hostage when she's sleeping
BDR 529 IL:	they rarely seem to mind either
GatorCandie:	"GatorCandie: no, sorry. I was just leaving you a message. But it didn't end up being what I wanted it to be."
GatorCandie:	I wrote that up there.
BDR 529 IL:	I see that, but that's the first that I'm seeing it
GatorCandie:	really?
BDR 529 IL:	it threw up some nonsense firewall message and I have been typing ever since—with no reply
"BDR 529 IL:	Consuela has taken you hostage, OR consuela has fallen asleep and you took her hostage"
"GatorCandie:	**why do you say that?"**
BDR 529 IL:	that's all I have
GatorCandie:	WOW
GatorCandie:	yes, it got a bit frustrating for me
GatorCandie:	when I was typing and you didn't seem to comprehend me.
BDR 529 IL:	I feel the same way!!!
BDR 529 IL:	someone is trying to keep us apart!!!
GatorCandie:	haha maybe it wasn't meant to be?
BDR 529 IL:	have you pissed off any Illumanati lately?

GatorCandie:	what would they want with me?
GatorCandie:	Nothing Will Tear Us Apart
BDR 529 IL:	…tear. Can I borow your tissue?
GatorCandie:	it's soaked, but sure
GatorCandie:	As I said, Consuela has left me
BDR 529 IL:	her loss
GatorCandie:	she thinks she had it hard
BDR 529 IL:	no no, that's what you're getting
GatorCandie:	I knew that was coming, heehee
BDR 529 IL:	yeah, it was left wide open
BDR 529 IL:	I couldn't resist
GatorCandie:	all by design, darling
GatorCandie:	I am a very good straight man
BDR 529 IL:	great, so I have to be the woman in this relationship?
GatorCandie:	No, please don't.
BDR 529 IL:	wheeew! Thank God
GatorCandie:	I dated a guy for 2 months who wanted me to spank him. I couldn't.
BDR 529 IL:	spank **HIM**??
GatorCandie:	yep.
BDR 529 IL:	that's a little backwards (no pun intended). Actualluy, yes, yes, the pun is officially intentional.
GatorCandie:	I never had sex with him.
BDR 529 IL:	yet he asked you to spank him?

GatorCandie: We had foreplay for like a month and then he told me he wanted me to spank him and I told him that I had to be moving along.

BDR 529 IL: Foreplay for a month?!?! You must have been exhausted!

BDR 529 IL: what else did you guys do for the first month??

GatorCandie: Not much I guess.

BDR 529 IL: wow, you must have seen a LOT of movies

GatorCandie: I had some guy friends and I used to cry on their shoulders, "he won't have sex with me."

GatorCandie: of course, it brought on the usual comments

BDR 529 IL: that's a dangerous thing to cry about on another guy's shoulder

GatorCandie: like men are interchangeable or something

GatorCandie: Well, it was a group of us.

BDR 529 IL: kinky

GatorCandie: and we all used to bitch about our sex lives

BDR 529 IL: "so one day…"

GatorCandie: no, there was no "one day" haha

BDR 529 IL: I know

GatorCandie: me with another girl—fine. Two guys?—I'm not so sure

BDR 529 IL: I would really like to be lying next to you right now

GatorCandie: pillow talking?

BDR 529 IL: among other things

GatorCandie: it would be nice. It has been a long time since I have slept with someone next to me.

BDR 529 IL:	It's nice to be playful in bed
BDR 529 IL:	not necessarilly sexual
BDR 529 IL:	just playful
GatorCandie:	how did you like my "interchangeable" comment? I thought that was funny
BDR 529 IL:	we are interchangeable.
BDR 529 IL:	we're all the same
GatorCandie:	you think? Tell that to some of my match. com stalker guys
BDR 529 IL:	my advice to you… find the one with the biggest weiner and you're all set
GatorCandie:	um, could I hold out for some talent too?
BDR 529 IL:	nope. Just weiners
GatorCandie:	nah
GatorCandie:	big weiner. What a concept
BDR 529 IL:	I don't think I have ever said, much less typed the word "weiner" in my life
GatorCandie:	say it out loud now. I dare ya
BDR 529 IL:	no. I'd like to keep my no weiner record in tact
GatorCandie:	have you named yours? If that's not too personal…
BDR 529 IL:	well, I like to call him Larry but he makes me call him Lawrence
BDR 529 IL:	haha. No, I haven't named him.
GatorCandie:	haha
GatorCandie:	it sounds like a weird B movie

BDR 529 IL:	I Like to Call Him Larry", Starring Merideth Baxter Birney as Larry
GatorCandie:	Tonight is Right for Love
BDR 529 IL:	is that your statement, ma'am?
GatorCandie:	...with Meredith Baxter Birney
BDR 529 IL:	A woman Scorned
BDR 529 IL:	I know My Name is Michael
GatorCandie:	are these TV movies she has been in?
BDR 529 IL:	no, these are TV movies that she shouldn't have been in or should I say, that shouldn't have been made, period.
BDR 529 IL:	ok, so, do I have a sexy Pamela message waiting for me?
GatorCandie:	um, no. There is one silly message and uh, well, two silly messages.
GatorCandie:	"Hello my name is Michael and I am Jesse's penis"
BDR 529 IL:	you have to come up with a better name than that for my penis
BDR 529 IL:	I'm looking at him now and he doesn't look like a Michael
GatorCandie:	Maybe if and when I meet your penis I'll be inspired with a better name for him.
GatorCandie:	Does he look like Shaft?
BDR 529 IL:	well, he's not black and he doesn't have leather pants
BDR 529 IL:	but other than that, yes
GatorCandie:	just checking
BDR 529 IL:	so, two silly voicemails and no sexy ones

BDR 529 IL:	silly is good too
GatorCandie:	sorry it's so late to ask this, but what are warm leatherettes?
GatorCandie:	I wanted to leave you a sexy message but you were IM'ing me and I started laughing so I sang "Lemon Tree"
BDR 529 IL:	hahahaha. Please, go ahead. I'll be as quiet as a mouse with his tongue cut out
GatorCandie:	I can't anymore…
BDR 529 IL:	just think about how I could do whenever I want to you. I can touch you and tease you and there would be nothing that you could do about it.
GatorCandie:	I love the "do whenever I want" part, but you seem to know that already
GatorCandie:	I am deliriously tired but I think I could turn myself on if I relied on old standbys
BDR 529 IL:	I think I know what you like
GatorCandie:	I think I know what YOU like and you're naughty
BDR 529 IL:	me, naughty? Nah
GatorCandie:	Do you realize that after all this typing I'm going to be seriously nervous when I talk to you on the phone?
BDR 529 IL:	that's why we can ease the tension with messages, until we eventually meet and are both engulfed in overwhelming waves of passion.
GatorCandie:	I mean, do people who talk this way to each other on the computer ever actually

	meet? And for that matter, do people on the computer actually talk to each other like this?
GatorCandie:	If we ever kiss, you would be the only Italian guy that I ever kissed.
GatorCandie:	Except my dad.
BDR 529 IL:	haha, it's just like kissing a normal person except with thicker hair and our pockets are filled with meatballs
GatorCandie:	haha
GatorCandie:	I'm not so sure, it might be even weirder
BDR 529 IL:	"IF" we ever kiss. I don't think I could forgive myself if I never got to kiss you
GatorCandie:	I only say "if" because who knows what the future holds?
BDR 529 IL:	that's true
GatorCandie:	You could get hauled off to jail, finally.
BDR 529 IL:	jail?? What did I do?
GatorCandie:	Well, I know what you were planning to do to me when we first met.
BDR 529 IL:	since when is buying someone dinner a crime? Unless it's at an Arby's of course. Then I think it's a misdemeanor.
GatorCandie:	just kidding though. It seemed like a funny statement actually. With the "finally" tacked on the end
GatorCandie:	what about the butchering and stuff? Have you forgotton about all of those threatening promises?
BDR 529 IL:	hey, that would be a legitimate transaction. You get crank out of the deal, remember?

BDR 529 IL:	or, I could just follow you home in my van one day
GatorCandie:	yes, but like all good stars and union members, I want more.
BDR 529 IL:	I'll see what I can do to sweeten the deal
GatorCandie:	I wish you were here
BDR 529 IL:	so… like I said yesterday, do you think it will be strange meeting for the first time, knowing what we know about each other?
GatorCandie:	yes.
BDR 529 IL:	"hey, how are you"? "Nice day" "Did you find the place ok"? …hmmmmm
GatorCandie:	when is he going to pull my hair?
BDR 529 IL:	hahaha
BDR 529 IL:	when do I get to put my hand around her neck?
GatorCandie:	haha
GatorCandie:	We are mostly normal people right?
BDR 529 IL:	I think we are totally normal
BDR 529 IL:	more normal than people who aren't honest about their desires
GatorCandie:	wow, shows how much you know
BDR 529 IL:	I want you so bad right now you have no idea
GatorCandie:	Yeah, I want to be the female lead in a trashy romance novel. The kind with bodices, whatever they are being ripped open on every other page.
BDR 529 IL:	ha
GatorCandie:	I've never had my shirt ripped off…

GatorCandie:	You are such a bad influence on me!
BDR 529 IL:	haha
BDR 529 IL:	see, now you're all ready to leave me a sexy message!
GatorCandie:	I cant, it wouldn't sound right.
BDR 529 IL:	I understand
GatorCandie:	Plus I believe I need dialogue with you first.
BDR 529 IL:	an old fasioned girl, ay?
GatorCandie:	I'm such an amateur
GatorCandie:	I hate to say good night…
BDR 529 IL:	Hate is such a strong word. I did it to you again, didn't I? I kept you up all night; I'm sorry. God night sweetie
GatorCandie:	God? Pretty presumptuous
BDR 529 IL:	God? No, Jesse. Good Night.
BDR 529 IL:	as I'm sure you have seen throughout the night…
BDR 529 IL:	my typing has gotten progressively worse.
BDR 529 IL:	ji
BDR 529 IL:	rheal
BDR 529 IL:	wehekcvhnd
GatorCandie:	iluji
GatorCandie:	ha, I like you.
BDR 529 IL:	I like you too
BDR 529 IL:	as a matter of fact.
BDR 529 IL:	goodnight sweetheart
BDR 529 IL:	swet dreams

BDR 529 IL: sweet

BDR 529 IL: swet god

GatorCandie: and to you. I'll be thinking your name.

BDR 529 IL: I wish that I could kiss you goodnight, but I
                   cant, so try and imagine that I did

GatorCandie: k, it's fuzzy.

GatorCandie: good night :-)

BDR 529 IL: :-)

BDR 529 IL signed off at 3:59:00 AM.

THE FIFTH DAY

BDR 529 IL: You have been on my mind all day

BDR 529 IL: Just so you know.

GatorCandie: Really? You too.

GatorCandie: I think that's cool! I was thinkin' my emails were simply not appreciated.

BDR 529 IL: Oh they are… Very much so.

BDR 529 IL: I woke up looking forward to getting your movies, but much to my surprise, nothing was there!

GatorCandie: Yes, I made the mistake of sending them together. Are you on your PDA?

BDR 529 IL: Yes I am

GatorCandie: Cool. So what did you get up to today? It rained up here for a little while but I managed to get out and about.

BDR 529 IL: It was sooo hot here today but I loved it. It was about 90 degrees by mid-day

GatorCandie: 90? That almost never happens here.

BDR 529 IL: Oh it was hot allright

BDR 529 IL: But nice because most of this summer has been very mild

BDR 529 IL: What were the movies of?

GatorCandie: Oh, it's me narrating my garden, being a little silly and over-proud.

BDR 529 IL: Hahaha, cute

GatorCandie:	"Here's my garden… those are my tomatoes… bla bla bla" It would only be interesting to someone who liked me.
BDR 529 IL:	I have a garden also. I keep it at the produce section of my local supermarket
GatorCandie:	cheater
BDR 529 IL:	Hehe…. I wish I got the movie!
GatorCandie:	You will eventually I bet.
BDR 529 IL:	I would love to see you and your garden
BDR 529 IL:	Hopefully I'll get the movie.
GatorCandie:	There is a chance you will not?? huh?
BDR 529 IL:	Well, what if we meet and you find me totally disgusting and my personality comparable to that of a grape?
GatorCandie:	Well, what if you meet me and find that I'm not skinny enough?
GatorCandie:	Bet that question scared ya.
BDR 529 IL:	it did not scare me
BDR 529 IL:	You are just perfect
GatorCandie:	I don't think I could find you disgusting and I hope this isn't a Cyrano De-bla-bla thing
BDR 529 IL:	Hahaha
GatorCandie:	Do you have a ghostwriter?
BDR 529 IL:	Yep, and when we meet he'll be hiding in the bushes
BDR 529 IL:	Ummm… If I were going to send you fake pictures, I would have surely chosen someone more attractive than me!
GatorCandie:	No, I meant your personality. Grape like?

BDR 529 IL:	No. I don't think that I'm any different than I am on here.
GatorCandie:	I've had a craving to listen to Steve Earle all day. Do you know him?
BDR 529 IL:	Steve Earl… rings a bell
BDR 529 IL:	But I'm not sure
GatorCandie:	So no misrepresentations then? That's good.
BDR 529 IL:	Sounds like you have been giving this a lot of thought
GatorCandie:	Giving what thought?
BDR 529 IL:	Do you suspect me?
GatorCandie:	of what?
BDR 529 IL:	Missrepresentation?
GatorCandie:	Not at all!!
GatorCandie:	Do you want to know what my secret fear is? Or should I save it?
BDR 529 IL:	No no… tell me
GatorCandie:	That I'll end up really, really liking you, like more than I do now.
BDR 529 IL:	Why would you fear that?
GatorCandie:	Um, I guess the answer could be boiled down to 300 miles.
BDR 529 IL:	400 miles actually
BDR 529 IL:	But… you never know what could happen
GatorCandie:	Well it's 400 to Long Island so I gave the other 100 the benefit of the doubt
BDR 529 IL:	When I get on the thruway, there's a sign that reads "Pamela: 397 Miles"

GatorCandie:	haha, Yeah, a reflective Pamela sign.
GatorCandie:	But I haven't even met you yet. I'm not much of a worrier. Just random thoughts
BDR 529 IL:	My fear is that we meet, and it's very akward due to how well we know each other already.
GatorCandie:	It would be easy if we decided that we didn't like each other actually and I don't get worried about that. I meet people I don't like every other day.
BDR 529 IL:	I'm sure we can overcome that
GatorCandie:	Oh yeah, I'm pretty disarming actually. I can force ease into any situation if I want to. I just act silly and crack stupid jokes.
BDR 529 IL:	"force ease"—haha
GatorCandie:	Yes, force ease. It sounds like some over the counter medicine
BDR 529 IL:	Haha… Lemme switch over to my laptop
GatorCandie:	k

BDR 529 IL signed off at 7:59:28 PM.

BDR 529 IL signed on at 7:59:53 PM.

BDR 529 IL:	ahh, that's better
GatorCandie:	haha, you "ring" when you sign on.
GatorCandie:	You really must listen to Steve Earle. It's the only thing that could keep me from listening to your CD right now.
GatorCandie:	Which it is, but it's not an insult. I haven't listened to him in a few months and I craved it today.
BDR 529 IL:	hehe

GatorCandie:	I am so digging it.
GatorCandie:	I missed you
BDR 529 IL:	I missed you too… I really did
BDR 529 IL:	all day
GatorCandie:	How long has it been since I was a teenager???
BDR 529 IL:	11 years, my dear
GatorCandie:	12 actually.
GatorCandie:	But thanks.
GatorCandie:	Oh, you should read my new profile on match. I was cracking myself up writing it.
BDR 529 IL:	31, ay? I only date 30-year-old girls. Sorry hun. Missed it by one year!
GatorCandie:	haha!
GatorCandie:	I know, there are alot of lonely 31-year-old girls out there.
GatorCandie:	Luckily for my ego, I'm not one of them
BDR 529 IL:	neither am I. I have never been a lonely girl.
GatorCandie:	That's a start, but if you were I would convert.
BDR 529 IL:	haha, now THAT'S love
GatorCandie:	Yeah, but if you looked like that as a girl, it might be a problem
BDR 529 IL:	well, if I looked like this as a girl then you wouldn't have to go through the trouble of converting to lesbianism! Providing that the version of me as a girl still had a penis.
GatorCandie:	that's true; and quite odd all at the same time.
GatorCandie:	I must perform a time sensitive task that will take me 60 secs. brb

BDR 529 IL:	ok
GatorCandie:	how long was it?
BDR 529 IL:	48 seconds
GatorCandie:	I figured you counted
BDR 529 IL:	I didn't. I guessed.
GatorCandie:	wow I'm good
BDR 529 IL:	yes, very
GatorCandie:	It would take me longer to 'splain what I did
BDR 529 IL:	splain baby, splain
GatorCandie:	Well, I don't know if everyone does this… Does your mom cook?
BDR 529 IL:	yes
GatorCandie:	ok, well when I was growing up and my mom made eggplant parmigian (WHY CANT I SPELL THAT WORD???) she sliced the eggplant,
GatorCandie:	salted it and pressed between towels and books to make them very thin and really tender.
BDR 529 IL:	k
GatorCandie:	That's what I just did. I sliced, salted and pressed my eggplant from my garden. But luckily I have a large slab of marble so no books.
BDR 529 IL:	and don't worry about your spelling of parmigiana. My spelling is horrible. Spell check ruined me! I was voted "Mr. Vocabulary" in the 7th grade, God damn it! Now, since the creation of spell check, I have forgotten how to spell the simplest of wodrs. Get it… wodrs—words. Hardy har?

GatorCandie: haha. Yes, I got it.

GatorCandie: Were you really voted Mr. Vocabulary??

BDR 529 IL: Yes, I was

BDR 529 IL: I have the medal to prove it!

GatorCandie: Wow, I think someone snidely bestowed that title on me recently.

GatorCandie: I have to dumb it down a lot of the time actually.

BDR 529 IL: jealous… um… what's the word I'm looking for…

BDR 529 IL: jerks?

GatorCandie: nah, if I want their trust, I have to mirror them, not make it about me.

GatorCandie: Sometimes I get fooled though and then realize I'm using the wrong vocabulary.

BDR 529 IL: you don't have to mirror them; just make sure they get a lot of low protien meals and keep them deprived of sleep

BDR 529 IL: they will follow your every command

GatorCandie: haha, is that your angel, umm… Angel? Angle?

BDR 529 IL: haha, yep. That's my angle allright

BDR 529 IL: an equalateral snow angel

GatorCandie: Did you read my new profile? I'd like your opinion? I think it will make you laugh, actually.

BDR 529 IL: ok, I'll go look

BDR 529 IL: looking to attract new guys?

GatorCandie:	No, but I've been wanting to write something like this for a long time, and our conversation about honesty inspired me
GatorCandie:	It won't attract anyone, believe me
BDR 529 IL:	I like it. Are you single? Interested in going out sometime??
GatorCandie:	haha, maybe. It depends
GatorCandie:	do you fit what I'm looking for?
GatorCandie:	are you "the one"?
BDR 529 IL:	well, I'm also into fake sexual fantasy van abductions
BDR 529 IL:	is this a problem for you?
GatorCandie:	haha
GatorCandie:	you've got the wrong girl; I like animals but only to eat
GatorCandie:	NOONE will wink at me now, haha
GatorCandie:	Dating Suicide!!
BDR 529 IL:	My name is Jesse. My hobbies include, rape fantasys, aggressive sex and long walks on the beach. I enjoy talking to Pamela for 9 or 10 hours a day and poking homeless people with pointed sticks. I also enjoy stranding animals, masturbation and golf.
GatorCandie:	HAHA
GatorCandie:	LMAO
GatorCandie:	Well, what are you waiting for?? Put it up there!
BDR 529 IL:	you know what… I will.
GatorCandie:	haha, I'd love it

BDR 529 IL:	think match will let it go through?
GatorCandie:	the rape thing might be a problem but we can work on that
BDR 529 IL:	we can work on rape???
BDR 529 IL:	when can we start?!?!
GatorCandie:	haha
GatorCandie:	"stranding animals", haha
BDR 529 IL:	I'm so glad you finally set up your webcam as promised. I have been looking forward to getting some pictures of you
GatorCandie:	I'm still laughing
BDR 529 IL:	hint… cough… wink… hint
GatorCandie:	I'm coughing too
GatorCandie:	I'm wearing glasses today. You're not missing anything.
BDR 529 IL:	I like glasses… got that sexy student thing goin'
GatorCandie:	mmm… perhaps
GatorCandie:	It's the "I'm not going to see anyone important today that I know of" look
BDR 529 IL:	oh, well, you should see me. I'm definitely not looking my bestest-est
BDR 529 IL:	I'm in a ripped black t-shirt and boxers
BDR 529 IL:	it's laundry day
BDR 529 IL:	in fact, I forgot to pick it up
GatorCandie:	"I have to rest my eyes because I've been straining them staring at a computer screen talking to Jesse in all of my spare moments" look

GatorCandie: Pick it up?? Geez

BDR 529 IL: eh… it's too late

BDR 529 IL: have you received any interesting winks lately?

GatorCandie: um… lemme check

GatorCandie: wnybam sent me an email that was incredibly boring

GatorCandie: I've got an email for ya…t his was so sad.

BDR 529 IL: ok, send it

GatorCandie: Subject: Your Keys are Here!~

"Hello Angel,

As I was galloping through the land in my Shining Armor, I was brought to a sudden Halt… a Lady stood near the water. As I approached she turned to me, her beauty struck me like a single daisy rising in a field of green.

When she turned to me she WINKED and I was completely disarmed and defenseless… I dismounted and began to speak when she held up her hand and said, "Halt", "I am Mischievous and adventurous by Nature and Demand Fruit with Whipped Cream" I scrambled to decipher this ancient riddle of passage and spoke with as much clearity as my nerves would allow".

I am the one who will stand by your side, with Love and Tenderness, Peace and Harmony will lead us to take the world as we walk through this troubled but beautiful land. I have a hand for you, come walk with me.…

I hope you enjoyed my jaunt into the mystical, fantasy of my dreams! Thank you for inspiring me to smile and look into your dreams. As I read your profile I was filled with a sense of warmth and understanding. As I continued to read I knew you were someone I wanted to share with and learn about.

I love your sense of humor, your positive outlook, your up-front perspective.

Hope I got your attention or atleast made you smile!

Here is my reg email if you are not a member....

emarti at juno com

Of course you would ignore the spaces and add the . between juno and com as this site tends to erase any other email addresses being shared.

If you have a picture to share I would be most grateful!

Anxiously awaiting your reply,
Marty.

BDR 529 IL:	wow. Wanna come to my place and play Dungeons and Dragons?
GatorCandie:	sure, Skippy
GatorCandie:	Did you see his picture??
BDR 529 IL:	yes...in the suit, right?
BDR 529 IL:	or was that a different guy?
GatorCandie:	no, different guy but he's wearing a suit too
BDR 529 IL:	oh. Ok, lemme go look
BDR 529 IL:	awwww, he seems like a nice guy

GatorCandie: haha

BDR 529 IL: I feel bad for making Dungeons and Dragons jokes now

GatorCandie: Skippy

GatorCandie: Is what he looks like

BDR 529 IL: yes, I can see that

GatorCandie: check this out...

GatorCandie: "hello, how are you? my name is Lee, I liked your profile on match and figured i'd write to you! If you'd like to talk sometime let me know, I can be reached at pumpkincraazzy69@aol. com , well Ihope to hear from you soon have a great day!!!!...bye hun

GatorCandie: ok the ridiculous thing is that he's 23 years old. As if!

BDR 529 IL: oh he's just your type

GatorCandie: which part? I didn't find any

GatorCandie: Oh the part where he's 2 inches shorter than I am? I missed that.

GatorCandie: I should get in touch right away!!

GatorCandie: I get really young guys winking at me all the time for some reason

BDR 529 IL: oh? Been on any midnight romps through the playground??

BDR 529 IL: I'm only 5'10 at best... Maybe 5'9 even... gulp!

GatorCandie: just squeaked through actually

GatorCandie: My cutoff is 5'8. I NEVER respond to men who are my height or shorter.

GatorCandie: I very rarely respond as it is anyway, haha

BDR 529 IL: actually, I have been lying. I am really 4'10, 350 lbs, have a wooden leg and hooks for hands

GatorCandie: hooks? kinky

BDR 529 IL: haha

GatorCandie: I know it sounds like I'm so critical, but these guys are so clearly not what I'm looking for and it's hysterical

GatorCandie: smart and funny—Is that so hard?

BDR 529 IL: oh come on… you need more than that

GatorCandie: Well, you're right.

GatorCandie: I'd give some of these guys a heart attack.

BDR 529 IL: HAHA

GatorCandie: Could you imagine me and Tragically Hip guy?

GatorCandie: I would run mental circles around him and his D&D buddies

BDR 529 IL: could you imagine, sweet, innocent Pamela. The two of you are out on a date, you have fun, meet again, have some drinks and go back to your place. Minutes later your date is running out the front door, his shirt ripped to threads and bite marks all over him

GatorCandie: hahaha

GatorCandie: hey, I am sweet and innocent!

BDR 529 IL: I know

GatorCandie: just kinky, too

BDR 529 IL: I know… that's what I like about you.

GatorCandie:	I'm glad you finally decided to stop blowing me off, haha
GatorCandie:	It's so funny in a way that Kris found your profile and suggested I email you.
GatorCandie:	She honestly wouldnt leave me alone about you.
GatorCandie:	And I was like, "listen I already sent him a funny email…it was all I could do…"
BDR 529 IL:	honestly, when I think of you, it's rarely about anything sexual. More cuddling and talking to you.
BDR 529 IL:	that's gonna make you vomit, isn't it?
GatorCandie:	no, not at all, because I feel the same way. Despite the obvious attraction I have for you.
GatorCandie:	What happened to turning everything into a sex thing?
BDR 529 IL:	I ususally do; and I'm sure somewhere in the back of my head those sex thoughts are bobbing around
BDR 529 IL:	for example, right now, I happen to be thinking very sexual thoughts
GatorCandie:	Oh, about your torn shirt and my teeth all over you?
BDR 529 IL:	just imagining how our bodies would feel pressed up against each other
BDR 529 IL:	how your lips would feel on me
BDR 529 IL:	how you would react to my lips and tongue on you
GatorCandie:	um, you shouldnt do this
BDR 529 IL:	why not?

GatorCandie: because you're sending me off into dangerous territory

BDR 529 IL: good

GatorCandie: my witty banter is faultering

GatorCandie: I'm actually thinking very bad things now.

BDR 529 IL: do tell

GatorCandie: I can't tell!

BDR 529 IL: oh yes you can

GatorCandie: It's too graphic.

BDR 529 IL: no its not, trust me

GatorCandie: haha

GatorCandie: ok, clean version

GatorCandie: I'm lying on my back, you're on your side, your hand on my bare chest, kissing my neck and my right leg is kind of between yours

GatorCandie: ok, I got through that with very few problems

BDR 529 IL: no, add the problems!

GatorCandie: sorry, I can't

BDR 529 IL: you can do anything you put your mind to, Pamela. Didn't your mom ever tell you that?

GatorCandie: haha, yes "do", not type

BDR 529 IL: typing is a form of doing

GatorCandie: I kind of thought about setting my mind to writing pornography at some point. Then realized it would bore most segments of the population

BDR 529 IL: I'll be your first subscriber

GatorCandie: and I could never bring myself to write the words, "hard, throbbing cock" haha

BDR 529 IL: haha—you just did!

BDR 529 IL: "GatorCandie: Im laying on my back, youre on your side, your hand on my bare chest, kissing my neck and my right leg is kind of between yours"

BDR 529 IL: I'm so turned on right now

GatorCandie: I love talking dirty but I have to be really super worked up for that. Maybe it's because of how worked up I get that I really like it.

GatorCandie: did I say kissing my neck??

GatorCandie: ha, silly girl, I meant biting

GatorCandie: Maybe that's just the number of minutes I've progressed in this thought stream

BDR 529 IL: ha, that could be

BDR 529 IL: kissing slowly turns into biting

GatorCandie: omg

GatorCandie: this is bad

GatorCandie: I have a very good imagination.

GatorCandie: I'm scared of you :-)

BDR 529 IL: imagine you and I are standing beside the bed. I pull your hair back with one hand and undress you with the other. I guide your head down onto the bed, your hair still in my hand, and spank you, whispering between each little spanking "do you want me to make you cum, Pamela"?

GatorCandie: ☒ speechless

BDR 529 IL:	⊠ erection
BDR 529 IL:	haha…. I'm sorry. So crude.
GatorCandie:	you're trouble and I'm afraid somewhat uncontrollable. I'm very very turned on.
BDR 529 IL:	now, now. You know that I can control you
BDR 529 IL:	because you know what you'll get if I can't.
GatorCandie:	I'm totally biting my lip and I can't think of anything to say
GatorCandie:	why can't you be here right now???
GatorCandie:	I can't think of anything I don't like about you.
BDR 529 IL:	I have a superfluous third nipple
BDR 529 IL:	just kidding
GatorCandie:	yuck!
GatorCandie:	that would turn me off in a big hurry. Actually, just thinking about it cooled me down quite a bit!
BDR 529 IL:	I knew it would
GatorCandie:	that's good
BDR 529 IL:	but now I just get to turn you back on again
GatorCandie:	…if you could see how big my smile is right now
BDR 529 IL:	I'd love to
GatorCandie:	and I am listening to this awesome song. I'm totally happy. Can't think of anything I'd rather do right now, except be closer to you
BDR 529 IL:	so, when you come into the dark bedroom on Tuesday night, I might tie your hands behind your back so I can spank you. Is that a problem?

BDR 529 IL: Damn! I write something totally dirty just as you say something totally sweet

BDR 529 IL: Now I feel like a complete jerk

GatorCandie: good! haha

GatorCandie: um, the tying up thing might be a bit advanced for me. Its been done, but never very well. I kind of hung up my spurs on that one, but my mind isn't closed to it at all.

GatorCandie wants to directly connect.

BDR 529 IL is now directly connected.

BDR 529 IL: oh I would tie you up ever so lightly; just enough for you to feel he silk on your wrists

BDR 529 IL: but then again, how could you reach around and touch me as I spank you if you're tied up

BDR 529 IL: ...I see your point

GatorCandie: Hahaha. I didnt mean that, but I do like to try to prevent it from happening.

GatorCandie: I am totally desperate to have you hear this song.

GatorCandie: But I cannot send it no matter what I do.

BDR 529 IL: I guess it wasn't meant to be

BDR 529 IL: burn it and send it to me

GatorCandie: By then the mood will be gone, but I don't have a problem with that. Do you have your napster back?

BDR 529 IL: no!!! It's terible... no file sharing for me until I can figure out this new Windows update nonsense

BDR 529 IL:	so…why was your friend so keen on getting us together?
GatorCandie:	She loved your profile, with the "doorstep" thing and obviously she knows me, so she was playing match maka
GatorCandie:	The cigar pic maybe put me off just a bit. I wrote her back and said "Did you see the pic with the cigar?? He's totally Italian looking!"
GatorCandie:	She's like, "yeah, but see how funny he is"?
BDR 529 IL:	What is so bad about Italian guys? I am ½ Italian. You are aware of this, are you not? And… YOU'RE ½ Italian too!
GatorCandie:	Most Italian types (men) that I've met just kind of want to squeeze you into this image of what they want, so I have avoided them ever since.
BDR 529 IL:	yeah, I guess I know what you mean. Hey, by the way, you don't mind if I call you Marie from now on, do you?
GatorCandie:	um, Anna Maria?
GatorCandie:	Anna Maria Josephine?
GatorCandie:	My grandfather's name is Rocco Sinisi
GatorCandie:	My Nana calls him "Rock"
GatorCandie:	or Roc
BDR 529 IL:	I think you have the wrong impression of Italian guys—for the most part anyway
GatorCandie:	Um, I grew up around them…
GatorCandie:	Dino Ferrante, Anthony Cardina, Francis Blandino

BDR 529 IL:	oh… Dino, Tony and Franky… Those guys are different.
GatorCandie:	I know what you mean, and here I am talking to you, but it's just what I've seen. They seem to have respect on the surface.
GatorCandie:	My sister dates Italian guys and she doesn't seem to mind them.
BDR 529 IL:	you make us sound like saltines… "eh, I don't mind 'em"
GatorCandie:	Her only long-term guy, Tommy Nocigliato was a fabulous guy
GatorCandie:	Really sweet.
BDR 529 IL:	By fabulous do you mean gay? haha
GatorCandie:	Fabby, baby
GatorCandie:	No, definitley not gay.
BDR 529 IL:	so let me ask you this…
GatorCandie:	k
BDR 529 IL:	whats your favorite drink?
GatorCandie:	margarita
BDR 529 IL:	hmmm… what's your second favorite?
GatorCandie:	or Mike's Hard Cranberry
BDR 529 IL:	ok… what's your favorite snack?
GatorCandie:	Yogurt
GatorCandie:	Fruit
BDR 529 IL:	do you like wine?
GatorCandie:	am I ruining everything? How can I say this? No, I don't like wine unfortunately.
BDR 529 IL:	not at all??

BDR 529 IL:	wow. You ruined everything. Hit the bricks, sista.
GatorCandie:	There have been very few wines that I like and they have always been white.
BDR 529 IL:	Racist!
GatorCandie:	Believe me, I would love to love wine. It's really right up my alley.
GatorCandie:	The whole wine tasting thing. But I simply don't like it! I keep trying though.
BDR 529 IL:	I like wine. I'm not a big drinker at all, but I do love wine.
GatorCandie:	I love champagne. Go figure.
BDR 529 IL:	mmmm…. I LOVE champange… maybe a little too much!
GatorCandie:	I especially like champagnes that have citrus notes.
BDR 529 IL:	oh no… You ruined it again
BDR 529 IL:	haha
GatorCandie:	haha
GatorCandie:	You like that mineral-ish flavour?
BDR 529 IL:	flavored champanges arent actually champange… they're sparkling white wine
GatorCandie:	I don't mean like I like Asti or anything
BDR 529 IL:	but…. to each their own
GatorCandie:	NO!! Not flavored champagne!!
BDR 529 IL:	I know plenty of people who've lived very full lives, having never once tasted wine.
GatorCandie:	NO!! Not flavored champagne!!

GatorCandie:	Just that subtle hint of citrus from the grapes.
BDR 529 IL:	ahh… gotcha
BDR 529 IL:	I like Moet White Star or Brut Imperial—very good champagne for the price.
GatorCandie:	its in there—citrus notes, I'm not crazy. Ive tried a bunch of different champagnes, never FLAVORED, haha
GatorCandie:	I'm trying to remember the Moet I bought for New Year's Eve last year. It was so yummy.
BDR 529 IL:	probably one of the two I mentioned. Moet is one of the most popular brands
GatorCandie:	I can't believe you thought I was talking about Lambrusco or Asti Spumanti!
BDR 529 IL:	hahah
GatorCandie:	I am mortified
BDR 529 IL:	I'm sorry, it won't happen again. I should have known better.
GatorCandie:	I haven't been living in a trailer park my whole life!
BDR 529 IL:	LMAO
GatorCandie:	I decided to reinvent myself…
BDR 529 IL:	wow… it worked
GatorCandie:	So I relearned English from scratch
GatorCandie:	Stopped eating Spam
BDR 529 IL:	yeah… you talks real good now
GatorCandie:	Stopped beating the neighbor's children with a shoe
BDR 529 IL:	see… a real redneck wouldn't ruin a perfectly good shoe

GatorCandie: threw out all of my 3 inch electric blue shoes

GatorCandie: with the spiky heels

BDR 529 IL: ha

GatorCandie: spandex? Gone.

BDR 529 IL: leg warmers?

GatorCandie: gone (I hear they're coming back though)

BDR 529 IL: that's what I hear

GatorCandie: Genny? Gone.

GatorCandie: That habit I developed of talking with a cigarette dangling from my lip? Gone.

BDR 529 IL: see… out of the blue I'm thinking about sex again

GatorCandie: yikes, what I'm saying is not condusive to that

BDR 529 IL: aww shit. A few friends just came over

GatorCandie: talk to you later, maybe?

BDR 529 IL: yes, definitely.

GatorCandie: k

BDR 529 IL: how late will you be online??

GatorCandie: unsure. I usually don't hang unless somebody I know is around. Send me an email if you're going to be on and I'll get it on my PDA

BDR 529 IL: ok sweetie, I will.

GatorCandie: bye

BDR 529 IL: bye

BDR 529 IL signed off at 9:57:42 PM.

Later That Same Night

BDR 529 IL: oh no, not you again

GatorCandie: I know!

BDR 529 IL: sheesh

GatorCandie: So, come here often?

BDR 529 IL: no, my first time

GatorCandie: What's your sign, hot stuff?

BDR 529 IL: my sign? Yeild.

GatorCandie: Very courteous.

BDR 529 IL: Thanks. I try to be helpful

BDR 529 IL: I'm on the cusp of "Yeild" and "Slow Children Playing"

GatorCandie: The rain was very hard today.

GatorCandie: I had my triple super duper wipers going.

BDR 529 IL: wow... tripple super duper?

BDR 529 IL: that's serious business

BDR 529 IL: I heard it was terrible and power went out in a few places

GatorCandie: Power went out?

GatorCandie: hockey helmet children?

BDR 529 IL: short bus children

BDR 529 IL: power went out in some places, not all obviously.

GatorCandie: and children scattered about

GatorCandie: in some places

BDR 529 IL: A poem for all

GatorCandie: all who like that sort of thing

BDR 529 IL: I'm... I'm touched

GatorCandie: touch of the flu?

BDR 529 IL: there are naked girls on my television and it appears that they have all "gone wild"

GatorCandie: someone ought to calm them down

GatorCandie: unless they want to take all of their clothes off

GatorCandie: Speaking of, Consuela took the day off to help her brother in the fields

BDR 529 IL: ooohhh… How many beans did they pick?

GatorCandie: She has not reported back to me, Senor.

BDR 529 IL: that's it… get the whip!

GatorCandie: Not that I would really understand her

GatorCandie: I'm obviously not a very good switch.

BDR 529 IL: I recomend 30 lashes

BDR 529 IL: give or take a lash

GatorCandie: thank you for your guidance

BDR 529 IL: I'm here for you Pamela

GatorCandie: but I'll run my short-skirted, under-priveleged helper any way I want.

BDR 529 IL: it sounds like you have things firmly under control

GatorCandie: haha, I imagine so.

BDR 529 IL: so did you have fun while you were out?

GatorCandie: It was cool. I had a tea slushy in leiu of caffiene. Did you have fun while you were in?

BDR 529 IL: yes, I had fun while I was in

GatorCandie: lieu

GatorCandie:	loo
GatorCandie:	Lou
BDR 529 IL:	I use lieu all the time
BDR 529 IL:	and I mostly get weird looks from people
GatorCandie:	It's better to be in than out sometimes.
BDR 529 IL:	I'd have to agree with you
GatorCandie:	At night anyway.
BDR 529 IL:	hey! You got dressed again
GatorCandie:	whaddya mean?
BDR 529 IL:	I can't see when you're typing
GatorCandie:	oh, I know. It's fun.
GatorCandie:	Fun for me anyway.
BDR 529 IL:	tease
GatorCandie:	You seem to know me perty well, Hoss.
BDR 529 IL:	yes ma'am
GatorCandie:	I'm only be a ma'am when I get my first mammogram.
BDR 529 IL:	or if you start working in a whiskey bar in Texas
GatorCandie:	People have been calling me ma'am since I was 18 years old and I'm tired of it.
GatorCandie:	finally tired of it, haha
BDR 529 IL:	give 'em what for, honey
BDR 529 IL:	starting with me
BDR 529 IL:	really let me have it
GatorCandie:	Actually, I get alot less ma'ams now that I don't wear suits everyday.

GatorCandie:	any day, actually.
GatorCandie:	I'm starting to get "miss" again.
BDR 529 IL:	would you prefer "…and five dollars is your change, baby"
GatorCandie:	no, I prefer "you sweet thang"
BDR 529 IL:	how 'bout "hot pants"
GatorCandie:	er
BDR 529 IL:	or "dribble drawers"?
GatorCandie:	haha, um I prefer "urban gorilla" to "dribble drawers"
BDR 529 IL:	I guess we'll stick with Miss
GatorCandie:	k. I'm game
GatorCandie:	new wink
BDR 529 IL:	let's see
GatorCandie:	mrportisroy
GatorCandie:	He's got the beginnings of a Frankenstein thing going.
BDR 529 IL:	hahahaha
GatorCandie:	I am a very tricky person to figure out right away; very complex and unpredictable. I think I have a great balance of character that is difficult to duplicate.
GatorCandie:	Sounds like a blast.
BDR 529 IL:	I was going to ask how complex you think I am
BDR 529 IL:	you know… from 1-5
BDR 529 IL:	5 being an all black jigsaw puzzel

GatorCandie:	Complex? Um, I believe you operate on a few different levels.
GatorCandie:	I think you probably have a lot on your mind, but tend to compartmentalize.
GatorCandie:	I read a biography on Neal Peart, the drummer of Rush. And I read the newspapers daily, as I am in that field of business.
BDR 529 IL:	A biography on Neal Peart?? Hahahaha
BDR 529 IL:	Also noted for being the world's shortest book
GatorCandie:	Yeah, he really hooked me with that one.
BDR 529 IL:	he's wacky
GatorCandie:	He's a card.
BDR 529 IL:	hey look… he has stickers on his face
GatorCandie:	Yeah, crazy!!!
BDR 529 IL:	woah… slooooow down partner
GatorCandie:	Wow, he's the fool for me. Now that I look at him, he's winked at me twice before, but he's not one of my regulars.
BDR 529 IL:	twice and not a regular
BDR 529 IL:	my heart goes out to you
GatorCandie:	I have people who wink at me once per month.
GatorCandie:	As soon as match will let them, it seems.
GatorCandie:	They must be salespeople or something.
BDR 529 IL:	we should hold a big party for all the annoying people who have winked at us and video tape the entire event.
BDR 529 IL:	it would be a great social experiment

GatorCandie:	I agree. How many hookups do you think?
BDR 529 IL:	Nitwit Interaction Experiment One (1)
GatorCandie:	Would my rejects be attracted to yours??
GatorCandie:	Are they compatible?
BDR 529 IL:	I think so… most men don't really care much
GatorCandie:	Just by the sheer fact that they were somehow attracted to us
GatorCandie:	Don't care about what?
BDR 529 IL:	don't care what the girls look like… if it gets late enough in the night, everyone will hook up
GatorCandie:	really?
BDR 529 IL:	not all, but most
GatorCandie:	I've never hooked up before so I don't know the things that happen.
BDR 529 IL:	do you realize how many zaney antics will be going on at this party?
GatorCandie:	Like, "ok, you take that one and I'll get the other one"
GatorCandie:	Oh, sure. I've been to some wild wild parties before.
BDR 529 IL:	oh I've been out and watched guys just walk from girl to girl in the bar until one of 'em bites
GatorCandie:	But what are they biting for? A one-night stand?
BDR 529 IL:	by 11 o'clock, everyone will have stickers on their faces
GatorCandie:	Who would bite for that?

GatorCandie:	haha
BDR 529 IL:	you'd be surprised how many girls do
GatorCandie:	I think I definitely would be. I couldnt imagine it.
BDR 529 IL:	I used to own a bar so I've seen it happen night after night
GatorCandie:	right, I imagine you have seen a lot of that sort of thing.
GatorCandie:	I mean, I've been attracted to people before, but not that much. And I have been propositioned before I guess. It used to happen constantly when I was married.
BDR 529 IL:	propositioned? How so? Right out of the blue?
GatorCandie:	I sold a phone to an 84 Lumber account guy, who started complaining about his wife and within minutes was asking me how I felt about my marriage, and if my husband treated me well.
GatorCandie:	But in a slimy way.
BDR 529 IL:	ick
GatorCandie:	Yeah, I told him it couldn't be better. I think sometimes the more money a guy has, the more he doesn't really care what people really end up thinking of him.
BDR 529 IL:	I didn't get any new winks today
GatorCandie:	aww poor Jesse
BDR 529 IL:	I know… nobody loves me
BDR 529 IL:	boo hoo hoo
BDR 529 IL:	weep

BDR 529 IL:	sniffle
GatorCandie:	Oh I'm sure you'll get some new winks soon. But you have to admit...
GatorCandie:	Your winks are probably much more appealing than mine.
BDR 529 IL:	only because you get winks from everybody!!
GatorCandie:	Oh, I forgot that that wink was a result of that ridiculous profile I put up, ha
BDR 529 IL:	how many times did you say your profile was viewed? 17,000
GatorCandie:	Yes, and it stopped counting for like 4 weeks.
BDR 529 IL:	wow
BDR 529 IL:	you're in demand
GatorCandie:	not really, I'm just another chick with a pic
BDR 529 IL:	we should sell advertising space on your shirt in your photos
GatorCandie:	I think that's an awesome idea actually.
BDR 529 IL:	you could have 5 pictures; that's 5 spots at $250 a week each spot
BDR 529 IL:	not bad
GatorCandie:	I've seen some gym trainer type girls who use it as a vehicle for marketing their businesses
GatorCandie:	I like the way you think.
GatorCandie:	Product placement
BDR 529 IL:	yep. Hell, you could be drinking a Coke or Pepsi in one of 'em
GatorCandie:	I don't really drink soda but I could sell out I guess!

GatorCandie:	Instead of the "Nice Rack" t-shirt, I'll wear something more productive
BDR 529 IL:	well... the first pic has to be the nice rack pic
BDR 529 IL:	lure 'em in
BDR 529 IL:	then... we hit 'em with the advertising
GatorCandie:	ha, I think you're allowed like 20 pics too
BDR 529 IL:	any placement directly before or after the rack pick is $350
GatorCandie:	haha
GatorCandie:	I actually did get an advertisement email from a guy... hold on a sec.
BDR 529 IL:	ok. You can even keep most of the revenue. I'll just take 10% of the gross weekly sales
BDR 529 IL:	Plus a 30% up front fee for the idea. That's 30% of the expected yearly sales, which I would expect to be approximately $5,000,000.
BDR 529 IL:	So please cut my check for $1.5MM now and make it payable to cash ("Cash" is a actual real first name). I'll expect it by then end of the week of I'll have to charge you a late fee of 1% compounded daily for every day that the check is late... starting today.
GatorCandie:	You drive a hard bargain but it's a deal. Check out this profile
BDR 529 IL:	by the way, that $1.5MM is WITHOUT figuring in the "Rack Pick" promo bonus
GatorCandie:	the nice rack thing was MY idea!! What the heck?
GatorCandie:	http://www.match.com/profile/showprofile.
BDR 529 IL:	aggghhh

GatorCandie: He sent me a fricken form letter!

GatorCandie: Hello my name is Rick and I wanted to let you know about the newest and hottest party band in WNY The Face Band. This band features former members of the Grille band and they perform music from 4 decades that range from rock, funk, pop, jazz, blues, disco and top 40. They can play anything! They even do covers of modern day artist like; Brittany Spears, Christina A, No Doubt and Outcast. They play this Friday Night at Evo Night Club on Transit road in Williamsville. You can check the band . Have a great day and I will see you at the show.

Rick

P.S. You look fantastic! I would of never guesses that you are 30. You could pass for early 20's.

BDR 529 IL: wow... what a loser. Seriously, I don't know what else to say.

BDR 529 IL: nice vest

GatorCandie: Are you sure you're not a music industry exec?

BDR 529 IL: haha

GatorCandie: you'd see me penniliess and broken in my nice rack t-shirt peddling fake silver on a street corner in the Village

BDR 529 IL: sounds ok so far... then I could take you in and make you my slave

GatorCandie: Wouldnt it already have amounted to that?

BDR 529 IL: I suppose

GatorCandie:	Working for peanuts?
GatorCandie:	I mean, I like peanuts, don't get me wrong.
BDR 529 IL:	I knew an elephant once who worked for peanuts
GatorCandie:	And I'm not trying to make you mad, missa jesse.
BDR 529 IL:	don't make me get ma belt, woman
BDR 529 IL:	now fetch me some cornbread
GatorCandie:	are you all set for beer?
BDR 529 IL:	what?
GatorCandie:	beer to go with the cornbread
BDR 529 IL:	no thank you, but what is the soup du jour?
GatorCandie:	it's the soup of the day
BDR 529 IL:	mmmm… that sounds good. I'll have that.
GatorCandie:	so I have an important question
BDR 529 IL:	ok
GatorCandie:	Manhattan Clam, New England Clam or Oh my God I would never eat either?
BDR 529 IL:	New England
BDR 529 IL:	but Manhattan does have its up side too
GatorCandie:	Now I get to tell you to hit the bricks! Very liberating.
BDR 529 IL:	ahh… must be a weight off your shoulders
GatorCandie:	I am so jealous of all the great seafood you downstaters get.
GatorCandie:	I used to eat Mako within hours of it being alive.

BDR 529 IL:	you should be! Part of our tax dollars go to constructing billboards in Buffalo just to taunt you with our good seafood
BDR 529 IL:	I went to my favrite restaurant the other day
BDR 529 IL:	Sal Anthonys on E. 13th st
GatorCandie:	What's that?
BDR 529 IL:	favorite
BDR 529 IL:	I hate seeing really bad typos too late
GatorCandie:	that wasn't too bad. I can't even picture E. 13th
GatorCandie:	typos are becoming part of my life lately
BDR 529 IL:	no it was bad… a really bad typo is one where the reader may believe that you really thought it was spelled that way
BDR 529 IL:	"favrite"
BDR 529 IL:	uuugh
GatorCandie:	Oh, I've only noticed one consistent error on your part.
BDR 529 IL:	I've gotten so bad
BDR 529 IL:	fire away
GatorCandie:	Um, the plural of a word ending in 'y' is usually 'ies'
GatorCandie:	such as fantasys or fantasies
BDR 529 IL:	ahh…. That must drive you up a wall
GatorCandie:	No, not really. I actually feel bad.
BDR 529 IL:	you feel bad?
GatorCandie:	Well, like you might have missed that and you think that's the way it's supposed to be.

GatorCandie: Now, if you were constantly screwing up, it wouldnt even phase me. But since you are obviously very on the grammatical and spelling ball, it makes me want to help.

BDR 529 IL: To tell you the truth, had I been paying closer attention, I would have picked it up

BDR 529 IL: I try to be pretty good with that sort of thing, but I tell ya, since the invention of Microsoft Word, it's all gone downhill

GatorCandie: oh, even better. I'm sure I make stupid mistakes all the time. like 'to' for 'too'

GatorCandie: Bill Gates is evil in all sorts of ways

GatorCandie: Here's another profile for you to look at— http://www.match.com/profile/showprofile.aspx

GatorCandie: Did I send you this guy? He almost scared the pants off me. He's new.

BDR 529 IL: wow… do you want me to let you go?

BDR 529 IL: he might be waiting for your call

BDR 529 IL: that picture with the tank top is priceless

GatorCandie: He might be. Did you see his second picture? oh my.

GatorCandie: The 4th pic is great. Probably the birth of his baby or something.

BDR 529 IL: ha

BDR 529 IL: "sometimes I make people laugh so hard their ribs hurt"

BDR 529 IL: from his profile

GatorCandie: really? I don't think I read it. I could make HIS ribs hurt, ha

BDR 529 IL:	haha
GatorCandie:	He's "FAITHFUL"
BDR 529 IL:	"I love the outdoors and tan easily"
GatorCandie:	what do you think happened there?
GatorCandie:	Yeah, don't tell me that tan comes from just the sun
BDR 529 IL:	I tan easily, even when I'm not outside
GatorCandie:	Right, even when the sun never shines for 6 months, I have a tan.
BDR 529 IL:	"Locally, I like fine dining restataraunts like Salvatores"
GatorCandie:	I love that pink tank top
BDR 529 IL:	I've seen that place—Salvatore's
GatorCandie:	There you go. That's just as over the top as your casinos.
BDR 529 IL:	no no no.... Salvatore's is WAY more ridiculous than the casino that I go to
GatorCandie:	Salvatore's is the gaudy, "high end" place in town. But its not even really in town, its in the burbs
GatorCandie:	I prefer the Chop House though
BDR 529 IL:	www.theborgata.com
GatorCandie:	"your happy place"
BDR 529 IL:	haha... such a scam
BDR 529 IL:	I love it
GatorCandie:	haha, they have the "wake up smiling" or the "up all night" packages. More like the "wake up groaning"

BDR 529 IL:	wake up? That would mean that you went to sleep at some point
GatorCandie:	the "too drunk to fuck" package
BDR 529 IL:	haha
BDR 529 IL:	it's amazing the amount of alcohol you can drink at that place
BDR 529 IL:	it's all free and they just keep bringing it and bringing it and bringing it
GatorCandie:	"Here at the Borgata, we have many packages designed to fit your unique needs, or we can design one just for you".
BDR 529 IL:	whatever you want
GatorCandie:	I know, I heard that about Casinos. But it isn't really free, is it?
BDR 529 IL:	if you're gambling, it's free
GatorCandie:	Right.
BDR 529 IL:	they pump oxygen into the gaming rooms to keep you awake, the drinks come out all night, there are no windows and no clocks
GatorCandie:	Sounds smart.
GatorCandie:	That room in the "Do not disturb" package looks super cool
BDR 529 IL:	They only have one of those rooms and I have yet to be able to get it
GatorCandie:	When I was training people, I had no clock.
BDR 529 IL:	the host there tells me that you need to take out a million dollar marker to get that room
GatorCandie:	What?
GatorCandie:	...ok

GatorCandie:	What's the trouble? I'll just make a call…
BDR 529 IL:	meaning, you're going to gamble one million dollars at that casino
GatorCandie:	haha
BDR 529 IL:	yeah… it's nuts
BDR 529 IL:	we usually get the room below that; the Piatto Suite. That's the one in the pictures that I sent you
GatorCandie:	I love how they put it in the marketing pics yet its mostly unattainable.
BDR 529 IL:	oh I've tried every trick in the book to get that room
BDR 529 IL:	no dice
BDR 529 IL:	no pun intended
GatorCandie:	have you really? haha
GatorCandie:	what are some of these tricks?
GatorCandie:	You can take the boy outta Brooklyn…
BDR 529 IL:	I offered a host $500 to LET me pay $1,500 a night for the room
GatorCandie:	haha
BDR 529 IL:	I had a friend of mine who is a host at the tropicanna call and say that we were high rollers coming in and they couldn't accomodate us
BDR 529 IL:	then I finally called the hosts boss and said look, there has to be a time when the room is not occupied, just RENT it to me
BDR 529 IL:	nope
BDR 529 IL:	nothing

GatorCandie:	wow it sounds like you've been up and down this. I'm sure you're more determined than ever.
BDR 529 IL:	hahaha… it's the point of the whole thing now
BDR 529 IL:	the room comes with a private chef!
GatorCandie:	oh, I totally understand AND agree, haha
GatorCandie:	and a Consuela?
BDR 529 IL:	I wouldn't doubt it
GatorCandie:	you MUST get into that room!!!
BDR 529 IL:	I know it's childish, but when we are all together, it's a lot of fun
GatorCandie:	It sounds it and it's not childish. When people put roadblocks in front of me, I try to fenagle them down.
BDR 529 IL:	last time we went down there we banged 'em for just about $10,000. I told the host if they want to make their money back, to give us the room so we would stay another night
BDR 529 IL:	he wouldn't
GatorCandie:	wow, that must burn your butt.
BDR 529 IL:	banged em… see, any casino talk brings me right back down to my street slang
GatorCandie:	that's fine, I'm witcha so far. No explaining needed yet.
GatorCandie:	a million dollars is a lot of money.
BDR 529 IL:	If I had a million dollars to gamble, I certainly would not be at the casino
GatorCandie:	Wow, a million dollars to gamble. hmm

GatorCandie: I would buy a person.

GatorCandie: haha

BDR 529 IL: I've already spent my first extra million…. a Hinckley Talleria. Quite possibly the world's finest sailing vessel

BDR 529 IL: I simply must have it

BDR 529 IL: www.hinckleyyachts.com

GatorCandie: sweet

BDR 529 IL wants to directly connect.

BDR 529 IL is now directly connected.

BDR 529 IL: I was going to send you a picture of my boat now…. but I don't think I have any on this computer

BDR 529 IL: sorry—I'm sure you're heart broken

GatorCandie: I would love to see it actually.

GatorCandie: Wow that's some boat!—The Hinckley.

BDR 529 IL: yeah… it's something else

BDR 529 IL: This is the one I have. Not the exact one, but the same model and year

BDR 529 IL: http://adcache.boattraderonline.com/6/4/0/726458240.htm

GatorCandie: awww poor baby, stuck with such an inferior boat

BDR 529 IL: honestly… mine is like a toy in comparison

GatorCandie: I see that, but it's a neat toy.

BDR 529 IL: yes

BDR 529 IL: wow… we forgot to talk about sex again

BDR 529 IL: what's going on here?

GatorCandie: Well, we were actually talking about other stuff.

BDR 529 IL: I know, but how is it that a girl I'm so attracted to makes me think about things other than sex?

GatorCandie: Which is ok too. Because I don't think we touched on anything so far since we met that I mind talking to you about, or that got boring

BDR 529 IL: uh oh

BDR 529 IL: this might mean I really like you

GatorCandie: You really like me!! You really, really like me!!

BDR 529 IL: hahaha

GatorCandie: You mean that doesn't happen?

BDR 529 IL: not very often

GatorCandie: 'lil Pam, exception to the rule

BDR 529 IL: hehe

GatorCandie: I know what you mean.

GatorCandie: But I usually don't keep talking. I just take off.

BDR 529 IL: so do I

BDR 529 IL: so… umm, do you like… stuff??

GatorCandie: Ok, you showed me your boat, so I'll show you my… yeah, some stuff.

BDR 529 IL: show me your? Your what?

GatorCandie: what's your favorite stuff?

BDR 529 IL: um… just stuff

GatorCandie: show you my… garden, which kinda pales in comparison in a lot of ways…

GatorCandie:	But I roto-tilled it myself, haha
BDR 529 IL:	my boat is not delicious
GatorCandie:	My tomatoes are! I really get excited about my garden, actually. Sense of personal accomplishment and all.
BDR 529 IL:	well let me see it then. Make it snappy.
GatorCandie:	I'm trying to make it snappy, don't worry bub
GatorCandie:	is it too early for me to call you bubbie or bubala
BDR 529 IL:	of course not
GatorCandie:	Can I just tell you that I miss knishes?
GatorCandie:	From a corner vendor with mustard, oh how I love them. And dogs.
BDR 529 IL:	no knishes there??
GatorCandie:	In the kosha section of a few supermarkets. They are packaged and stuff. And they're from Brooklyn, but it's not the same.
BDR 529 IL:	no, it's never the same
GatorCandie:	…and it never will be again
GatorCandie:	I think you got the picture of my annoying garden
BDR 529 IL:	it looks nice
BDR 529 IL:	did you get a lot of vegatables?
GatorCandie:	oh, if I don't make fried green tomatoes, I'll have ripe tomatoes coming out of my ears in a week or so. I've been getting 1 tomato a day so far, but it's going to be out of control soon
BDR 529 IL:	mmmm

GatorCandie:	But I've had spinach, lettuce, beets radishes and I'm about to harvest string beans. Urban farmer girl
BDR 529 IL:	mmm mmm mmm
BDR 529 IL:	sounds good
BDR 529 IL:	now I'm hungry again
GatorCandie:	oh yeah and my little eggplant, which was pretty good
GatorCandie:	I know, I'm afraid to remind myself of my sparse cupboard by going into the kitchen
GatorCandie:	I didn't eat at the coffee shop, so I'm up the creek without a nice boat.
BDR 529 IL:	I still have not gone shopping
GatorCandie:	I wish I had ground beef—I'd make sloppy joes.
BDR 529 IL:	it's almot time for breakfast anyway
GatorCandie:	Good point. I wish I had eggs
GatorCandie:	I have a funny diner story.
GatorCandie:	Do you know the Towne Restaurant?
GatorCandie:	Right on the corner of Elmwood and Allen
BDR 529 IL:	yes
BDR 529 IL:	I think so
GatorCandie:	Some buddies and I went there at 5 am one time and I was feeling silly so I took all the little special cards out of their slip covers and I distributed them, and we played go fish with them until the waitress got to us. She was horrified.
BDR 529 IL:	haha

BDR 529 IL:	who won
GatorCandie:	She got to us way before we could declare a winner.
GatorCandie:	She won. She got all of them in a hurry.
BDR 529 IL:	hahaha
BDR 529 IL:	are you banned for life???
GatorCandie:	no, as a matter of fact we were regulars every Sunday morning at about 4 or 5 for 4 months or so.
GatorCandie:	And she worked there all the time. But I guess all of our good tips and sweetness stood for nothing.
BDR 529 IL:	she'll remember your kindness the next time someone unscrews the sugar lid
GatorCandie:	Imagine what would happen if I were vindictive
BDR 529 IL:	oh no
BDR 529 IL:	I wouldn't even want to imagine
GatorCandie:	So tell me about this CD I'm listening to darlin'
BDR 529 IL:	what would you like to know
GatorCandie:	Or talk about sex. Either way.
BDR 529 IL:	haha
GatorCandie:	struck with a sudden disinterest
BDR 529 IL:	yah.... the lyrics are ok but could use some work
BDR 529 IL:	I don't know... I guess I'm just burnt out on it
GatorCandie:	I like that line, actually.

GatorCandie:	I bet you have heard it over and over and over
BDR 529 IL:	and over and over
BDR 529 IL:	and played it over
GatorCandie:	and over?
BDR 529 IL:	and over
BDR 529 IL:	haha
GatorCandie:	I hear Toadies, sorta
BDR 529 IL:	Never really listened to them
GatorCandie:	Rubberneck is pretty good. Some of the songs are a little hard. But there is one song that totally gets my motor running because of the lyrics.
BDR 529 IL:	what song?
GatorCandie:	Tyler
BDR 529 IL:	hmmm... don't know it. If I ever get my file sharing stuff sorted out, I'll download it
GatorCandie:	I *think* its kind of about rape, but I'm not sure
BDR 529 IL:	you can make it be about whatever you want
GatorCandie:	Hey, I don't want you to think I'm totally obsessed with that by the way. I've never actually done it.
BDR 529 IL:	haha... I don't. A fantasy is just that—a fantasy. If it happened in reality it would be considered an occurance.
GatorCandie:	Your lead singer sounds angry
GatorCandie:	Hes got that growl going

BDR 529 IL:	a bit... I think the vocals need to be turned down a bit and he needs to let some space go without singing
GatorCandie:	So far I agree.
GatorCandie:	So if I comment on the CD, am I in danger of insulting you?
BDR 529 IL:	not at all
BDR 529 IL:	comment away my dear
GatorCandie:	I think you guys have a ton of potential and I think there might be a few too many rhymes and cliches
BDR 529 IL:	yeah... I agree
BDR 529 IL:	I don't even hear the lyrics when I listen to it
GatorCandie:	I'm just the guy on the street though.
BDR 529 IL:	I just do it for fun. I don't think MTV and invites to P-diddy's are on the way
GatorCandie:	You're obviously all talented.
BDR 529 IL:	why thank you
BDR 529 IL:	I like track 5
GatorCandie:	Yes, I like the guitar work on track 5
BDR 529 IL:	it gets a little boring but the end is pretty cool
GatorCandie:	I could definitely hear that song on the radio
BDR 529 IL:	listen for the riff, man. Waaaaait for it...
BDR 529 IL:	wait for it.....
GatorCandie:	uh, like, yeah I'm waiting (flips her hair back with other hand on hip)
BDR 529 IL:	mmm... sounds sexy
GatorCandie:	It's the DOORS! Right on your 3rd track

BDR 529 IL: and track 9 is my favorite to play live

GatorCandie: ooohh I like it already

BDR 529 IL: :-)

GatorCandie: there's some color in this one

BDR 529 IL: yeah… I like it

GatorCandie: You're great.

BDR 529 IL: haha….. you're not so bad yourself lil lady

GatorCandie: why thank you cowboy

BDR 529 IL: <—— tips hat

GatorCandie: I can see the fedora

BDR 529 IL: haha

BDR 529 IL: it says 10 gallon but it's really just an 8 and a half

BDR 529 IL: don't tell anyone

GatorCandie: little man

GatorCandie: Have you ever heard the band Treat Her Right?

BDR 529 IL: no

GatorCandie: It was Mark Sandman's gig before Morphine.

BDR 529 IL: oh really? Any good?

GatorCandie: Totally different from Morphine

GatorCandie: Yeah, theyre good. They have some great lyrics. One of their songs is "King of Beers" and another is "Junkyard"

GatorCandie: Its a little redneck-y believe it or not.

BDR 529 IL: in a Primus kind of way or really redneck-y?

GatorCandie:	I'm trying to think of a good comparison, but because they kind of defy category, you don't hear stuff like that on the radio.
GatorCandie:	Lets see, there is a guitar with a twang in it.
GatorCandie:	11 is sinister
BDR 529 IL:	yeah... I like that also... it works well into track 12....
BDR 529 IL:	theres a little Pink Floyd guitar part in there
GatorCandie:	Good energy on track 12.
BDR 529 IL:	that's usually our closer
BDR 529 IL:	we had a song that we used to play and it was really boring, so I brought a deck of cards with me to a show one day and played a game of solitare while playing it... it was great cause it was so subtle... Chris (the singer) turns around, see's it and just bursts out laughing on stage
GatorCandie:	haha where did you lay out the cards?
BDR 529 IL:	the drums were set up next to a big shelf on the left side with a bunch of PA monitor equipment on it. Thre was some free space to play cards on there.
GatorCandie:	6 is the song I referred to when I mentioned energy
BDR 529 IL:	oh. yeah... it's cool, but can get grating after hearing it a few times
BDR 529 IL:	ha... that's the only song on the album from when we were kids
BDR 529 IL:	we wrote that song about 12 years ago
GatorCandie:	I really like the beat.

BDR 529 IL:	:-)
GatorCandie:	You guys should change it up and yell oi instead of hey, ha
BDR 529 IL:	hahaha… "oi". I haven't heard that word in a while
GatorCandie:	Oh, this song gets better and better
BDR 529 IL:	honey, I hate to do this, but I should really get to bed
BDR 529 IL:	I'm never going to wake up tomorrow. Scratch that—I will most likely wake up but it will be later than it should be.
GatorCandie:	k. sweet dreams darlin'
BDR 529 IL:	you too my dear
BDR 529 IL:	will I see you tomorrow?
GatorCandie:	Why? Will you be in Buffalo?
GatorCandie:	'cause I'd see ya in a heartbeat
BDR 529 IL:	unfortunately no. Will I type with you tomorrow?
GatorCandie:	When? Same time? Like 8ish?
BDR 529 IL:	Sure, sounds good to me.
GatorCandie:	ha, k. It's been nice talking with you. sd, lu bubye
BDR 529 IL:	goodnight honey
BDR 529 IL:	I like you
GatorCandie:	lu too bye
BDR 529 IL:	whats sd, lu
GatorCandie:	sweet dreams, like you
BDR 529 IL:	oh, stupid me.

Gatorcandie: iluji

BDR 529 IL: ilytps

Gatorcandie: hee, bye sweetness

BDR 529 IL: bye bye

BDR 529 IL direct connection is closed.

BDR 529 IL signed off at 4:26:40 AM.

Looking back at this, I'm fairly certain that she was trying to say that she loved me. That might sound quite egotistical, especially because it had only been a few days, but that's how it works sometimes. And I'd be lying if I said that I didn't feel the same way at the time. Saying "like you" was a safe way to test the "I love you" waters. We both felt very strongly towards one another right away, and it was hard not to say I love you; but at the same time, not only had it only been a few days that we knew each other, but we had never even met in person or even talked on the phone! So how on earth could either one of us realistically say I love you under those circumstances? Both of us knew that something was happening. We were feeling something that neither of us had ever felt before and neither of us knew how to express it or deal with it. Everytime we spoke, it would last for hours and hours, talking until morning. Signing off at 4:26 a.m. was not uncommon for us, despite the fact that neither of us were really night owls.

WHAT ARE WE?

BDR 529 IL: Good morning sunshine

GatorCandie: Hey darlin, good morning :-)

BDR 529 IL: Or good afternoon I should say

BDR 529 IL: I'm still in bed if you can believe it

GatorCandie: It's morning to you.

GatorCandie: I can, I got up only 2 hours ago.

BDR 529 IL: Yep... just opened my eyes

BDR 529 IL: And you were the very first thought I had

GatorCandie: I haven't left my place yet today.

GatorCandie: Same here. I'm working on a CD for you.

BDR 529 IL: Cool

BDR 529 IL: Can I ask you something?

GatorCandie: Sure.

BDR 529 IL: is it possible to have fallen in love with you when I haven't even met you yet

GatorCandie: it's doubtful but possible. Are you telling me that you're in love with me?

BDR 529 IL: I suppose not. It doesn't seem possible for that to have happened yet, does it?

GatorCandie: probably not but it's a sweet sentiment. I share a similar dilemma with you. :-)

GatorCandie: um, could be that you haven't been able to just be yourself in awhile with a girl? maybe?

BDR 529 IL: maybe. I'm not sure. I just know that I think about you all the time.

BDR 529 IL: which is probably due to the fact that we talk to each other comnstantly. I don't have any time to think about anything else! haha

GatorCandie: I like you too. I like you alot. Like, a really lot, lot.

GatorCandie: It's this internet thing a bit, maybe. We're only seeing the good things about each other. I don't mean to over-analyze though

BDR 529 IL: You might be right

BDR 529 IL: It's about 1 degree in here I think. I'm freezing!

GatorCandie: It's about 75 degrees in here.

BDR 529 IL: It's the air conditioning that's keeping me in bed

GatorCandie: I'm actually positive you're better in person.

BDR 529 IL: Positive?

GatorCandie: Yep.

BDR 529 IL: What nakes you so sure?

GatorCandie: Because I think your delivery has more punch in person.

GatorCandie: Punch, as in Hawaiian

BDR 529 IL: Forget in-person. You should try me with the raspberry vinigarette. I'm delicious.

GatorCandie: Hahaha. I know I'm better in person.

BDR 529 IL: Nothing I like more after a hard day's work than a nice warm glass of Hawaiian Punch

GatorCandie: So a friend of mine was publishing an underground literary magazine

BDR 529 IL: ok

GatorCandie:	And he knew how much the word "creamy" gave me the willies for some reason…
GatorCandie:	So he sends me a copy, and lo and behold the centerfold is all white space, saved for the word C R E A M Y in the middle, haha
GatorCandie:	ick
BDR 529 IL:	Haha
GatorCandie:	That word always kind of bugged me for some idioc reason.
BDR 529 IL:	Now that I think about it, creamy is a little icky… when talking about food anyway.
GatorCandie:	When talking about most things!
GatorCandie:	You make me feel all silly and teenager-ish by the way.
BDR 529 IL:	Oh yeah? Wanna cut class tomorrow and make out?
GatorCandie:	sure, why not. No one will know
GatorCandie:	do you like… stuff?
BDR 529 IL:	Ha… um, yeah… stuff is cool
GatorCandie:	dude, I totally don't want to go to school tomorrow
BDR 529 IL:	Let's ditch, man
GatorCandie:	yeah, we can do "stuff"
BDR 529 IL:	Cool
GatorCandie:	haha
GatorCandie:	wow, that is painful.
GatorCandie:	That's like the conversation I had with Mr. Nugget, and it wasn't my fault.

BDR 529 IL:	Poor poor Mr. Nugget
GatorCandie:	oh my God!! My match experiment turned out to be much worse than I feared!! Hysterical… next time you're on your laptop I'll show you. It gets worse and worse, like notsoevilwhatever guy
GatorCandie:	Sometimes I wonder how people get along.
BDR 529 IL:	How so?
GatorCandie:	Along in the world, I mean.
BDR 529 IL:	'splain Lucy
GatorCandie:	It's frightening that I share the same town as these people.
GatorCandie:	The winks I got. Total riot.
GatorCandie:	They top everything that came before.
BDR 529 IL:	I don't believe that
GatorCandie:	It's really true. One guys screen name is farmlivin1970. Can you believe it??
GatorCandie:	Just call me Daisy Mae
BDR 529 IL:	Oh no. Haha
GatorCandie:	Well like I told you, it has some entertainment value.
BDR 529 IL:	You should give him a call. Imagine the garden you'd have then!
GatorCandie:	I would rather just appreciate what I have and be grateful. :-)
GatorCandie:	So what's on your agenda today?
BDR 529 IL:	First—get out of bed
GatorCandie:	must… get… coffee. CONSUELA!!!

BDR 529 IL:	Yes, coffee is a must
BDR 529 IL:	Then, I was going to play music for a little while
BDR 529 IL:	My coffepot made me some all on it's own at 9am and I wasn't even there to appreciate it.
GatorCandie:	I haven't had any coffee yet. All I have in the house is Folgers and I would be disappointed expecting coffee and tasting that, so fahgetaboudit
GatorCandie:	I know, I have this really fancy shmancy coffee maker and I never use all of the neat features it has. It warms the carafe, sings me songs, has neat lights and buttons.
BDR 529 IL:	Mine says goodmorning to me then slaps me accross the face. German engineering—ya can't beat it.
GatorCandie:	wow, those Germans are crazy.
BDR 529 IL:	you bet they are.
GatorCandie:	You can get it to stop doing that, you know…
BDR 529 IL:	No….I kinda like it
BDR 529 IL:	Humbles me first thing in the morning
GatorCandie:	funny story #56,842
GatorCandie:	I was having brunch in a very nice bar type place with my ex and two of the guys that work for him for some bizarre reason one day…
GatorCandie:	And I must of said something like, "that would get you slapped" so he said he wanted me to slap him, right there in the restaurant. So after about a half hour, I did, haha. I

	guess you'd have to be there, but it was very amusing. He LOVED it.
BDR 529 IL:	haha. People seem to love to get hit by you.
GatorCandie:	We all thought he was a total nut.
GatorCandie:	I believe that is the last story that involves me hitting anybody.
BDR 529 IL:	You know, if you were lying in bed with me right now, I would keep poking you until you made me some coffee
BDR 529 IL:	Just so you know
GatorCandie:	You would?
BDR 529 IL:	Yes
GatorCandie:	That's okay. I like being poked and I enjoy coffee.
GatorCandie:	oh and how people love to get hit by me—I have NO idea why those things have occurred.
BDR 529 IL:	Haha
GatorCandie:	It was over a span of like 12 years.
BDR 529 IL:	Abuse!!
GatorCandie:	NO, haha. I hit the guy in the restaurant because it was like a dare and it was so completely freaky. He got all quiet and smiley after it too :-)
BDR 529 IL:	Haha
GatorCandie:	So you would poke me until I made coffee? I'm rethinking the poke part.
GatorCandie:	careful…
GatorCandie:	I'm unsure if I would like that. You'd have to show me the details of the poke beforehand.

BDR 529 IL:	it would be a fun, playful yet annoying kind of poke
GatorCandie:	I would laugh, squirm and try to get away I think.
BDR 529 IL:	There IS NO ESCAPE. Avtually there is an escape; to the kitchen to make coffee.
GatorCandie:	Oh yes there is! I have devised a pain free and foolproof way to get away. I had to insert "pain free" just to try to shed this reputation that I'm getting.
BDR 529 IL:	Haha
GatorCandie:	It's a little strange, but it works almost everytime.
BDR 529 IL:	Do I get to hear it?
GatorCandie:	Um, well I'd like your opinion on that one. If you were me, would you tell me?
BDR 529 IL:	Not a chance
GatorCandie:	haha, so what's your advice?
BDR 529 IL:	I say tell me
GatorCandie:	of course you do!!
GatorCandie:	That seals it.
BDR 529 IL:	Ok… this is crazy. I have to get out of bed!
BDR 529 IL:	And take a shower
BDR 529 IL:	And not be a bum
GatorCandie:	It is nearly 1:30, ya bum
BDR 529 IL:	Ha
GatorCandie:	k, have a great day!
BDR 529 IL:	You too honey. I'll talk to you a little later on

GatorCandie: k. get clean and caffeined.

BDR 529 IL: Will do

GatorCandie: see ya

BDR 529 IL: Bye

BDR 529 IL signed off at 1:28:49 PM.

OUR FIRST FIGHT

GatorCandie: hey, sailor. I've been talking about you.

BDR 529 IL: so that's why my ears were burning.

GatorCandie: you could see what I wrote about you if you like.

BDR 529 IL: good things, I hope?

GatorCandie: For good or ill, you have mail.

BDR 529 IL: I'll go look

BDR 529 IL: "at least I might get a chance to get to sleep early"

BDR 529 IL: :-(

BDR 529 IL: all my fault

BDR 529 IL: what a bastard I am

GatorCandie: I didnt send it to make you feel bad.

GatorCandie: I just didn't want to go through it all a second time, so I just forwarded you the email.

BDR 529 IL: I know

BDR 529 IL: I'm not married, by the way!

BDR 529 IL: :-(

She was upset that I wasn't around for the rest of the day. Obviously, she also mentioned to her friend that she thought I was married.

BDR 529 IL: I'm sorry, I was sailing the high seas today. I sold my boat so I was out on it for one last final cruise.

GatorCandie:	You sold it?
BDR 529 IL:	yep
GatorCandie:	How come?
BDR 529 IL:	I was planning on selling it this fall. I usually do (sell a boat in the fall and buy a new one in the spring)
GatorCandie:	gotcha
BDR 529 IL:	after the cruise on my boat, I wen't for a ride on a friend's boat out to Long Island. We had to leave it at his house out there.
GatorCandie:	and you hitched home?
BDR 529 IL:	no, he drove us back here (like a maniac I might add)
GatorCandie:	white knuckles all the way huh?
BDR 529 IL:	I closed my eyes and hoped for the best
BDR 529 IL:	so, what bothers you about me
GatorCandie:	um, nothing bothers me about you. As you can see (I think, but I cant remember exactly what I said) I like ya. I guess I was disappointed you werent online today, but oh well…
BDR 529 IL:	I know. I walked in the door only a few minutes ago.
BDR 529 IL:	it was a long day to say the least
GatorCandie:	Sounds it. I had a pretty good day.
BDR 529 IL:	I read your other email. Which friend had the baby?
BDR 529 IL:	have you mentioned her to me?

GatorCandie: Yeah, my neurotic friend. I love her to death. We went to high school together, too. Kris and Eri could not be further apart on the color wheel but they are totally awesome friends.

GatorCandie: They were NOT friends with one another in high school.

BDR 529 IL: so you're a fake aunt!

BDR 529 IL: congratulations!

GatorCandie: Auntie Pam

BDR 529 IL: Auntie Pam has a nice ring

BDR 529 IL: Congratulations again.

GatorCandie: er, I had nothing to do with it, but thanks!

BDR 529 IL: do you get a lot of spray-on-oil Pam jokes? Like from those old commercials—"Put a little PAM, on it".

GatorCandie: haha, absolutely none

GatorCandie: Never, but only close people really call me Pam or Pami. They can pick, I'm pretty laid back about it.

BDR 529 IL: wow, so I'm your first

GatorCandie: Yes, and Ill be marking this moment down in my diary.

BDR 529 IL: mark the date with a heart… Dear Diary, today was a very special day. Jesse made an obstcure and terrible 70's TV commercial refference abpout my name. At first it felt weird but then I started to like it

BDR 529 IL: obscure and about—not obstcure and abpout

BDR 529 IL: damn it

BDR 529 IL:	I'm a mess tonight
GatorCandie:	tired?
BDR 529 IL:	discombobulated. Hours on a boat and I feel like I'm still rocking about.
GatorCandie:	"I put it on, I paraded and luxuriated in it, then I hocked it at the corner consignment shop" but it was sweet nonetheless
BDR 529 IL:	yes, indeed

I have no idea what the above was in reference to, although I assume that it had something to do with the e-mail that she had sent to me earlier that day.

GatorCandie:	I love the series about Horatio Hornblower.
BDR 529 IL:	be right back. Need… water… must… have… water.
GatorCandie:	I never thought I'd get to mention it so I jumped on it when you said "hours on a boat"
BDR 529 IL:	I'm back
BDR 529 IL:	oh thats good water
GatorCandie:	Polish Park Water?
BDR 529 IL:	no, Smelly Finger Springs
BDR 529 IL:	It's the best
GatorCandie:	ha
BDR 529 IL:	I could really go for a nice MLT right now
GatorCandie:	Only if the Mutton is very lean and sliced thin.
GatorCandie:	Didn't boat guy feed you?
BDR 529 IL:	Boat guy? Haha, no. It was an in and out operation
GatorCandie:	Yeah, sounds familiar.

GatorCandie: that was funny!

GatorCandie: I think.

BDR 529 IL: yes, it was funny. I just read it and laughed but I'm trying to change my clothes and type at the same time

GatorCandie: k, then I'll be right back because there's some stuff that needs to be done here.

BDR 529 IL: but I'm all changed now.

BDR 529 IL: and in record time

GatorCandie: agggggghhhhhh

GatorCandie: Just getting it out of my system

BDR 529 IL: vent honey

BDR 529 IL: I can take it

GatorCandie: I think I'm done.

BDR 529 IL: thats it??

GatorCandie: What more do you think I should do? Do you have any advice? haha

GatorCandie: I'm just a little upset because I really wanted to talk to you today and you weren't around. Then I started talking to Kris and she made me feel a little angry at you about it for some reason.

BDR 529 IL: Hmmmm. Well I absolutely HATE oral sex so if you really wanna get back at me…

GatorCandie: haha, got it.

GatorCandie: My revenge NEVER has ANYTHING to do with sex. That would be a disaster for me.

BDR 529 IL: uh oh

GatorCandie: what?

BDR 529 IL:	does that mean I can expect revenge in a different form?
GatorCandie:	no, not at all. We're not dating and we hardly know each other. Technically, I shouldn't be at all concerned that you weren't around.
GatorCandie:	I just missed ya.
BDR 529 IL:	seeing you type that was revenge enough
BDR 529 IL:	;-(
GatorCandie:	As for the whole sex/revenge thing, it never happens. I hear some women do it, and I don't understand it even a little.
BDR 529 IL:	I was just kidding about the sex thing. I didn't expect sex revenge… and I do not hate oral sex… at all
GatorCandie:	I didn't think so. I figured it was a reverse psychology ploy.
BDR 529 IL:	and I'm sorry of you were worried about me. I really am. But things were kind of out of my control today
GatorCandie:	Oh, it's fine. Actually Kris really kind of got me riled more than anything. I was just like, "dunno".
GatorCandie:	But then she's like, is he married? And I'm like ummm what the fuck?? I don't know?? Eh, forgetaboutit
BDR 529 IL:	hahahaha
BDR 529 IL:	I told you, I am married… to several women
BDR 529 IL:	remember?
GatorCandie:	oh right. Can you remind me why we're still talking then?? haha

BDR 529 IL:	I thought you wanted to be one of my wives?
BDR 529 IL:	you can be the one I sleep with. The others can just work in the fields.
BDR 529 IL:	:-)
BDR 529 IL:	wife... haha... no normal woman would tolerate me
GatorCandie:	"Smart, pretty girl with lots to offer seeks to be the wife of a man with 5 other wives; living on a compound that's run by a man from downstate"
BDR 529 IL:	wow, what are the chances that we'd find each other?!?!
GatorCandie:	I know, and then you come along.
GatorCandie:	that's what my profile used to say, but you should have seen the crap I got back then.
BDR 529 IL:	so you've been getting some pretty bad winks?
GatorCandie:	oh my God!!
GatorCandie:	so funny and so scary at the same time
BDR 529 IL:	lemme see lemme see!!
GatorCandie:	k. hold on
GatorCandie:	http://www.match.com/profile/showprofile.aspx
GatorCandie:	Look at this guys pictures.
BDR 529 IL:	a ha ah ha aha ahaha aha a
BDR 529 IL:	oh my Lord & Taylor
GatorCandie:	yes, I know
GatorCandie:	it's almost embarrassing, but it's not my fault
BDR 529 IL:	he is a riot

GatorCandie:	I know it. I hope I never meet him on the street though. Buffalo is a small town.
BDR 529 IL:	yikes
GatorCandie:	Here's another—http://www.match.com/profile/showprofile.
BDR 529 IL:	Well let us see; "I am 6ft. 1 large framed. I still have my own hair which life added some white too"
BDR 529 IL:	"I would like to meet and keep a family type"
GatorCandie:	keep a family type?
BDR 529 IL:	"I am hoping that you have a job (big or little). and take care of your self"
GatorCandie:	what a loser! See what Im up against? See why I like you so much? haha
BDR 529 IL:	"last read: western outdoors mag."
GatorCandie:	I am SO not his type in SO many ways. Actually, all of the ways.
BDR 529 IL:	man, if one normal guy comes around, I'm done for
GatorCandie:	Another—http://www.match.com/profile/showprofile.aspx
BDR 529 IL:	Want me to call him and tell him that it's OK to be gay?
BDR 529 IL:	and that he shouldn't hide it anymore.
GatorCandie:	This would be a playground situation.
GatorCandie:	He barked up the wrong tree.
BDR 529 IL:	if he had bigger breasts, I might date him!
BDR 529 IL:	I hope you know I'm kidding

GatorCandie:	I did get a wink from a normal guy, but actually most guys are normal. Just not for me. Here he is… and of course I know youre kidding.
GatorCandie:	http://www.match.com/profile/showprofile.aspx
GatorCandie:	Except he's not normal, because he's in some sort of militia, haha
GatorCandie:	I DON'T "value my health" by the way, so I'm out anyway.
BDR 529 IL:	he's not in a militia, silly, he's in the Army.
BDR 529 IL:	he seem's pretty good. If you wind up hating me, I say give him a call.
GatorCandie:	I know, I just figured I'd be very left wing and call it "some sort of militia"
BDR 529 IL:	wow… that IS left wing!
GatorCandie:	It was just a joke!!
BDR 529 IL:	I know!!!!
BDR 529 IL:	you're so touchy tonight
BDR 529 IL:	I can tell you're pissed at me.
GatorCandie:	Am I?
BDR 529 IL:	keep away from my ribs and/or face
GatorCandie:	haha
GatorCandie:	Sorry if I seem touchy, I don't feel that way.
GatorCandie:	But take a step closer and you're done. ;-)
BDR 529 IL:	so, why don't you like him? He's the right age, good looking, in shape… what's the problem?
GatorCandie:	You really want to know?

BDR 529 IL:	yes
GatorCandie:	Let's say he wasn't a soldier, because that would be an easy answer, actually…
GatorCandie:	By the way, are you trying to hook me up with another guy or something?
BDR 529 IL:	ha… no, not at all. I'm just trying to understand you better.
GatorCandie:	Well, I know that anything I say from here on will make me look like a picky bitch, but ok.
BDR 529 IL:	no it won't… go ahead
GatorCandie:	"I strive to be a better man, trying new things. I enjoy helping others, and I won't hesitate to open your door for you"
BDR 529 IL:	ok, 'splain.
GatorCandie:	Um? Shouldn't we all be striving in our own way? It sounds like he's selling something.
GatorCandie:	I mean, I put some positive things about myself in my profile too, but they were things I did, not these amorphous concepts like "enjoy helping others". I could just see a Sunday morning at the soup kitchen or something.
BDR 529 IL:	yes, I can see your point
BDR 529 IL:	and I think I've actually seen that guy at the soup kitchen before. I go for the soup. What can I say… they make good soup!
GatorCandie:	Also, I go either way with self-deprecation.
GatorCandie:	Sometimes it turns me off, and sometimes its tolerable.
BDR 529 IL:	I smell like a pirate

GatorCandie:	I really prefer someone who is confident, not always putting himself down for sport
BDR 529 IL:	hey, sometimes it's a defense mechanism!
BDR 529 IL:	wanna hear a pirate joke
GatorCandie:	I know and I do that too, totally. But he's putting it in his profile! Yes, actually I do want to hear a pirate joke.
GatorCandie:	She's driving me nuts?
BDR 529 IL:	she?
GatorCandie:	Sorry, that's the punchline to my pirate joke.
GatorCandie:	Please go on.
BDR 529 IL:	ok
BDR 529 IL:	here goes
BDR 529 IL:	there is a pirate, famous for his record of victories over his foes
BDR 529 IL:	one day he is talking to a deck hand
BDR 529 IL:	the deck hand asks him
BDR 529 IL:	"sir, you are so brave. I only hope one day to be like you"
BDR 529 IL:	"but I must ask, I notice everytime we go into battle, you put on your red shirt"
BDR 529 IL:	"why is that?" the deck hand asks.
BDR 529 IL:	the pirate replies
BDR 529 IL:	"well son, if I ever get wounded during a battle, I don't want the men to see my blood and be discouraged"
BDR 529 IL:	"what a noble idea" says the deck hand

BDR 529 IL:	a few days pass the the pirate and his crew sail right into an ambush from a rival group of pirates
BDR 529 IL:	they were out numbered by the hundreds
BDR 529 IL:	the deck hand runs to find the Captain
BDR 529 IL:	"Captain, Sir, they're coming right for us and they're about to attack!"
BDR 529 IL:	"should I get your red shirt"? the deck hand asks.
BDR 529 IL:	the Captain looks to see how vastly out numbered they are and replies
BDR 529 IL:	"No, maybe you oughta get my brown pants".
GatorCandie:	haha
BDR 529 IL:	but it sounds much funnier in a pirate voice
BDR 529 IL:	and with a parrot on my shoulder
GatorCandie:	aye, matey, that it does.
GatorCandie:	Like the Pink Panther movie
GatorCandie:	Where he keeps blowing the parrot back up.
BDR 529 IL:	I love Peter Sellers. Well, love is a strong word. I like his work.
GatorCandie:	Me too.
GatorCandie:	old, salty sea captain
BDR 529 IL:	we should make it a point to get to bed by 2:00 a.m. tonight
BDR 529 IL:	I cannot sleep until noon again!!
BDR 529 IL:	I have to prepare for my trip
BDR 529 IL:	so many things to do tomorrow

GatorCandie:	k, good idea. So I have a question though… oh yes, your trip.
BDR 529 IL:	you have questions… I have answers
GatorCandie:	Well, seeing as how I have never explained what goes through my head when looking at someone's profile.
GatorCandie:	I realize it can seem a bit harsh. However, don't you do something somewhat similar? Or am I outta bounds?
BDR 529 IL:	oh no. I reject almost every wink I get.
BDR 529 IL:	I was just curious as to what exactly turned you off to that particular guy.
GatorCandie:	And he didn't "turn me off" per se, he just didn't really interest me, you know?
BDR 529 IL:	I understand completely
BDR 529 IL:	and I'm gald!
GatorCandie:	gald?
GatorCandie:	oh, glad.
GatorCandie:	ha
BDR 529 IL:	haha
BDR 529 IL:	yes… I'm very gald
BDR 529 IL:	see, I told you I'm a mess today.
GatorCandie:	But not very bald.
GatorCandie:	I have to wake up at about 6 tomorrow.
BDR 529 IL:	tehy say taht you dnot need to see the enrtie wrod, jsut a qiuck galnce at the fisrt and lsat lettres are enuogh for the mnid to copmrehend the wrod
GatorCandie:	haha, but it does take a bit more effort

BDR 529 IL:	a little
GatorCandie:	that must have been hard to type
BDR 529 IL:	a bit
GatorCandie:	So a pirate walks into a bar with a steering wheel in his pants and the bartender say's…
GatorCandie:	"I can't help but notice you have a steering wheel in your pants, Mr. Pirate" says the bartender.
GatorCandie:	The Pirate replies: "aye, she's driving me nuts"
BDR 529 IL:	hahahaha… I forgot the punchline and you said it only 10 minutes ago
GatorCandie:	HA…ha…ha
GatorCandie:	It's much better with a pirate voice.
BDR 529 IL:	yes
GatorCandie:	Well it's 2am; just enough time to say some nice things to you.
BDR 529 IL:	awww
GatorCandie:	1. I didn't really realize how much I liked you until this evening when you were gone.
BDR 529 IL:	awww
GatorCandie:	2. I think you're very handsome'
BDR 529 IL:	double awww
GatorCandie:	3. I like you… and stop it!! haha
BDR 529 IL:	haha
BDR 529 IL:	you're the coolest
GatorCandie:	like a penguin but not as smelly

BDR 529 IL: penguins are smelly? And here I thought it was my butler that smelled so bad.

GatorCandie: haha. I've always wanted a pet penguin. A butler? No Consuela?

BDR 529 IL: he hates it when I call him Consuela

GatorCandie: Haha, but he puts up with it for the paycheck.

GatorCandie: Sexual harrassment is everywhere.

BDR 529 IL: paycheck?? Oh man, no wonder he's been so pissed at me.

GatorCandie: haha!

GatorCandie: hey, don't think I'm awful :-)

BDR 529 IL: now why would I think that?

GatorCandie: my whole "rip apart everyone's profile" thing

BDR 529 IL: oh I do the same thing

BDR 529 IL: it's fun

GatorCandie: ok, but I'm really a sweetie to my friends and to other people I like.

BDR 529 IL: I didn't mean anything by what I said... just trying to get inside your head a little

GatorCandie: I feel burdensome guilt and I have no karma to burn

GatorCandie: and only my Stepfather was Jewish!!

GatorCandie: The menorahs should not have had such a profound affect on me

BDR 529 IL: help an old lady across the street tomorrow and you'll have enough left over for some shoplifting tomorrow night

GatorCandie: haha, good because that's what I had planned

GatorCandie:	But I could postpone 'til you get here…
BDR 529 IL:	hmmm
GatorCandie:	and that could be our first adventure together. A night in the hooskow.
BDR 529 IL:	think they'd let us share a cell if we get caught?
BDR 529 IL:	prison sex… even better than make-up sex
GatorCandie:	maybe if you bribe them. It is sorta like a hotel room
GatorCandie:	only one of us would know about prison sex, apparently.
BDR 529 IL:	that's what I've heard
GatorCandie:	sure.
GatorCandie:	well…
GatorCandie:	…deep subject
BDR 529 IL:	yah?
BDR 529 IL:	I've only been to prison once… and that old lady was asking for it… dressin' all sexy like that… flashing her girdle all over the place!
GatorCandie:	haha, I'm exhausted and I don't want to start a new topic or anything
GatorCandie:	haha! That hussy.
GatorCandie:	floosy
BDR 529 IL:	that's what I said!!!
GatorCandie:	Guess it didn't fly.
BDR 529 IL:	nope. I did a 10 year hitch in the pokey
BDR 529 IL:	just got out last week
GatorCandie:	Oh? Didja get any cool jailhouse tats, man?

BDR 529 IL: one. I wanted it to say mom but the guy wasn't paying attention, so it says wow

BDR 529 IL: still cool though

GatorCandie: Sometimes I wish I didn't get a tattoo.

BDR 529 IL: you'll have to show me one day

GatorCandie: I'd be glad to. It used to be a shriveled cat and whenever anyone asked to see it, they would be like, "what is it?"

BDR 529 IL: well now I know so I won't ask

GatorCandie: So I used to tell them it was a squirrel, haha. You should have seen their faces.

BDR 529 IL: I'll just say, "what a beautiful shriveled cat" tattoo you have there.

GatorCandie: Kris fixed it this year, so no more squirrel

BDR 529 IL: I was once at a party and a girl asked me if I had any tattoos

GatorCandie: yes?

GatorCandie: Is that the usual icebreaker?

BDR 529 IL: I told her that I have the faces from "family Ties" tattooed on my back.

BDR 529 IL: you know—all of their faces with the cloud background at the end of the opening credits.

GatorCandie: haha, did she believe you?

BDR 529 IL: I think she did believe me for a while.

BDR 529 IL: that's my usual reply when asked about tattoos. I sometimes tell people I have a tattoo of a chicken cutlet.

GatorCandie: LMAO

GatorCandie: Nobody ever imagines that I have a tattoo. Usually they only kind of see it in the summertime.

GatorCandie: Hahaha… chicken cutlet

BDR 529 IL: thankfully, there are still a few days of summer left, so I can still see it.

GatorCandie: It's on my back above the place where jeans used to come up to. Now it's in a strange spot.

BDR 529 IL: ok, we're 19 minutes over 2:00 and I still smell like a pirate.

GatorCandie: k, goodnight matey

BDR 529 IL: goodnight my sweet

BDR 529 IL: I will type with you tomorrow

GatorCandie: ok. Have a good day.

BDR 529 IL: you too honey

BDR 529 IL: don't hate me

GatorCandie: I don't think I could

BDR 529 IL: good

BDR 529 IL: neither do I

BDR 529 IL: goodnight Pami.

GatorCandie: g'night Jesse

BDR 529 IL signed off at 2:22:15 AM.

THE STORY CONTINUES

BDR 529 IL signed on at 1:46:00 PM.

BDR 529 IL: hello cutie pa-tutie

GatorCandie: hello handsome guy

GatorCandie: busy today?

BDR 529 IL: yes, very

GatorCandie: I got up at 6:30

BDR 529 IL: you beat me. I was up at 7:00

GatorCandie: I've put on 40 miles so far today and now I'm back, doing billing. Thanks for your moral support with the parrot :-)

I think I sent a little note along with it. The truth is that I couldn't get her out of my head. From the second I opened my eyes in the morning to the last few moments before I fell asleep each night, there she was, mingling around in all of my random thoughts. I'd be thinking of a shopping list and she would find her way in milk, eggs, Pam, bread. I never had this happen to me before. Not since my very first girlfriend way back in high school, Kathleen. She was the only person that I ever loved and we dated for almost five years. Since Kathleen, every other girl in my life was either just a passing fancy or strictly physical attraction. Until now, until this person that I barely know popped into my life. It's funny how things happen like that—in an instant, everything changes.

BDR 529 IL: where have you been driving??

GatorCandie: I went to a building department for a permit and set a new employee up with an I9 and W4 in Hamburg.

BDR 529 IL:	ah
BDR 529 IL:	where are they building??
BDR 529 IL:	gimme some inside info!!
GatorCandie:	I'm afraid I have nothing exciting to tell you. This is strictly residential additions in the 'burbs of the Southtowns.
BDR 529 IL:	ahh
BDR 529 IL:	I think I got propositioned by a 15 or 16-year-old girl today
GatorCandie:	wow, circumstances?? Are you still hanging around the High School summer sessions despite that order of protection?
BDR 529 IL:	haha. I was walking in to pick up my laundry and this girl was sitting on the curb outside. She asked me for a cigarette. I said she shouldn't smoke and went inside. When I came out she says, "do you want to hang out for a while"?
GatorCandie:	Can you believe a 15 year old was born in 1989?
BDR 529 IL:	I know, it's crazy
GatorCandie:	She did? Wow, that's bold.
BDR 529 IL:	so anyway, she's here making me lunch.
GatorCandie:	haha
GatorCandie:	Go get em Tiger!!
BDR 529 IL:	haha—you know I'm only joking.
GatorCandie:	freak
GatorCandie:	:-)

BDR 529 IL:	I said, "you wouldn't want to hang out with me, I'm very boring"
GatorCandie:	That's not what Pami thinks, but she's boring too I guess.
BDR 529 IL:	haha. I don't think you're boring
BDR 529 IL:	and neither am I
BDR 529 IL:	but what was I supposed to say to her
GatorCandie:	Wow, when I was that age I would never have said anything like that to an "older" guy.
BDR 529 IL:	ugghh… older
BDR 529 IL:	:-(
BDR 529 IL:	I so hate being an "older guy."
GatorCandie:	You should have told her about your van rape fantasies, stranding animals and so forth…
BDR 529 IL:	then I would have been sending you this message from jail! And besides, you're the one with the rape fantasy; I just added the van for to give it a hint of kidnapping.
GatorCandie:	haha, true.
GatorCandie:	Maybe she would have gone with you.
BDR 529 IL:	yeah, haha… I couldn't believe it—a cute little white girl at that. I wanted to drag her home to her mother by her ear. I'm not saying that there are no attractive 15-year-old girls out there. That would just be lying and any man who disagrees is simply lying as well, but to act on such a thing is a totally different story.
GatorCandie:	I can honestly say that no 15-year-old boy has propostitioned me in the last 14 years
GatorCandie:	Really. Kids nowadays.

GatorCandie: You must look pretty young.

BDR 529 IL: I don't think she cared about my age. And I must admit that it was a boost to my ego, but this kid had issues. I could tell that she was looking for trouble.

BDR 529 IL: and I can't imagine that I looked too attractive today, wearing my old army shorts and a Meile Auto Parts T-Shirt

GatorCandie: Scary in a way, isnt it? She's going to get hurt. :-(

BDR 529 IL: possibly. I probably should have taken her home with me just to keep her out of harms way. What'll probably happen is some of her friends will come along and she'll wind up hanging out with them.

GatorCandie: Ok, maybe she won't get hurt. That's a good way to think about it.

GatorCandie: I kinda got propostioned by the new guy I processed, but I get the same questions all the time.

GatorCandie: Have you picked up your cleaning?

BDR 529 IL: yes. Its all here—all happy, pressed and folded.

GatorCandie: Yay. Good for you.

GatorCandie: I get, "So, are you married?"

BDR 529 IL: oh geez. By anyone good at least?

GatorCandie: And because its construction and because none of it is their business and because I don't really HAVE to be nice, I usually answer in one or two words to each question.

BDR 529 IL: haha

GatorCandie:	No, never anyone really good. I know what they're making and it doesnt really interest me. Sorry to sound elitist but these are framers mostly—few skills, limited vocabulary.
BDR 529 IL:	what about me? I only make about a dollar a day picking cotton in the fields.
GatorCandie:	If I know you, you found a way to make an additional profit off that cotton.
GatorCandie:	"So, let me get this straight… You're starting your third job this year, you have no car and you're making $11 bucks an hour. Would you like me to pick you up after work and go back to your parent's or is my place fine for you?"
BDR 529 IL:	HAHAHAHAHA
GatorCandie:	haha, obviously I'm stereotyping.
BDR 529 IL:	one of my bum friends asked me to borrow $6,000 the other day. Can you believe the nerve?
BDR 529 IL:	he doesnt work, by the way
GatorCandie:	$6000.00 wow
GatorCandie:	and you know you would never get it back. It's too much to part with.
BDR 529 IL:	28 years old and he lives off of a credit card that his mother pays for.
GatorCandie:	sorry to say this…
GatorCandie:	LOSER
BDR 529 IL:	I would get it back; I just wouldn't give it to him. Not because I'm mean but because he's lazy. And I would get it back in drips

and drabs... a few hundred here, a few hundred there.

GatorCandie: Yeah? You think he would pay you back?

BDR 529 IL: I told him that if he had gotten a job a year ago, this wouldnt be a problem now

BDR 529 IL: he bartends two days a week and he complains about that!

GatorCandie: $6000 clams is a bit too much to lend to anyone, much less an under-employed bartender. But bartenders make good money, sometimes. I don't know how some people survive.

GatorCandie: Does your band generate income?

BDR 529 IL: no, not good money. He works two day shifts a week

GatorCandie: days, ugh

BDR 529 IL: he is IN the band!!!

GatorCandie: I put the pieces together...

BDR 529 IL: well, when we play shows, we make about $300 or so (whatever the door pulls in), but I never ask for any of that

GatorCandie: Well, you obviously don't deserve it, since you have another source of income, haha

GatorCandie: Wanting your share would just make you greedy.

BDR 529 IL: I just don't feel like dividing the $300 4 ways, minus gas money, tolls, the bar tab and all that other nonsense is worth it. After all is said and done we're talking about $30 or $40 bucks each.

BDR 529 IL: drives me up a wall

BDR 529 IL: that's the way they are… "I paid for gas and that .35 cent toll before, so I'm owed…"

BDR 529 IL: grrrrr—We're fucking adults for Christ's sake. Suck up the $3 in gas that you used.

BDR 529 IL: ok, I'm done ranting.

BDR 529 IL: now I'm listening to When Doves Cry

BDR 529 IL: hahaha

GatorCandie: I hear ya sweetie, but Prince won't make them any less cheap. haha

BDR 529 IL: haha

BDR 529 IL: thats one thing I can't stand, cheap people.

BDR 529 IL: I can understand being frugal, but these bastards are just plain cheap!

GatorCandie: I know, I have a funny cheap story for you if you have an extra second

BDR 529 IL: I have unlimited seconds for you.

GatorCandie: I dated this guy for about two minutes and decided he was just going to be a "friend," so…

GatorCandie: After the appropriate amount of time had gone by, where he got the idea that we weren't seeing each other (like 4 months, haha)

GatorCandie: I rang him up to see if he wanted to go to the homeshow because he likes that kind of stuff. So we met and I asked if he already got his ticket.

GatorCandie: And he said, yes, he had stolen it from the billboard showing the different kinds of tickets and their prices. Sure enough, one

	of the pink tickets they had taped up there was gone...
BDR 529 IL:	oh no
GatorCandie:	and this guy makes better than decent money! I was like, uh, ok... but that's why I decided I didn't like him anyway. Frugality yes, but cheapskate stuff no.
BDR 529 IL:	ha, yeah. It always amazes me how amazingly stingy people can be.
GatorCandie:	He told me he parked really far away to avoid paying for parking. That was actually the last time we hung out.
BDR 529 IL:	oh God
GatorCandie:	Bizarre, the guy pulls over 100k a year and... whatever. haha
BDR 529 IL:	you wanna hear crazy? This summer, I rented a beach house in Cape Cod with some frends. Anyway...
BDR 529 IL:	one of my pain in the ass bum friends came up for a couple of days
BDR 529 IL:	the house was a big 4-bedroom house
BDR 529 IL:	plenty of room
GatorCandie:	k
BDR 529 IL:	come 2am, he says he's going to sleep
BDR 529 IL:	I say, "Ok, goodnight"
BDR 529 IL:	and I see him walking out to his car
GatorCandie:	huh?
BDR 529 IL:	I ask, "Where are you going"?

BDR 529 IL:	he says he's sleeping in the car cause he didn't want to have to chip in for the house at all
GatorCandie:	HAHA
BDR 529 IL:	I wouldn't have asked him for money for the house
BDR 529 IL:	but I let him sleep in the car anyway
GatorCandie:	I'm sure you wouldn't have, haha! Hilarious. What a freak, sleeping in the car.
GatorCandie:	I have a philosophy about that stuff anyway.
BDR 529 IL:	do I get to hear it?
GatorCandie:	If you're in on the initial dealie, you chip in and be done with it. If you then subsequently invite someone, it's implied that you're a guest.
GatorCandie:	Like with drugs, haha
GatorCandie:	what a horrible example!
BDR 529 IL:	yes, I agree; however, if I were that guest, I would definitely offer to pay something and when the NORMAL person refused, I would buy a bottle of wine or something for the house.
GatorCandie:	Oh, definitely, like a good guest should do.
GatorCandie:	Bring something to the party. Of course.
GatorCandie:	I can't believe he slept in the car!! Priceless. Did you get pictures?
BDR 529 IL:	haha. I don't think so... lemme look
BDR 529 IL:	nope
GatorCandie:	ahh, oh well. He must have redeeming qualities.
BDR 529 IL:	yes, they all do. Otherwise I would stop talking to them completely.

GatorCandie:	Yes, I have shed friends before. Its a gradual thing, isn't it?
BDR 529 IL:	not for me… see ya later, jackass
BDR 529 IL:	haha
GatorCandie:	I had a really good guy friend while I was married, and after we broke up, he somehow thought that we would start dating or something. He got all moody and pouty and it was silly so I had to stop talking to him. It was kind of a bummer.
GatorCandie:	Like now that I was single, we could finally be together. A legend in his own mind, haha.
BDR 529 IL:	yeah, well I have news for you that you probably already know. Any guy friends that you have want to have sex with you
GatorCandie:	Um, mebbe. But I can just hang with the guys and hold my own. After they get over the "no were not dating or having sex or anything" thing, most of 'em adjust pretty well.
GatorCandie:	be right back, k?
BDR 529 IL:	k
GatorCandie:	sorry darlin I'm back in colors
BDR 529 IL:	be right back
GatorCandie:	haha
GatorCandie:	k
BDR 529 IL:	ok, I'm back in colors too
GatorCandie:	haha, I imagine that since we are both working, this will happen periodically
BDR 529 IL:	yes, haha.

GatorCandie: So I've had some good guy friends over the years. I had a very poignant moment once with one of them while camping in Chicago and staying up all night talking about, um, stuff.

BDR 529 IL: and he didn't make the moves?

GatorCandie: Nope. His name was Larry and he was fat but a good friend. Plus I was married and I made it clear to everyone that I was not available. It was actually fun. Larry was part of this scooter thing and I just wanted an escort to see Chicago.

BDR 529 IL: his name "was" Larry? He's no longer named Larry? Heehee.

GatorCandie: So they had their silly scooter rally and I drove to Chicago. Okay—his name IS Larry. Haha.

GatorCandie: Then I came back to the campsite at about 2ish and we had our long talk in this cornfield in the middle of nowhere.

BDR 529 IL: about anything special?

GatorCandie: um, how creepy it would be if a clown popped out of the cornfield... but other than that, the meaning of life, love, just what everyone talks about I guess. I mean, we had driven in my convertible to Illinois and laughed our butts off the whole way, so we became closer after that.

BDR 529 IL: that's nice

GatorCandie: Yeah, and he was a skinhead so he got a pretty bad burn, haha.

BDR 529 IL:	be right back (again)
GatorCandie:	He did the whole skinhead thing—Docs, suspenders and the whole bit. I did not "approve", but he was my friend. I didn't look like the typical girl at the rally, ha.
BDR 529 IL:	boots and braces
BDR 529 IL:	I knew a few skins in my day. Not racist skinhead guys but the "working class crusader" types. Most people don't know that all skinheads are not racist assholes.
GatorCandie:	yeah, pork pie hat. All that—and yes, I agree about the skinhead thing and people not knowing.
GatorCandie:	He actually inspired me to buy my lambretta.
BDR 529 IL:	grrr... brb again
GatorCandie:	no prob!
GatorCandie:	They're really good people if they adhere to the root philosophy of being a skinhead.
BDR 529 IL:	back
GatorCandie:	I kept typing so you have catching up to do *G*
BDR 529 IL:	yes, I agree that most skinheads are ok, but I'm past the point of "wearing my image" and I think that everyone our age should be past that point as well.
BDR 529 IL:	or at least getting close
GatorCandie:	Oh, I have never looked any different than a white girl from Long Island.
BDR 529 IL:	hehe

GatorCandie:	Maybe I wore concert t-shirts, but I never did the costume thing
GatorCandie:	brb
BDR 529 IL:	hun, I'm sorry but I have to go for a while. I still have a buch of stuff to do.
GatorCandie:	k. talk to ya later
BDR 529 IL:	ok good. I'll be back in a little while
BDR 529 IL:	have a good day, sweetness ⋠
GatorCandie:	you too

BDR 529 IL signed off at 3:02:32 PM.

Later That Day, The Story Continues to Continue

BDR 529 IL signed on at 5:21:42 PM.

BDR 529 IL:	ugghh… a good day turned into a bad day
GatorCandie:	really? I'm sorry. How?
BDR 529 IL:	work stuff—very annoying
GatorCandie:	Out of your control?
BDR 529 IL:	to an extent
BDR 529 IL:	I'll spare you the details, unless you want to hear them
GatorCandie:	Go ahead if you want to vent.
BDR 529 IL:	ok…
GatorCandie:	But only if you want to :-)
BDR 529 IL:	on the side, I am part owner of a small trucking company. Today, one of our trucks blew an engine in the middle of a huge job.
GatorCandie:	ok…

BDR 529 IL: at the same time, it started to rain at another job and another truck, a big tri-axle got stuck in the mud.

GatorCandie: sounds expensive

BDR 529 IL: The stuck truck is no big deal. My brother has a wrecker that can pull it out.

GatorCandie: so a blown engine

BDR 529 IL: but the other truck is NEEDED for tomorrow

BDR 529 IL: so we have to get a truck from a guy we know and send it out tomorrow, but I still don't know if that is possible

GatorCandie: How about an engine? Not a chance huh?

BDR 529 IL: I am usually pretty silent in the day-to-day operations, but my partner is away on vacation. My friend Sal that I told you about.

GatorCandie: Well he better get his ass back here, haha

BDR 529 IL: yes! The engine is already out and being worked on, but it will be another week at least until it's done.

GatorCandie: Hopefully you break even.

BDR 529 IL: I have some more bad news. I had to cancel my trip tomorrow so I could arrange to have the other guys trucks on site OR make sure the guys run heavy loads and hope the DOT doesn't get them for being over-loaded.

BDR 529 IL: no, it's not a money issue; it's a credibility issue

BDR 529 IL: this job has to be done this week.

GatorCandie: oh definitely but it doesn't hurt to not lose money.

BDR 529 IL: well, we didn't lose any money so far. Let's see what the story is with the truck first.

GatorCandie: Sounds like you did all you could do, and running heavier loads will be great as long as you don't get stopped.

BDR 529 IL: yeah, but if the truck gets stopped, its a big deal.

GatorCandie: oh I know

BDR 529 IL: I really can't complain. I never really have to get involved in this business at all. I handle most of the paperwork, legal issues—forms, compliance and whatnot and my partner runs the business. There are a lot of people involved. My brother's friend bought one of the trucks and the others are owned by Sal. My brother is paying his friend back for half of the one truck with the profit that the truck generates. I put in a lot of money for parts, paperwork, permits, etc.

BDR 529 IL: So there's my brother, his friend, Sal and me. Really there are two separate companies but we all work together. The problem is that I shell out money hand over fist for all kinds of things—parts, lettering, permits, legal stuff like forming the corporation… thousands of dollars and I never see a penny.

GatorCandie: are you union?

BDR 529 IL: no

GatorCandie: do you operate in NYC?

BDR 529 IL:	sometimes in the Bronx, but we have a few union guys that can run down there if need be
GatorCandie:	Niagara Falls up here is like NYC for unions. Its tough and some non-unions won't even go there.
BDR 529 IL:	yeah, it can be a hassle if you don't know the right people. Fortunately, Sal seems to know everyone!
GatorCandie:	Who are the right people? What do you mean?
BDR 529 IL:	we know a guy who runs a pretty big construction outfit in the Bronx. When we run loads in the city, we use his union drivers
GatorCandie:	oh yeah. Definitely, and some of the larger concrete guys just use unions in the Falls. It's hard to sneak around up there. You know, it would be very hard to tie this into sex in any way whatsoever.
BDR 529 IL:	loads?
BDR 529 IL:	hmmm…..
GatorCandie:	…with any degree of grace, I mean Hahaha.
BDR 529 IL:	haha, yes, with any grace it's nearly impossible.
GatorCandie:	SORRY YOU HAD A TOUGH DAY!! :-\
BDR 529 IL:	its ok. No big deal
GatorCandie:	brb Jesse
BDR 529 IL:	I'm mainly pissed cause I had to cancel my trip
GatorCandie:	bummer for me too

BDR 529 IL: I will reschedule very soon, maybe even this week

GatorCandie: cool!

This was a really big deal, although neither of us let on as to how upset we were. This was to be our first meeting in person! Looking back, I think that part of me was relieved because I had become very nervous about meeting her in person. I suppose that I was fearful that she would be disappointed with me, my looks, whatever. I was just very nervous and I was terrified about ruining what we had already established.

BDR 529 IL: it really started to pour today

GatorCandie: Well you had such great weather all weekend. It's good for a Monday to be rainy. They're usually not the best of days anyway.

BDR 529 IL: true dat

GatorCandie: word

BDR 529 IL: sorry if I'm quiet here and there, I'm trying to settle some stuff

GatorCandie: Same here. Don't worry, I'm still working a little but I can keep talking, just more s l o w l y

BDR 529 IL: it's pitch black outside

BDR 529 IL: like it's the middle of the night

GatorCandie: that bad? Good day for a book... and soup from the local kitchen.

GatorCandie: Have you done your food shopping?

BDR 529 IL: I actually went shopping today!

GatorCandie: haha

GatorCandie: scary

GatorCandie:	I always eat all the really good stuff first
GatorCandie:	Although my definition of "good stuff" isn't always shared by most people.
BDR 529 IL:	I just put it all away and haven't had a chance to eat any of it yet
GatorCandie:	whoa—weird fax coming in
BDR 529 IL:	weird?
BDR 529 IL:	what's weird about it?
GatorCandie:	Well, something I wasn't expecting. So since everything is so black & white with me, (ha) if its not expected, it's weird.
GatorCandie:	I'm sure all the pieces will fall into place eventually.
BDR 529 IL:	I have faith in you
GatorCandie:	Really? Excellent. That's 7 out of 10, if you don't count my mom. She's on the fence, actually.
BDR 529 IL:	hahahahahaha
GatorCandie:	Poke her with a sharp stick though, and she caves.
BDR 529 IL:	they all do
BDR 529 IL:	that stick has powers, I tells ya
GatorCandie:	Yes, I used to have a magic wand that was all pink and iridescent, but I think I might make the switch to a plain old pointed stick.
BDR 529 IL:	nothin beats a pointed stick
GatorCandie:	Did you get the pointed stick reference, by the way? I never asked.
BDR 529 IL:	Please… Don't insult me! Monty Python

GatorCandie:	sorry for asking
BDR 529 IL:	"what if he has a pointed stick"
BDR 529 IL:	hehe
GatorCandie:	exactly, haha
GatorCandie:	soooo funny
GatorCandie:	me with the Lambrusco, you with the Monty Python
BDR 529 IL:	hahahaha
GatorCandie:	Do you remember Magic Garden? I have to ask.
BDR 529 IL:	oooohhhhh… the chuckle patch
GatorCandie:	I LOVED the Magic Garden, ha. Only people from New York seem to know it. Must have been local.
BDR 529 IL:	I think most of PBS was pretty local back then
GatorCandie:	Kris has one of thier "releases," haha
GatorCandie:	brb darlin'
BDR 529 IL:	hun, I've got to run
BDR 529 IL:	I'll be back in a bit
BDR 529 IL:	I miss you ⨀
GatorCandie:	oh, k, gotcha. Talk to ya later
BDR 529 IL:	see ya in a little while, Pami.
GatorCandie:	Catch ya lata Jesse

BDR 529 IL signed off at 6:05:56 PM.

NEW YORK PIZZA

GatorCandie:	Jesse!
BDR 529 IL:	Pamela!
GatorCandie:	Can you talk? Are you busy?
BDR 529 IL:	sure, I'm just cleaning up a few things around my desk
GatorCandie:	I'll leave you to it. I just signed on, so if you feel like chatting, beep me up.
BDR 529 IL:	of course I feel like chatting
BDR 529 IL:	that's why I came online
BDR 529 IL:	to chat with you
BDR 529 IL:	so... beep beep beep
GatorCandie:	⊠ warm & fuzzy
BDR 529 IL:	⌁
BDR 529 IL:	how was the rest of your day?
GatorCandie:	It was great! But I forgot to eat, so now I'm kinda stuck. I ordered a pizza. Yuck.
BDR 529 IL:	oh I'm sorry... I've had buffalo pizza. They really shouldn't even call it pizza.
GatorCandie:	Yeah, you have a point. It's been awhile since I've had real NY pizza. Maybe it would rekindle the romance for me.
GatorCandie:	Nice and thin, crispy.
BDR 529 IL:	eh... even near me in the 'burbs the pizza stinks... its Brooklyn, the Bronx, Manhattan or nothing. Granted, the pizza near me is

	WAY better than Buffalo pizza but still not the real thing.
GatorCandie:	Believe it or not, there was a pizza place in Point Lookout that made the best pizza I ever had.
GatorCandie:	Angelo's I believe.
BDR 529 IL:	obviously you haven't had good Brooklyn pizza
GatorCandie:	I lived in Point Lookout for a while… it was the best.
GatorCandie:	I have a Brooklyn boy story, actually.
GatorCandie:	When I was 17, my mom hooked me up with a job at a nightclub called Escapes in my hometown.
GatorCandie:	brb k?
BDR 529 IL:	k
GatorCandie:	k sorry
BDR 529 IL:	you're NOT SORRY!!
GatorCandie:	ok, IM NOT SORRY!! But i'm cute…
BDR 529 IL:	yes, you are
BDR 529 IL:	☒
GatorCandie:	thanks
BDR 529 IL:	no, thank you
GatorCandie:	no, no, thank you
GatorCandie:	thank YOU
BDR 529 IL:	so… continue
GatorCandie:	k

GatorCandie:	So I worked there during the day, taking reservations for bachelorette parties and such, due to the "all male revue" (which to this day I have never seen, ha)
BDR 529 IL:	poor girl
GatorCandie:	ick. I have an insider's secret…
GatorCandie:	They're like 85% gay.
BDR 529 IL:	ha. not surprising
GatorCandie:	Who cares? I'm not going to get all hot over a guy that's not mine any way.
GatorCandie:	So…
GatorCandie:	The people who owned it, sold it to 3 Brooklyn boys who figured they'd give it a go. They were kind of yucky, but whatever.
GatorCandie:	Anyway, they brought all their buddies from the trades to come do work there. So there was a lighting guy who wouldn't stop bugging me, I mean like 4 weeks in a row until I went out with him.
GatorCandie:	So I told him I didn't really do the club thing too much so if he wanted to go to a movie, that would be fine. Anyway, I'll cut this short:
GatorCandie:	At the end of the night, after his pager had gone off like a million times and he had to go to payphone after payphone, I asked him if he was a drug dealer.
BDR 529 IL:	haha …and?
GatorCandie:	⌧ Long Island Girl
GatorCandie:	No, he wasnt a drug dealer.
GatorCandie:	He was a "gun dealer" haha

BDR 529 IL:	no! really?
GatorCandie:	yes, really.
GatorCandie:	And he told me that I was a nice girl, and that I should probably stay away from him and quit the club.
GatorCandie:	So he didn't have to tell me twice.
BDR 529 IL:	wow. He was right, I'm sure
GatorCandie:	So I quit him and the club, haha. A friggin' gun dealer. I told him my heart couldn't take it. He seemed like a nice Irish guy, but whatever.
BDR 529 IL:	hahaha… that's odd
GatorCandie:	Funny huh? All the luck.
GatorCandie:	Why is it odd?
BDR 529 IL:	it's just an odd story
GatorCandie:	Not really, considering that I was working for a nightclub. But the previous owners had owned that place forever.
BDR 529 IL:	Buffalo used to be mostly Italian about 20 or 30 years ago
BDR 529 IL:	for some reason
GatorCandie:	I live in a very Italian neighborhood.
GatorCandie:	My last name used to end in a vowel, so I fit right in.
GatorCandie:	My old landlady used to live right next store and she had red velvet and icons all over the place.
BDR 529 IL:	haha

GatorCandie:	The headboard of her bed was red velvet. She told me I shouldn't walk around the house naked and I told her to stop spying on me.
BDR 529 IL:	I've got the velvet headboard beat!
GatorCandie:	do tell
BDR 529 IL:	A kid I knew growning up...
BDR 529 IL:	his name was Rob
BDR 529 IL:	his parents had a headboard... horrible ornate brass
BDR 529 IL:	and on the left side...
BDR 529 IL:	a picture of his father
BDR 529 IL:	and on the right, his mother
BDR 529 IL:	nuilt into the headboard
BDR 529 IL:	one of those cloudy white background pictures
GatorCandie:	on the headboard? ha
GatorCandie:	yikes.
BDR 529 IL:	yes, a big oval picture surrounded in turned brass—cheaply made and inferior quality brass I might add. In fact, it probably wasn't even real brass at that!
GatorCandie:	I would not want a picture of myself in my headboard
BDR 529 IL:	it was hilarious
GatorCandie:	good Lord and Taylor, as you say
BDR 529 IL:	haha
GatorCandie:	I'm stealing that btw.
BDR 529 IL:	what's mine is yours, sweetie

BDR 529 IL:	I'm kind of a design snob
GatorCandie:	really
GatorCandie:	I know what I might have.
BDR 529 IL:	I can't stand when people think they have good taste
GatorCandie:	Well I'll tell you right now that I do have good taste. I just can't always afford it, haha
GatorCandie:	So I make due. I am a bit spartan by design actually.
BDR 529 IL:	I would bet heavy that you DO have good taste, but I'm sorry, I cannot take your word for it
BDR 529 IL:	everyone thinks they have good taste
GatorCandie:	You are right.
GatorCandie:	I can tell you that I have nothing hideous in my place. That I know.
BDR 529 IL:	hideous is ok sometimes when done with humor in mind
GatorCandie:	…except this dress that I must have been on drugs to buy.
GatorCandie:	It's like a pea green with a Chinese motif all over it with a Mandarin collar.
GatorCandie:	What the heck was I thinking?
BDR 529 IL:	haha
GatorCandie:	I actually don't like hideous things.
GatorCandie:	brb…
BDR 529 IL:	I had a bartender, Jessica, who used to wear dresses like that all the time
BDR 529 IL:	you left me!

GatorCandie:	No, but I am very angry
BDR 529 IL:	why??
GatorCandie:	I'm sorry.
BDR 529 IL:	whats wrong?
GatorCandie:	There was like a ton of honking outside my house and it turned out to be the Pizza Guy. I asked him if they told him anything, and he said no.
BDR 529 IL:	told him anything?
GatorCandie:	I hate to inconvenience everybody in my neighborhood for a pizza.
GatorCandie:	I said to the order taker, "Please walk it up" and so instead this poor guy is down stairs, lights on, engine running honking his horn for 10 minutes. I finally went down to see what was going on.
BDR 529 IL:	they don't usually come to the door??
GatorCandie:	I'm so upset that I've woken everybody up.
BDR 529 IL:	eh… they'll live
GatorCandie:	Well, I don't eat much pizza, although I know the owner who wasn't there tonight and now that I think about it, I've never had pizza delivered here.
GatorCandie:	But it's easy stuff. I'll be fine, I just hate to be the disruption in such a quiet neighborhood when I'm not even drunk.
BDR 529 IL:	well, to make up for it I suggest you get liquered up and start a ruckus
GatorCandie:	yes, I have a TV Id like to smash, haha
BDR 529 IL:	perfect

GatorCandie:	sorry. So Jessica used to wear bizzarre dresses all the time?
BDR 529 IL:	yeah… that's all there is to the story
BDR 529 IL:	haha
GatorCandie:	btw, if I get angry, I do it then I'm done.
BDR 529 IL:	I like to bottle mine up and then take it out on old ladies
GatorCandie:	they're asking for it anyway; in one way or another
BDR 529 IL:	finally… someone who understands me. haha
GatorCandie:	Who loves ya, baby? Who's got your back?
GatorCandie:	No, I'm really asking, haha
BDR 529 IL:	hahahaha
GatorCandie:	just kidding!!
GatorCandie:	Wow I'm super funny tonight.
BDR 529 IL:	you're on a roll
BDR 529 IL:	I'm on a bagel
GatorCandie:	cream cheese?
BDR 529 IL:	but of course
GatorCandie:	I love you!!
BDR 529 IL:	hahaha
BDR 529 IL:	no you don't
GatorCandie:	Nobody understands me.
GatorCandie:	In this moment I do.
GatorCandie:	I feel very joyful.
BDR 529 IL:	it must be the pizza talkin'
BDR 529 IL:	actually, that's the one thing I'm sure its not

GatorCandie:	and, gasp…
GatorCandie:	They did not cut it into slices. That kinda gets under my skin a bit.
BDR 529 IL:	?????
BDR 529 IL:	they didn't slice it?
GatorCandie:	No, a lot of places in Buffalo don't actually.
BDR 529 IL:	Seriously? I can't see one single advantage to not clicing a pizza for the customer! Not one.
BDR 529 IL:	once at a local seafood restaurant, the waitress dropped an entire bowl of lobster bisque on my brother's head
BDR 529 IL:	and I mean, not a little bit
BDR 529 IL:	the whole thing
GatorCandie:	no way!
BDR 529 IL:	right on his head
GatorCandie:	on purpose?
BDR 529 IL:	no she dropped it
BDR 529 IL:	he didn't move, motion, yell or anything
BDR 529 IL:	calmly and slowly, he just took some bread from the basket on the table and starting dabbing it on his face to sop up the soup and ate it
BDR 529 IL:	it was the best reaction you could have possibly had to a situation like that.
GatorCandie:	how awful! Waitress there's a whole lot of something in my soup.
GatorCandie:	haha!!!
GatorCandie:	That's so awesome.

BDR 529 IL: yeah, it was seriously funny

GatorCandie: I imagine I wouldn't move either.

BDR 529 IL: brb

GatorCandie: you just want revenge :-)

GatorCandie: And since I deserve it, I will sit here and wait for you, not moving. Except maybe to eat some pizza.

GatorCandie: eBay Watched item ending soon!— Lamborghini: I'd better hurry up and decide if I want it or not, haha

BDR 529 IL: get two, honey

GatorCandie: ha, it's actually not all that and a bag of raw carrots.

GatorCandie: Here'http://cgi.ebay.com/ebaymotors/

BDR 529 IL: yeah, I don't even really like them. They're a bit ostentatious

GatorCandie: It kind of looks like a bug

BDR 529 IL: it does!

GatorCandie: But check this out…

BDR 529 IL: ugghh…I'm sorry, I hate the Viper

BDR 529 IL: and I hate the Corvette too—not my style

BDR 529 IL: my dad had a '66 Jaguar XKE convertible

GatorCandie: But look at that particular Viper. It's not bad looking

GatorCandie: Change the wheels and gas cap…

GatorCandie: The Vanquish is totally awesome.

BDR 529 IL wants to directly connect.

BDR 529 IL is now directly connected.

GatorCandie: Is it the same as the 67?

BDR 529 IL: a little different. His had chrome webbing over the headlights

She sent me a picture to see if what she was looking at was close to what my dad had.

BDR 529 IL: yeah, that's pretty close

GatorCandie: Plenty of sex appeal, that's for sure.

I sent her a picture of my 1968 Caddy.

BDR 529 IL: look at THAT hot rod

I'm joking here, because although the Caddy is really cool looking, it was so giagantic that it's far from being a "hot rod". Nevertheless, I loved it.

GatorCandie: I hate to say it's totally cute, but it really is

GatorCandie: yikes

BDR 529 IL: the picture is totally compressed

GatorCandie: it's all bunched up. What is it?

BDR 529 IL: it's the back of my car at the beach house

GatorCandie: I was going to say it looks german

BDR 529 IL: open it in another window... it will look normal

BDR 529 IL: actually, don't bother. haha

GatorCandie: But I guess the wheels MIGHT have tipped me off had I been paying attention

BDR 529 IL: ha

GatorCandie: That is one long car when its not all looking like a cabrio, haha

BDR 529 IL: yeah…its big

I then sent her a picture of another Caddy—an on 40s Caddy. They were *huge*!

BDR 529 IL:	now THAT'S a car
BDR 529 IL:	look at the second pic down on the left
GatorCandie:	You could definitley have boom boom in that car, I mean if you were into that sort of thing :-)
BDR 529 IL:	oh we sure could
GatorCandie:	Now I'm going to make you dislike me for sure…
GatorCandie:	I have never developed a true appreciation for Cadillacs. Please don't be mean to me!!
BDR 529 IL:	not all Cadillacs, but the 1960 Coupe Deville convertible is a thing of beauty
BDR 529 IL:	look at that grill
GatorCandie:	What the heck do you need a boat for? You could go sailing in that! heehee
BDR 529 IL:	yep
BDR 529 IL:	haha
GatorCandie:	I do like the grille
GatorCandie:	You could open a diner in that car
BDR 529 IL:	haha
GatorCandie:	Don't be mad at me!!
BDR 529 IL:	of course I'm not, silly
GatorCandie:	I hope you're not pouting or anything. I'd have to kiss it right off your lips.
BDR 529 IL:	☒ melting
BDR 529 IL:	cadi…what??

GatorCandie:	☒
GatorCandie:	You're sweet. Are you really this sweet?
GatorCandie:	Or are you going to let me sleep in the car?
BDR 529 IL:	nope... I'm a cold-blooded killa
BDR 529 IL:	my other wives are sleping in the car... maybe I can slip you in the trunk?
GatorCandie:	haha
GatorCandie:	I don't think I would like that, unless I had a reading lamp and an air mattress, that is.
GatorCandie:	oh, and something to read, and Consuela.
BDR 529 IL:	I could work that out
BDR 529 IL:	nothins too good for my lady
GatorCandie:	I can tell!
GatorCandie:	**breaking newsflash** brought to you by Kermit THE Frog
BDR 529 IL:	hahahahaha
GatorCandie:	But wait!! You havent heard the **breaking newsflash** !!
BDR 529 IL:	I'm waiting
GatorCandie:	Laura Branigan (she sang 'Gloria' in the 80s) is stone dead.
BDR 529 IL:	I knew that this morning!!!
GatorCandie:	That's all I know.
BDR 529 IL:	newsflash my ass!!
BDR 529 IL:	haha
GatorCandie:	AND YOU DIDN'T TELL ME???
GatorCandie:	what the heck?

BDR 529 IL:	I thought fo sho you knew
BDR 529 IL:	brb
GatorCandie:	k
GatorCandie:	me too. I need a drinkie
GatorCandie:	beatcha
BDR 529 IL:	back
BDR 529 IL:	you won
GatorCandie:	I'm so competetive!
GatorCandie:	you just watch me, haha
GatorCandie:	Ok, so Laura Branigan died in East Quogue. Did you know that?
BDR 529 IL:	I do now
GatorCandie:	I'm sure you're wondering why we are not finished talking about Laura Branigan
GatorCandie:	and I can't say why.
BDR 529 IL:	I think you're in love with her
GatorCandie:	I would really like to hear her sing MY name, ha
GatorCandie:	But Gloria's alias was actually Pamela—a little known fact.
BDR 529 IL:	hmmmph—I didn't know that
GatorCandie:	see? Neither does anyone else.
GatorCandie:	You're the first person to have heard it! Lucky you!
BDR 529 IL:	wow... did Laura know?
GatorCandie:	um, it is not known.
BDR 529 IL:	wow... even SHE didn't know. Now THAT'S a secret

GatorCandie:	like the magic 8 ball says, "shake me later" or something to that effect.
BDR 529 IL:	shake me later? Hahaha It's "Ask Again Later".
BDR 529 IL:	but if you'd like a good shake…
BDR 529 IL:	lemme know
GatorCandie:	is it? I'm still going to say "shake me later" though; it has a nice ring to it
GatorCandie:	shake rattle and roll
BDR 529 IL:	fine by me. I'm on board.
GatorCandie:	two new emails, neither even worth trying to laugh at
BDR 529 IL:	ooh ooh… lemme see!!
GatorCandie:	really? No pics though…
BDR 529 IL:	eh, it's not fun without pics
GatorCandie:	From: thunderballz32
	Subject: hi there
	Hi! I read your profile and you seem to be an exciting person. Well I suppose I should tell you a little about me, I am an honest, fun, and caring individual. I am a 25-year-old dental student at UB. I like to watch and play sports. I am 5'8" tall and I have an athletic build. I like to travel and do anything fun. I am signed up for match.com because I am sick of the bar seen and I want to meet some new and exciting people. I do have some pictures I can send if you would like to see them. If you want to know more about me feel free to ask.
GatorCandie:	the bar "seen"
GatorCandie:	ME? An exciting person? Haha, that's funny

GatorCandie:	I would never write to someone "you seem like an exciting person"
BDR 529 IL:	haha. Agreed.
GatorCandie:	From: torbay
	Subject: Hi
	Hi, how are you? I'm kind of new at this but thought it would be worth a try. I'm sick or bars/clubs and all that those places entail. Have you been on this site long? Well, here's alittle about me. I'm 34. I have a very easy going personality and great sense of humor. I like just about any sport, playing, watching, or attending. Day trips or long weekend getaways are a must. My two favorite places would have to be NYC or Toronto. Also just staying home making a nice dinner over a bottle of wine is nice also. Presently, I'm working on my Master's degree in World History. Well, I guess that's enough about me for now. I'd love to hear more about you and your interest. I do have a picture to send if you'd like. Hope to talk with you soon and Good luck. Bye.
GatorCandie:	That's a real draw for a girl, by the way: "I like just about any sport, playing, watching, or attending."
BDR 529 IL:	wow. He can balance his dinner on a bottle of wine?
GatorCandie:	haha, that's talent or poor grammar, one of the two
BDR 529 IL:	he's super duper

GatorCandie: skippy

GatorCandie: I haven't even checked my winks. I stopped having them sent to my email a long time ago.

GatorCandie: OH NO!! haha

GatorCandie: a new crop haha

BDR 529 IL: I haven't gotten any really funny ones lately. Just too boring to mention

BDR 529 IL: YES!

BDR 529 IL: jackpot

BDR 529 IL: I better come snatch you up before you find some hunk up there

GatorCandie: Give me an example of one though! I'm so curious who else wants you.

GatorCandie: Shall I grab the freakiest one first?

BDR 529 IL: yes!!

BDR 529 IL: anababe27

GatorCandie: It's so hard to choose. You should just go on my site and take a peek.

GatorCandie: but is it more fun this way?

BDR 529 IL: yes. I like to get 'em one by one so we can talk about 'em

GatorCandie: k

GatorCandie: Here ya go—http://www.match.com/profile/showprofile.aspx

BDR 529 IL: ahahahaha

GatorCandie: it's sooooo bad!

BDR 529 IL: why do people have to wear their lives on their sleeves

GatorCandie:	my dream vacation has always been to see the Jesus Statue
GatorCandie:	what???
BDR 529 IL:	HAHAHAHAHAHAHA
GatorCandie:	I like Italian food, especially my mothers
GatorCandie:	ugh, I'm sure it's good but…
BDR 529 IL:	ha… ok… next!
GatorCandie:	icky
GatorCandie:	Click da link, yo—http://www.match.com/profile/showprofile.aspx
GatorCandie:	holy pointy chin bearded geek batman! how did he get into my winks?
BDR 529 IL:	wow, that's some picture!
GatorCandie:	The Mardi Gras or the bearded guy?
BDR 529 IL:	both!
GatorCandie:	I have yet another for you, ha
BDR 529 IL:	shoot
GatorCandie:	http://www.match.com/profile/showprofile.aspx
GatorCandie:	on occasion a bald guy might be sexy. This one isn't. period.
BDR 529 IL:	oh no
BDR 529 IL:	is he from the future?
GatorCandie:	ha!
GatorCandie:	He's from never as far as I'm concerned.
BDR 529 IL:	hahaha
GatorCandie:	here—http://www.match.com/profile/showprofile.aspx

BDR 529 IL:	"I need the following in a woman: b r a i n s ; intellect (not they same…dig?)"
GatorCandie:	Is that what he said?
BDR 529 IL:	yes
GatorCandie:	um, ok
GatorCandie:	This other guy is a bit of a regular. He is the Manager at Hooter's and he's 5'8
BDR 529 IL:	which one?
GatorCandie:	"I'm a restaurant manager at Hooter's, and some of the people I've dated in the past were uncomfortable with that. They have a misconceived notion of what it is, but I assure you…work is just work. If I was interested in any of them, would I be here ?"
BDR 529 IL:	oh wow.
BDR 529 IL:	this is from the profile of the guy from the future… it's not worth cutting and pasting. Just read the whole thing.
BDR 529 IL:	"I am a low key, down to earth, public school teacher. I thirive on the wonder and curiousity natural to all children and I go to bed each night delighted that when I wake I get to do it all over again. I need the following in a woman: brains; intellect (not they same… dig?); a great loud laugh; the wherewithall to go midnight bowling, the fair, the opera and a chinese buffet all within the span of 24 hours and still not want to kill me; the curiousity to watch a lunar eclipse and the daring-do to entertain the thought of sky-diving; oh

	yeah…and the truly under-appreciated skill of swearing creatively. Dig it?"
GatorCandie:	Hep cat. Cool, I "dig it", daddy-o
GatorCandie:	A 24 hour renaissance man
BDR 529 IL:	he's a keeper
GatorCandie:	a crypt keeper?
BDR 529 IL:	weirdo
BDR 529 IL:	there are some real 'beauts out there
GatorCandie:	they all are!!
GatorCandie:	then of course I got the requisite "normal" guy
GatorCandie:	Click—http://www.match.com/profile/showprofile.aspx
BDR 529 IL:	eh
GatorCandie:	"I have two words for you… KAREOKE BABY!!! I also enjoy getting hot and sweaty on the dance floor in a cool club. I don't mind having a drink from time to time either."
BDR 529 IL:	I'm truly amazed. Oh and by the way, that means he's a drunk
GatorCandie:	haha, you think so?
BDR 529 IL:	haha, maybe. Here's one for you—Click the link.
GatorCandie:	She is pretty scary. That's a heck of a lot of pink she's got going there.
BDR 529 IL:	oh man, no kidding
GatorCandie:	Wow, shes only 25 and she looks like she's 40.
BDR 529 IL:	I think she's lying about her age. Or should I say I HOPE that she's lying about her age.

GatorCandie: haha, "benefit of the doubt" doesn't enter your vocabulary, huh?

BDR 529 IL: maybe, but I doubt it

GatorCandie: "I will travel anywhere, anytime as long as I can shop."

GatorCandie: ????

GatorCandie: How bizarre to say that!

BDR 529 IL: at least she's honest... "Pay for me and I'll fuck you"

GatorCandie: As if she's been thrown down the stairs for shopping

GatorCandie: oh... is that what that means? I thought it was like, don't get in my way

BDR 529 IL: I didn't even read the whole thing

GatorCandie: that's actually all it said.

GatorCandie: I don't think like that, so I thought she might have had a bad experience with "mall face"

GatorCandie: You know, when you're at the mall and only one of you wants to be there?

GatorCandie: guys develop "mall face"

BDR 529 IL: I have to admit... I love to shop

GatorCandie: really? um, I could take it or leave it actually

BDR 529 IL: most people don't like it, but I really do

GatorCandie: But! If I was with someone I liked, and not on a mission, it would be fun.

BDR 529 IL: I'm a suit hog

GatorCandie: You wear suits?

BDR 529 IL:	at least I was for a while. I've gotten it out of my system for a bit
BDR 529 IL:	I wear suits when the occasion calls for it or for important meetings
GatorCandie:	yes, I remember. I used to wear suits all the time. I got a bit crazy with them and now I have an entire closet full that I never wear.
GatorCandie:	Which is actually fine, haha
GatorCandie:	Nobody calls me ma'am anymore.
BDR 529 IL:	I don't get called ma'am much either
GatorCandie:	"I love to read (ususally trashy romance novels but I will throw a good mystery in there sometimes). I like to hang out with fun people, as long as I'm having fun, I'm happy."
GatorCandie:	Let me guess…
GatorCandie:	she's not very smart.
BDR 529 IL:	bingo
GatorCandie:	Is this what you usually get? ha
GatorCandie:	I think we should definitely throw a party.
BDR 529 IL:	I've gotten a few cute girls, but none nearly as cute as you
GatorCandie:	aww
GatorCandie:	(lies)
BDR 529 IL:	un-lies!
GatorCandie:	There are lots and lots of girls cuter than me, just not with my particular combination of qualities, haha
BDR 529 IL:	you are super cute in my eyes, but I would have to agree with you—you are one of a kind.

GatorCandie:	Speaking of qualities, hanging from a street sign is not as easy breezy as it looks.
BDR 529 IL:	haha, looks like you had some help getting up there
GatorCandie:	No, actually it was near a fence that I climbed up to get there, but I was really hanging and it was very cold and the sign was sharp. So I'm like, "Kristen, take the freaking picture!!" (smiling the whole time)
BDR 529 IL:	ha
GatorCandie:	thanks; I really appreciate it when you compliment me. As opposed to not appreciating it.
BDR 529 IL:	sonnybabby77
BDR 529 IL:	shes cute, but just didn't do it for me
GatorCandie:	She seems sweet.
BDR 529 IL:	yah
GatorCandie:	I'm not jeapordizing my karma on her. She seems like a nice person, but I do see what you mean.
BDR 529 IL:	:-)
GatorCandie:	Catch her in a few months and see if she likes girls. haha
BDR 529 IL:	nice karma save!
BDR 529 IL:	hahaha
GatorCandie:	Her "Likes"—Tattoos, Body piercings, Skinny dipping, Flirting, Thrills, Erotica, Candlelight, Thunderstorms
GatorCandie:	She's wild, actually.

BDR 529 IL:	yeah, there's a devil behind that angel
GatorCandie:	tattoos and body piercings?
GatorCandie:	wow, those didn't make my list.
BDR 529 IL:	neither am I. On men anyway. I wouldn't get either
BDR 529 IL:	but it can be sexy on a girl if done right
GatorCandie:	I have gone back and forth about getting a belly button ring and I believe I finally landed on "nah"
GatorCandie:	I agree about that, I just don't really want to mark myself up anymore. That probably sounded odd.
BDR 529 IL:	no, not odd at all
GatorCandie:	I kind of like myself this way and don't want to make any statements about myself unless I'm actually saying it.
BDR 529 IL:	you mean you're NOT getting that tattoo of me on your behind??
GatorCandie:	um, did I make a promise in a weak-kneed moment?
BDR 529 IL:	you were drunk; I took advantage.
BDR 529 IL:	but yes, you agreed.
GatorCandie:	So, I need some advice on this one...
GatorCandie:	Should I follow through even though I was taken advantage of?
BDR 529 IL:	about the tattoo??
GatorCandie:	Yes, the tattoo of you, haha
BDR 529 IL:	yes, follow through indeed
GatorCandie:	Or were there other promises??

BDR 529 IL:	yes, a whole lot of promises. I have a list.
GatorCandie:	do tell! I'm dying to hear it!! What have I done?
BDR 529 IL:	it's easier to show
BDR 529 IL:	ever hear of a Chinese basket job??
GatorCandie:	uh-oh… no
BDR 529 IL:	yeah well, I get one of those…
BDR 529 IL:	the list goes on and on.
GatorCandie:	hey!! Hold the phone bub!
GatorCandie:	lmao
BDR 529 IL:	you agreed to be my oral sex alarm clock for a month.
BDR 529 IL:	lots of other stuff too
GatorCandie:	let's see, Chinese basket makers and porn sites come up on google. Are we going to China? haha
BDR 529 IL:	I made that up
BDR 529 IL:	I think it's a line from a movie but I can't remember
GatorCandie:	Did you really? Because there is a website that refers to it. You are truly prolific.
GatorCandie:	http://www.ii-dya.com/bizzzzarre-divx.html
GatorCandie:	ick don't bother, I just wanted you to see what it said
GatorCandie:	FREE bizarre divx and free Chinese basket job!
BDR 529 IL:	wow… free!!
GatorCandie:	So what is it? I must know.

BDR 529 IL: we'll figure it out as we go along

GatorCandie: I just learned what snowballing was about 2 weeks ago via a very circuitous route. I LOVE learning new things! ha

BDR 529 IL: I'm still in the dark

BDR 529 IL: what is it?

GatorCandie: snowballing?

BDR 529 IL: yes

GatorCandie: Oh, I'm so glad someone else doesnt know what it is.

GatorCandie: It has something to do with sharing a guy's ejaculate, either with him (?) or another person. Such as in a situation where three people are having sex with one another.

BDR 529 IL: HIM?!?!?!? Ummm... errrr... Yikes!

GatorCandie: haha, I don't know. Look it up my brother.

GatorCandie: LMAO

BDR 529 IL: I believe you, but if we ever get to that point, don't EVER do that!!

GatorCandie: haha! Don't worry.

GatorCandie: I don't usually pick sex as a good time for practical jokes.

GatorCandie: laughing yes, jokes no

GatorCandie: I like mine though, so why don't guys like thiers??

GatorCandie: guys are so picky

BDR 529 IL: Hahaha. It's just a big turn off

BDR 529 IL: guys, NOT girls

GatorCandie:	That's fine, I'm totally kidding and even though I've never tried it, I somehow intuitively understood that.
GatorCandie:	Not sure exactly how.
BDR 529 IL:	it seems obvious
GatorCandie:	Yes, I guess so. You're making me feel all frisky though. Not exactly "motor running", but I am paying attention to how this conversation is going.
BDR 529 IL:	no motor running??? Usually all I have to do is say two or three words and the girl's clothes come right off.
GatorCandie:	have you said the right two or three words though?
BDR 529 IL:	no, they are in German and I don't speak German, so, it can be difficult at times.
GatorCandie:	I'll take you shopping?
BDR 529 IL:	haha
GatorCandie:	Well this girl can't be bought without at least a hair pull and a neck bite.
BDR 529 IL:	well thats a given
GatorCandie:	Oh, I put that little scenario I told you about into motion this morning and it was good.
BDR 529 IL:	what scenario?
GatorCandie:	Oh, where I'm lying down and you're next to me, etc
BDR 529 IL:	oh yes, elaborate
GatorCandie:	I have to turn this song off for that…

GatorCandie:	um, I am lying in bed on my back and you're lying on your side next to me, your hand on my bare breast, your teeth lightly grazing my neck, and my legs are kind of wrapped up in yours.
BDR 529 IL:	mmm
BDR 529 IL:	sounds like heaven so far
GatorCandie:	Sorry, I'm shy.
BDR 529 IL:	you shouldn't be shy with me
GatorCandie:	Shy in this neighborhood of conversation anyway
GatorCandie:	I'm kind of bummed that you won't be around tomorrow. I was looking forward to graduation day.
BDR 529 IL:	I know... I was too
BDR 529 IL:	I have to admit; I made all these stupid arrangements
BDR 529 IL:	then I was getting nervous
GatorCandie:	about what?
BDR 529 IL:	about how it would go
GatorCandie:	you and I?
BDR 529 IL:	yes
BDR 529 IL:	when I said stupid arrangements
BDR 529 IL:	I didn't mean meeting you
GatorCandie:	So you're a chicken cutlet?
BDR 529 IL:	uggh, I just read that back and saw how it looked
BDR 529 IL:	I meant I made special arrangements for when you came by to see me

GatorCandie:	No, it wasn't misconstrued.
BDR 529 IL:	oh… good
GatorCandie:	You did?
BDR 529 IL:	nothing special. Just something I thought was funny
GatorCandie:	haha, that's cool.
GatorCandie:	But it wont be because… kabosh
BDR 529 IL:	yeah
GatorCandie:	I do hope to meet you sometime though. I am not nervous really.
BDR 529 IL:	sometime??? I hope it's sooner than sometime
GatorCandie:	You just keep calling me cute and I think I am and other people think so too, but I'm all stuck on this model you're dating.
BDR 529 IL:	First off, I haven't seen her in a while and second, she WAS a model; she's not currently a model and lastly, why would that intimidate you?
GatorCandie:	I don't know, I guess because I went for modelling and everyone always encouraged me and I was rejected.
GatorCandie:	poor me!!
GatorCandie:	haha
BDR 529 IL:	yeah… boo hoo. Please… you're beautiful, smart, funny… you have absolutely everything going for you.
BDR 529 IL:	I would get kicked out of that modeling agency so fast my shoes would fall off

GatorCandie: I'm sure my life turned out tons better than it would have if I ended up getting roped into that.

GatorCandie: They said I had a look shared by lots of other girls taller than me, and I was overweight. Which was a shocker, at the time.

GatorCandie: I was like 115 pounds, ha

BDR 529 IL: you mean you weren't 85 lbs???

GatorCandie: All of my friends and family were like, that's fucked, dude. So I went on with my life. I was only 14.

BDR 529 IL: oh geez…14??

BDR 529 IL: too young

GatorCandie: Well, I wanted to grow up fast. Like all little girls I guess.

BDR 529 IL: I'm going to go to sleep soon. I have to be up early tomorow

GatorCandie: you go, Jesse.

BDR 529 IL: but I definitely think you should complete the scenario

BDR 529 IL: in full and uncensored detail

GatorCandie: No, you should. You are much, much better at it than I, and we are on the same kinky page.

GatorCandie: And you don't mind being vulgar, whereas I obviously have a hard time with it.

BDR 529 IL: that's why you need to do it. You need to overcome your fear!

GatorCandie: No, let me stay this way! I like it here!

BDR 529 IL: what a wimp!!

BDR 529 IL:	hahahaha
GatorCandie:	No, just a bit on the submissive side in bed. But I rock. True porn star material right here.
BDR 529 IL:	I love the submissive side, but tell me more about the "true porn star material"
GatorCandie:	Well, I'm kind of loud and I like to express the affirmative as often as possible.
BDR 529 IL:	go on
GatorCandie:	And I love to do anything as long as it feels good to someone (ha) rather than get truly snobbish about it.
BDR 529 IL:	anything?
BDR 529 IL:	hmmm
BDR 529 IL:	wheels turning
GatorCandie:	mostly, ha
GatorCandie:	There is something that I've done that is totally off the deep end.
BDR 529 IL:	oooohhhh… sounds interesting
GatorCandie:	That sounds truly awful when written down.
BDR 529 IL:	good
BDR 529 IL:	haha
GatorCandie:	I peed once while I was having sex. It was something I tried to do and it took a lot of patience, but it was incredibly worth it. I can't even tell you how good it felt. I know it may sound a little strange.
BDR 529 IL:	wow. I can't even imagine how you would get your body to do that
BDR 529 IL:	haha

GatorCandie: It took a lot of patience.

BDR 529 IL: I bet

BDR 529 IL: while he was inside you?

GatorCandie: Words really can't describe what a unique feeling it was. It's not something I NEED to do though, ha.

BDR 529 IL: if it makes you feel good, it makes me feel good

GatorCandie: Yeah, I was on top and he was pressing on my stomach. It took like 15 minutes though, to get there.

BDR 529 IL: sounds interesting

GatorCandie: Me and my crazy ideas. I think I read somewhere that it felt good, so there I was "I want to try that!"

BDR 529 IL: haha

BDR 529 IL: and it worked…who woulda' thunk

GatorCandie: Interesting, yes. I guess you'd have to be there to understand it.

BDR 529 IL: I can see it, bit its obviously different for a girl than a guy

GatorCandie: It's not like this great amount. It's tiny, almost like a girl who's really wet.

BDR 529 IL: yeah

BDR 529 IL: you're going to make me go to sleep with a hardon and no Pamela to help!!

GatorCandie: I think I tried mentally like 5 times before I ever got to the point where I was comfortable enough to do it

BDR 529 IL: haha

BDR 529 IL: practice pee?

GatorCandie: Well it's definitely not "right" to pee anywhere but the bathroom, so it takes some mental gymnastics to make it work. Do you have a big pete?

BDR 529 IL: at the moment, yes

GatorCandie: That makes me so happy!

GatorCandie: You still don't think I'm a total freak! Or you do and you like it! Either way.

BDR 529 IL: I don't think you are any freakier than I am

BDR 529 IL: I think we would have lots of new things to try

GatorCandie: Sorry about the hardware though. OK, before you go to sleeps, what makes you freaky?

BDR 529 IL: you!

GatorCandie: oh go on

BDR 529 IL: neither of us are obviously into regular, 10 minute, lay there sex

BDR 529 IL: we are into… well, different things

BDR 529 IL: and it's hard to find someone that totally "fits" with you

BDR 529 IL: in all respects

GatorCandie: I have bared 75% to you and so you have to tell me something now!

BDR 529 IL: we are into the same things

BDR 529 IL: you like to be submissive? That's a big thing with me

BDR 529 IL:	I like that—YOU being submissive that is, not the other way around.
GatorCandie:	I have some other freakier things in my head, but I'll wait for you to find them.
GatorCandie:	Ok I have a pointed stick question. Are you sadistic?
GatorCandie:	BDR 529 IL: and it's hard to find someone that totally "fits" with you
GatorCandie:	Do you think I fit with you?
BDR 529 IL:	yes, I think you do. Sadistic? Only when its a mutual thing
GatorCandie:	um, vague alert!
GatorCandie:	I mean, do you want to see me cry?
BDR 529 IL:	no, not for real. I would never want to see you sad or in any real pain.
BDR 529 IL:	but if we were playing around, I could get into it
GatorCandie:	It's never happened, but I'd follow you most places I think. I think we might fit too. In lots of ways I mean.
BDR 529 IL:	I agree
GatorCandie:	But I don't want to be sad or in real pain.
GatorCandie:	ha, that's not my thing.
BDR 529 IL:	hey I just remembered, you never set up your webcam!
GatorCandie:	Neither did you!
BDR 529 IL:	I know, but my webcam is old, I don't have the software and I don't even know if it still works

GatorCandie:	bla bla
GatorCandie:	gooses and ganders
BDR 529 IL:	you have a brand new one, just waiting to show me your pretty face.
GatorCandie:	I was actually guessing that you didn't. Good bluff, wouldn't you say?
BDR 529 IL:	that I didn't what?
GatorCandie:	Didnt set it up.
GatorCandie:	I will work on it, but I spend so much time in my office on the computer that as soon as I get the chance, I get the flock out of here.
BDR 529 IL:	well, here you are with nothing to do. What a perfect opportunity.
GatorCandie:	Nothing to do but sleep!
GatorCandie:	OK, how long 'til you think you'll make it to Buffalo?
BDR 529 IL:	hopefully, this week
BDR 529 IL:	if not prob next week
GatorCandie:	Then, in the tradition of Monty Hall, I will make you a deal. Wanna hear it, here it go:
BDR 529 IL:	I'll take what's in the box!
GatorCandie:	When I set up my webcam, you have to spend at least 15 minutes on the phone with me. HORROR OF HORRORS!!
BDR 529 IL:	ok, it's a deal.
GatorCandie:	…he said, grudgingly!!
BDR 529 IL:	no, I just like talking to you here—but the phone will be good too.
GatorCandie:	I like your voice.

BDR 529 IL:	I like yours too
GatorCandie:	And in light of today's alteration of events and the uncertainty of the future, I will mail you that CD.
BDR 529 IL:	so sweet
GatorCandie:	really? Thank you. I loved the voice mail you left me. As a matter of fact, I don't think I erased it and I should find it and play it again. You were very funny.
BDR 529 IL:	I was?
GatorCandie:	yes. I'm trying to find it now.
BDR 529 IL:	yeah, where I kept talking long after we were disconnected? haha
GatorCandie:	It was so cute.
GatorCandie:	there you are!
GatorCandie:	"but just so you know, I continued talking for like 2 minutes before I realized the phone had hung up"
BDR 529 IL:	☒
GatorCandie:	"so I should be back there in like 5 minutes, ok talk to you then"
GatorCandie:	I love your voice!
BDR 529 IL:	oh stop
GatorCandie:	I'm so glad I met you. ☒
GatorCandie:	well, kind of met you.
BDR 529 IL:	aww
BDR 529 IL:	well, you KNOW how glad I am that I met you!
BDR 529 IL:	or at least you should know.

GatorCandie: I guess I do. We are different from other people, I think.

BDR 529 IL: I think so too.

GatorCandie: And we are more tired lately than other people too.

BDR 529 IL: yes, is it bedtime?

BDR 529 IL: do you want the right side or the left side of the bed?

GatorCandie: I guess so. I do love talking to you. And always the left side.

BDR 529 IL: uh oh

GatorCandie: haha!

GatorCandie: great minds

GatorCandie: we'll see what happens. (That's me, not conceding to anything)

BDR 529 IL: you can have the left side my dear....

GatorCandie: I guess you would have to make me so tired and blissed out that I wouldnt care. ☒

BDR 529 IL: I was going to say I'll just push you over when you fall asleep

GatorCandie: (what a jerk)

BDR 529 IL: hahaha

GatorCandie: Oh, did I type that out loud??

BDR 529 IL: yes you did!!!

GatorCandie: How could I??

BDR 529 IL: fool

GatorCandie: Don't know a good thing… but wait, yes I do!

GatorCandie: The left side of the bed is a good thing!

BDR 529 IL: it is. And I should put myself there right now

GatorCandie: Can I ask you one more question before you
                   go to sleep or have I hit my quota?

BDR 529 IL: no no, go ahead.

GatorCandie: k

GatorCandie: Do you go around winking at girls a lot?
                   Just curious.

BDR 529 IL: I did, but I have stopped entirely in the past
                   few days

BDR 529 IL: if ya know what I mean.

GatorCandie: Everybody seems to pale in comparison to
                   you ☒ future relationship suicide!!

BDR 529 IL: hahaha. Oh stop. You know I feel the same
                   way about you, so it's joint relationship
                   suicide

GatorCandie: I hope you have sweet dreams, Jesse. I like you.

BDR 529 IL: sweet dreams, Pamela.

BDR 529 IL: I really like you.

GatorCandie: k bye, me too.

BDR 529 IL: goodnight sweetness

BDR 529 IL: talk to you tomorrow

BDR 529 IL: ly

GatorCandie: lytoo

BDR 529 IL direct connection is closed.

BDR 529 IL signed off at 1:47:24 AM.

ANOTHER DAY ANOTHER CHAT

BDR 529 IL: oh no, not YOU!

GatorCandie: I feel the same way!

GatorCandie: thpppt

BDR 529 IL: haha

BDR 529 IL: how are you doing?

GatorCandie: Great. Et vous?

BDR 529 IL: pretty good

BDR 529 IL: just came home to take care of a few things

GatorCandie: fair to middle?

BDR 529 IL: no, fair to midland

BDR 529 IL: want a George Bush belt buckle??

GatorCandie: I haven't left my house yet today. Um, no, but I'll remember your generosity if I ever get upset with you.

GatorCandie: I will definitely remember this moment, don't worry.

BDR 529 IL: hahaha

GatorCandie: Do you really have a George Bush belt buckle?

GatorCandie: Or are you just trying to think of the perfect thing for me?

GatorCandie: fishing around?

BDR 529 IL: I saw a commercial selling them on CNN

GatorCandie: Did you ever see that jibjab thing?

BDR 529 IL: jibjab? No.

GatorCandie:	do you have a spare minute?
BDR 529 IL:	yes, I even have a spare tire
GatorCandie:	www.jibjab.com—sound must be turned on
BDR 529 IL:	oh yes, I saw this
GatorCandie:	well, they're selling related clothing now.
BDR 529 IL:	sweeeet
GatorCandie:	"liberal wiener" thong
BDR 529 IL:	haha
GatorCandie:	I'm watching, I cant help it
GatorCandie:	I'm such a slacker
BDR 529 IL:	you can't say nuclear!
BDR 529 IL:	he really can't
GatorCandie:	I know he can't
BDR 529 IL:	slap... what'd I do?
GatorCandie:	I love Bill Clinton
BDR 529 IL:	man... I just had a sneezing fit
BDR 529 IL:	wheeeew
GatorCandie:	salut
BDR 529 IL:	why thank you
GatorCandie:	salut is what my stepfather used to say
GatorCandie:	I say mazel tov!
BDR 529 IL:	ha
GatorCandie:	or maybe l'chaim I can't remember
GatorCandie:	l'chiam? Yikes.
GatorCandie:	should I send this CD to your Ramapo address?
BDR 529 IL:	yes

BDR 529 IL:	I'm gonna make some coffee
BDR 529 IL:	brb, ok?
GatorCandie:	k, fine. Could you get me some? Milk no sugar?
BDR 529 IL:	I only have Half & Half
BDR 529 IL:	you'll have it and LIKE it!
GatorCandie:	typical, but that's fine, haha
BDR 529 IL:	brb
GatorCandie:	k
GatorCandie:	brb
BDR 529 IL:	k
BDR 529 IL:	and yes, I do have milk for you
BDR 529 IL:	I forgot that I went shopping
BDR 529 IL:	so HA!
GatorCandie:	That's good because I have no milk. The last of it went into my coffee this morning.
BDR 529 IL:	muuahhhahahahahaha
GatorCandie:	That was a long time ago. Evil laugh?? Other people's misfortunes, ok got it.
GatorCandie:	remember how mine are off limits?
BDR 529 IL:	oh yes, my mistake.
GatorCandie:	"BDR 529 IL: oh... don't get me wrong... the misfortune of others is hilarious
GatorCandie:	just not yours?
BDR 529 IL:	exactly
BDR 529 IL:	now you're on the trolley
GatorCandie:	my misery is not so funny either, actually

GatorCandie:	keep that in mind
BDR 529 IL:	ok. Yours and mine—off limits"
BDR 529 IL:	woah
GatorCandie:	what?
BDR 529 IL:	that was from a while ago!
GatorCandie:	haha, within minutes of meeting actually
GatorCandie:	Are you kidding?? I'm going to court-of-law this stuff later.
BDR 529 IL:	taking me to court for being too cool??
GatorCandie:	and cute.
BDR 529 IL:	guilty as charged
GatorCandie:	that's what I like to hear.
BDR 529 IL:	brb, coffee is ready
GatorCandie:	you know you're a hottie, and you're dangerous.
GatorCandie:	k
BDR 529 IL:	k
GatorCandie:	BDR 529 IL: "I own a company that manually masturbates horses in captivity
GatorCandie:	liar, horses don't need that
BDR 529 IL:	well, they don't need it but they like it"
BDR 529 IL:	it's all true.
GatorCandie:	Maybe they would rather just have sex with each other.
BDR 529 IL:	nope.
BDR 529 IL:	This stuff makes for interesting reading actually. I haven't gone back until now to look at it.

BDR 529 IL: It would be fun to re-read. Send me what you have and I'll send you what I have. I saved pretty much every conversation that we've had thus far.

GatorCandie: I'll send what I have in a bit. I didn't save every conversation we ever tho, so…

BDR 529 IL: no, I need it now!

BDR 529 IL: just kidding

BDR 529 IL: later is fine

GatorCandie: It may be a bit discombobulated

BDR 529 IL: that's ok

GatorCandie: I need it now too, but what's a girl to do?

BDR 529 IL: JOHNSON, I want that report on my desk FIRST THING tomorrow morning!

GatorCandie: Hey, coffee is for closers.

BDR 529 IL: hahaha

BDR 529 IL: A B C

GatorCandie: I don't see any closers here.

GatorCandie: What a dark and depressing movie.

BDR 529 IL: I know, like Death of a Salesman meets… umm… something

BDR 529 IL: hello? Mrs. Nyborg??

GatorCandie: meets um, you're right… something. Something dark

BDR 529 IL: "Grace, draw me $10,000 in petty cash please"

GatorCandie: I'm finding something, ha

BDR 529 IL: ok

GatorCandie: "We don't gotta sit here and listen to this."

"You CERTAINLY don't pal, 'cause the good
news is—you're fired."

BDR 529 IL: "the winner gets a car, the loser gets fired"

BDR 529 IL: oh I forgot, second place is a set of steak
                  knives

GatorCandie: "You never open your mouth until you know
                  what the shot is."

GatorCandie: "Patel? Fuck you. If fucking Shiva handed
                  this guy a million dollars, said "Sign the deal!"
                  he wouldn't sign. And the God Vishnu too.
                  Fuck you, John! You know your business, I
                  know mine. Your business is being an asshole.
                  When I find out whose fucking cousin you
                  are, I'm going to go to him and figure out a
                  way to have… you're a—fuck you."

GatorCandie: haha, it's been a while since I've seen that
                  movie, and that's fine with me

BDR 529 IL: that's so funny… "Patel". I have dealt with
                  many Patels in my day

GatorCandie: I bet you have.

GatorCandie: they are so shifty! LOL Sorry. It's just how
                  I feel.

GatorCandie: They never give you the straight story. They're
                  always driving you around hell's creation,
                  feeding you misinformation. um sorry again,
                  haha

BDR 529 IL: I remember once I rented an apartment to
                  a family of Patels. They owned a Dunkin
                  Donuts franchise. Nice people. I told him that
                  the only way he was getting this apartment is

	if he brought me 4 large Coffee Coolatas… jokingly of course
BDR 529 IL:	the next day, he brought them in!
BDR 529 IL:	he was a pretty smelly guy, so I didn't even drink them but it was so funny that he actually brought them! I told him that I was only joking and that I was so sorry that he misunderstood me.
BDR 529 IL:	he said that he knew that I was joking but he wanted to bring them for me anyway. Nice fellow—smelly but very nice.
GatorCandie:	The guy I knew owned a Seven Eleven or two. I'm sounding really racist, but I'm not. I just don't like doing business with them.
BDR 529 IL:	you are too a racist
BDR 529 IL:	admit it!
BDR 529 IL:	go on with your story.
GatorCandie:	ok maybe a little
BDR 529 IL:	haha
BDR 529 IL:	you racist pig!
GatorCandie:	Well you know I grew up in Merrick
GatorCandie:	100% white…
BDR 529 IL:	near Seaford??
GatorCandie:	sorta near Seaford. On the same train line.
BDR 529 IL:	that's where we sailed the boat to the other day
GatorCandie:	"Next stop, Ron-KON-kama"
BDR 529 IL:	I love saying Ronknokoma almost as much as saying Hohokus

GatorCandie:	Yes, Seaford is between Wantagh/Bellmore and Freeport
BDR 529 IL:	yep, I know exactly where that is
GatorCandie:	haha! I've never heard of Hohokus, but yeah, Ronkonkama is a great word/name.
BDR 529 IL:	give Hohokus a chance—it's tons of fun to say
GatorCandie:	I had never really even seen black people until my mother took me to the movies…
BDR 529 IL:	oh stop it. There are plenty of black people in Wantagh—all over Long Island for that matter. Don't start getting all hillbilly on me now!
GatorCandie:	Well, long story short, when I was a kid, I always though black people smelled like popcorn.
BDR 529 IL:	butter or chedder?
GatorCandie:	Actually, to this day I still really believe that.
BDR 529 IL:	Black people are just fine by me. Growing up in Brooklyn, I was fortunate enough to have friends of every ethnicity that you could possibly imagine. And, I would much prefer to live in an all black neighborhood over a "white bread", mid-western town full of racist and ignorant white people. I like diversity in my neighborhoods.
BDR 529 IL:	On a separate note, I have a newspaper from 1902 and it has a classified ad that reads "1,200 Acres in Suffolk County: $12,000."

BDR 529 IL: I wish I had a time machine! Ten bucks an acre in Suffolk… could you imagine what that would be worth today?

GatorCandie: A time machine would be great, wouldn't it?

BDR 529 IL: oh it sure would! My goodness—10 bucks an acre and figure that you could easily subdivide each acre into four ¼ acre lots. That's 4,800 buildable lots in Suffolk! Take away 800 lots for roads and whatnot—that still leaves you with 4,000 buildable lots!

GatorCandie: I'd go and make sure I never lost all those transistor radios I did when I was a kid. It always used to really piss my mom off

BDR 529 IL: good plan

GatorCandie: if I was a better daughter, I'm sure she would look a lot younger than she does now.

BDR 529 IL: hahaha

BDR 529 IL: wanna hear about a horrible rip off!!

GatorCandie: sure!

BDR 529 IL: my fathers mother, my grandmother, her maiden name is Mayo…

BDR 529 IL: the Mayo's were one of the owners and founders of the company that produces and supplies ALL of the denim to Levi's. They still do to this day, by the way.

BDR 529 IL: well anyway…

BDR 529 IL: my grandmother's father died very young

BDR 529 IL: 26 years old

GatorCandie: wow

BDR 529 IL:	and in those days, women had nothing to do with business—they were pretty much always kept in the dark and/or out of the loop.
GatorCandie:	k
BDR 529 IL:	so, needless to say, when my grandmother's father died, they cut his wife off completely—like she never existed. They were already pretty wealthy and on their way to being SUPER wealthy.
BDR 529 IL:	so my grandmothers mother had to live on whatever cash was left, which wasn't much at all. Sold the house, which wasn't yet paid for and basically became relatively poor. They never saw another penny after he died and the company still operates to this day.
GatorCandie:	bummer
BDR 529 IL:	yah
GatorCandie:	so
GatorCandie:	Is that the story?
BDR 529 IL:	thats it… I got jipped outta my Levi money!
BDR 529 IL:	I could have been a pants billionaire!
BDR 529 IL:	actually, they were the main suppliers of the textiles to Levi and then bought into the actual Levi company several years later. So they own a piece of Levi's as well.
GatorCandie:	I wonder how they would feel now if they could come and see what a bitch Walmart is making out of them…
BDR 529 IL:	I'm sure they feel fine
BDR 529 IL:	bastards

GatorCandie: So you feel cheated?

BDR 529 IL: yes and no. I mean... I like pants!

GatorCandie: Nice pants.

GatorCandie: this is a bootstrap kinda country, kid

BDR 529 IL: ha

GatorCandie: I like pants too!

BDR 529 IL: and, here's another rip off

BDR 529 IL: my mother's 2nd cousin is Ann Bancroft...

BDR 529 IL: Ann Bancroft is married to Mel Brooks, one of my idols

BDR 529 IL: and I never got to meet him! I don't want anything from them. I just wanna meet the guy. I mean, it's Mel Brooks! He's the best! How cool would it be to be able to chitchat with Mel??

GatorCandie: Oh, now that is a major bummer.

BDR 529 IL: I know, he's the best!

GatorCandie: My rip-offs seem to be much smaller than yours, haha.

GatorCandie: "Did you bullshit today?"

GatorCandie: "Did you try to bullshit today?"

BDR 529 IL: whats that from?

GatorCandie: um... the unemployment line...

GatorCandie: trying to remember...

BDR 529 IL: Life Stinks?

GatorCandie: no, it can't be. Is it?

GatorCandie: It's the movie set in Roman times

BDR 529 IL: oh, History of the World?

GatorCandie: YES, thank you God!

GatorCandie: One of my favorite movies, not Mel Brooks, is um

GatorCandie: The Frisco Kid

BDR 529 IL: Hahaha, yeah that's a great movie!

GatorCandie: I would love to see that again.

GatorCandie: "Come here Chicken! I don't want to hurt you, I just want to eat you"

BDR 529 IL: "ok, so I take a right at the tree, then I go straight as piss for two days, then, make a QUICK left"

GatorCandie: haha!!

GatorCandie: straight as piss

BDR 529 IL: I think Mel Brooks had something to do with that movie, didn't he?

BDR 529 IL: he must have

GatorCandie: "What do you call this part of the horse?

Avram :   The tuches!

Tommy :   Well, you just keep your eyes on this took-iss, and don't take them off 'till we get to San Francisco! "

BDR 529 IL: ha

GatorCandie: dunno if he had anything to do with that movie. I'll check

GatorCandie: …nothing to do with Mel Brooks

GatorCandie: Robert Aldrich

BDR 529 IL: ever see Casino?

GatorCandie: No, but I saw Oceans 11

BDR 529 IL:	ugghh… not the same!!!
BDR 529 IL:	damn you!
BDR 529 IL:	lol
GatorCandie:	wha? haha
BDR 529 IL:	Oceans 11 has nothing at all to do with Casino
BDR 529 IL:	except for the fact that they are IN a casino, there are absolutely no other similarities.
GatorCandie:	I realize that…I was just kidding!! geez
BDR 529 IL:	I know…Im playing with you
GatorCandie:	Lighten up, missa jesse
GatorCandie:	"Greed, deception, money, power, and murder occur between two mobster best friends and a trophy wife over a gambling empire."
GatorCandie:	I have a question…
BDR 529 IL:	ok
GatorCandie:	as a rule I don't like Italian guys (no offense)
GatorCandie:	and I've never been in a casino
GatorCandie:	and mob movies don't move me…
GatorCandie:	What's in it for me to see this 'Casino' flick?
GatorCandie:	Is it funny?
GatorCandie:	Are there naked women?
GatorCandie:	haha
BDR 529 IL:	the characters are funny
BDR 529 IL:	have you seen Goodfellas?
GatorCandie:	of course, as a matter of fact I dated a guy that my friends nicknamed Spider. Not in a good way, of course

BDR 529 IL:	it's a lot like Goodfellas
GatorCandie:	Then why watch it? Sorry, just being a brat.
BDR 529 IL:	by the way, another weird fact about me, I know the two little girls who play Henry and Karen Hill's kids in that movie.
GatorCandie:	"I got a leg! I found a wing!"
BDR 529 IL:	"whataya like Henry, the leg or the wing"
BDR 529 IL:	haha
GatorCandie:	it's been awhile. That's my favorite part of the movie.
BDR 529 IL:	the knowing the girls story is a strange story
BDR 529 IL:	wanna hear it?
GatorCandie:	let it rip, baby
BDR 529 IL:	ok, here we go
BDR 529 IL:	I answered an ad in the paper for a "business assistant" and went for the interview to a house in Piermont (near my house)
BDR 529 IL:	I met with a woman named Wendy and she baked gourmet cookies in her house, which she obviously resold for profit—thus, the business. So I got the job. I was about 16 years old.
GatorCandie:	k
BDR 529 IL:	it started out small but within a short amount of time, they were being sold to high end stores like Bergdorf Goodmans and Bloomingdales, Zabars, etc.
BDR 529 IL:	anyway
BDR 529 IL:	it was only Wendy and I working there.

BDR 529 IL:	she had two young daughters
GatorCandie:	right.
BDR 529 IL:	Ruby and Violet
BDR 529 IL:	thus the name of the company
BDR 529 IL:	Ruby et Violette
GatorCandie:	k
BDR 529 IL:	those are the girls in the movie …Ruby and Violet
BDR 529 IL:	anyway
BDR 529 IL:	so I'm working for this lady at 16
BDR 529 IL:	she lives in a beautiful house overlooking the Hudson River.
BDR 529 IL:	she's a total socialite—knows everyone, has tons of money from God knows where. She was divorced so it was just her and the girls in the house, (and me most times).
BDR 529 IL:	after working with her for a few months, she would ask me to watch her house for her for days on end while she jetted off to… wherever.
BDR 529 IL:	and pay me for it!
GatorCandie:	cool
BDR 529 IL:	a 16-year-old kid living in a cool house and getting PAID for it
GatorCandie:	fun!
BDR 529 IL:	eventually, with my help, her company grew and we moved the operation to a factory on Long Island
GatorCandie:	really?

BDR 529 IL:	So now, I'm just about 17 years old and Director of Operations of this company
GatorCandie:	no way!
BDR 529 IL:	yeah… pretty weird
BDR 529 IL:	but cool
BDR 529 IL:	so….
BDR 529 IL:	I start to realize that she knows a lot of famous people
BDR 529 IL:	one day Lorainne Bracco came to the house
BDR 529 IL:	she played Karen from Goodfellas by the way.
GatorCandie:	ok
GatorCandie:	When you were 17?
BDR 529 IL:	one day, Harvey Keitel comes by to pick up Stella, his daughter. I had no idea this was his daughter mind you.
GatorCandie:	wow
BDR 529 IL:	in the next year, Robert Deniro (Bobby as she called him), and a handful of other famous people would be in and out of this house
BDR 529 IL:	I was meeting everyone. Meeting as in hello and goodbye but meeting them nonetheless.
BDR 529 IL:	it was pretty cool
GatorCandie:	fun
BDR 529 IL:	yeah, it was a blast
GatorCandie:	New Yorkers are good people
GatorCandie:	Did that make sense?
BDR 529 IL:	uh… yes?

GatorCandie: I mean, no matter their station, if someone is New York they're pretty cool.

BDR 529 IL: yeah... so I know I come out with a lot of weird shit, but I promise its all true. Sometimes people think I'm making this shit up because I have such off the wall stories.

GatorCandie: People think you're lying?

GatorCandie: Why would someone lie about that?

BDR 529 IL: its not like I go around telling everyone these stories, but when I do, it usually comes off like bullshit

BDR 529 IL: like on a resume—Director of Operations for a multi-million dollar company at age 17?

GatorCandie: It must be your delivery. It doesn't sound like bullshit to me.

BDR 529 IL: uhhh... most people don't believe that one

BDR 529 IL: meeting Harvey Keitel, Robert Dinero, etc.... people think that's bullshit too

GatorCandie: No, I can see the progression. It makes sense.

GatorCandie: Do you know them?

BDR 529 IL: well, it's not like we hang out or anything.

BDR 529 IL: but I have met them both several times

GatorCandie: You know what would sound like bullshit?

BDR 529 IL: what?

GatorCandie: 11 inches haha

GatorCandie: THEN we'd have problems. Otherwise I believe you.

BDR 529 IL: hahaha... nope, I'm a full inch and a half hard

GatorCandie: oh uh 'brb'

BDR 529 IL: ha

GatorCandie: oh, you think I'm joking? Are you still here??

BDR 529 IL: an inch and a half isn't enough for you??

GatorCandie: haha, I don't like the way this conversation is going, and I'm casting about desperately to change it back to the way I would like it to be

BDR 529 IL: hahaha

BDR 529 IL: how would you like it to go?

GatorCandie: LMAO

GatorCandie: Well, you said it would be cool to see me cry and you're missing it, haha

BDR 529 IL: HAHAHA

BDR 529 IL: awwww, I never said it would be "cool" to see you cry.

GatorCandie: I know, I was just taking a shortcut to the humor

BDR 529 IL: Ahh. That makes sense. So how big does a guy need to be to please you?

BDR 529 IL: foot? Foot and a half?

GatorCandie: hahahaha

GatorCandie: Not "big"

GatorCandie: Normal works for me.

BDR 529 IL: I can see you sweating from here "is he too small? Too big? Is it crooked?"

GatorCandie: Abnormal does NOT work, but I've been lucky there. The men I have fallen in love with have been normal.

GatorCandie: crooked would be ok, haha

BDR 529 IL: I have a friend we call tripod

GatorCandie: why?

BDR 529 IL: think about it

GatorCandie: oh, haha

GatorCandie: how would you all know?

BDR 529 IL: because he pulls it out every chance he gets…
                 crude little bastard

GatorCandie: I had a friend named Karl who loved his
                 penis very much.

GatorCandie: Exactly!! He used to pull it out and put it on
                 the table at parties, ha

BDR 529 IL: yes, same guy

BDR 529 IL: in a hot dog bun, etc, etc.

GatorCandie: yes, etc, etc.

GatorCandie: He LOVED his penis.

GatorCandie: He used to show us the amateur porn he
                 made with unsuspecting one-night stands.

BDR 529 IL: oh no!

GatorCandie: he was a bad boy.

BDR 529 IL: there was a girl in our highschool who made
                 a porn tape with her boyfriend. The tape got
                 circulated all over the place and eventually
                 made its way to the firehouse where her
                 father worked. They popped the tape in one
                 day and the father had no idea what he was
                 about to see…. neither did any of the other
                 guys

GatorCandie:	oh no! The guy I know "offered" me once. I decided I'd rather just admire him from very far away.
BDR 529 IL:	oh come on... you did him, admit it.
GatorCandie:	nope. I already had a good idea what it would be like. I'd already seen the penis—there was no mystery.
GatorCandie:	we were good friends and used to commiserate about our sex lives and stuff, but no sex between us.
BDR 529 IL:	I think you would like my penis once you got to know him. In fact, you can try it for 30 days and if you're not completely satisfied, you can return it for a partial refund
GatorCandie:	30 days? That's a long time!
BDR 529 IL:	yeah, it's a good deal
GatorCandie:	so you think I would like your penis?
BDR 529 IL:	sure you would. He's very easy to get along with
GatorCandie:	millions of happy customers?
BDR 529 IL:	billions!
GatorCandie:	haha
GatorCandie:	So no one has ever laughed at your penis?
BDR 529 IL:	not yet, but there's still time
GatorCandie:	If it hasn't already happened then I doubt it will.
BDR 529 IL:	you have to be a pretty cold-hearted girl to laugh at a man's penis. To his face anyway.
BDR 529 IL:	did you laugh once, Pamela??

GatorCandie:	well, in front of him, yeah
BDR 529 IL:	oh my God. What did he say??
GatorCandie:	no! Like you said, you'd have to be cold-hearted to do that in front of him. I would never.
GatorCandie:	There was a guy I was smitten with once…
GatorCandie:	his name was Brian…
GatorCandie:	he was about 6'4 and was super smart and pretty funny. He knew lots of great obscure stuff
GatorCandie:	We dated around for 2 months but never had sex.
GatorCandie:	He used to tell me about tantric sex, which to this day I don't understand, but he said he could do it and it kept him going for hours.
BDR 529 IL:	yeah yeah, I've heard that before
BDR 529 IL:	ok… go on
GatorCandie:	Well, we finally had sex, and
GatorCandie:	his penis was very small
GatorCandie:	and a shocking shade of pink
BDR 529 IL:	how small? Like reeeeallllly small
GatorCandie:	and he came in 5 minutes
BDR 529 IL:	wow
GatorCandie:	it was so awful
GatorCandie:	and this was after my previous boyfriends who were like all-stars
BDR 529 IL:	awww… poor fella
GatorCandie:	yes, reealllly small.

GatorCandie:	I'd say abnormally small probably.
BDR 529 IL:	deformed small? Like two inches small?
GatorCandie:	Maybe four inches ratcheted all the way
GatorCandie:	But don't forget the weird shade of pink.
BDR 529 IL:	oh that's not THAT terrible. I thought you meant really amazingly small
BDR 529 IL:	like a little bump or something
BDR 529 IL:	pink… hmmm
BDR 529 IL:	that's odd
GatorCandie:	Pink, like a dog.
GatorCandie:	I don't like pink.
BDR 529 IL:	no… pink is not good
GatorCandie:	It was an earth shattering experience because I really liked him, like a whole lot.
GatorCandie:	But I broke up with him almost immediately.
BDR 529 IL:	awww…. I feel bad for him
GatorCandie:	Yeah, I think he loved me and I feel really bad too.
BDR 529 IL:	I'll have to send you my penis' portfolio so you can decide if he is worthy
GatorCandie:	Hey, don't get all weirded out! Sorry I mentioned it.
GatorCandie:	I don't want you to have this impression that I rate people or anything. I'm not even that experienced!
BDR 529 IL:	I'm not. I'm just kidding
BDR 529 IL:	I think your penis stories are amusing

GatorCandie:	At my age, the amount of guys I've been with is almost appalling actually.
BDR 529 IL:	what's the official number?
GatorCandie:	appallingly small.
BDR 529 IL:	like Brian's penis?
GatorCandie:	um the number… give me a sec, it does require thought.
GatorCandie:	7 is what I counted, but somebody is missing. So 8.
BDR 529 IL:	one sec
GatorCandie:	k
GatorCandie:	are you choking?
BDR 529 IL:	sorry
BDR 529 IL:	I'm back
BDR 529 IL:	helloooo….
BDR 529 IL:	my darling???
GatorCandie:	hi
BDR 529 IL:	why hello (deep sexy voice)
GatorCandie:	hello baby
BDR 529 IL:	ha
GatorCandie:	so are you officially here?
BDR 529 IL:	semi-officially bordering on officially
GatorCandie:	is eight normal, a lot, appalling?
BDR 529 IL:	eight is normal I suppose
GatorCandie:	eight almost seems like a lot of people, but it feels like not a lot at all over 16 years.
BDR 529 IL:	no, eight isn't bad at all

GatorCandie: quality, not quantity. I try to be sure.

GatorCandie: Brian was a huge snag and a waste of placement in the eight.

BDR 529 IL: so really its 7.5 people.

GatorCandie: Yes, I only slept with him once and his penis was small so 7.5 is fairly accurate.

GatorCandie: He was a huge Bettie Page fan

BDR 529 IL: oh, so he was gay also?

GatorCandie: You would be number nine—ala Beatles

GatorCandie: haha, I can't believe I said that!!

GatorCandie: You bring out the bad in me.

BDR 529 IL: hahaha

BDR 529 IL: good!

GatorCandie: Here's something that would interest you...

GatorCandie: I used to have a collar.

BDR 529 IL: haha, and you don't anymore?

GatorCandie: no silly. What would I do with it? Wear it in public?

BDR 529 IL: no, but I would think you would keep it for special occasions.

GatorCandie: Such as?

BDR 529 IL: meeting me for one

GatorCandie: I think it would be strange wearing that one with someone else, don't you?

BDR 529 IL: true. We will have to get you a brand spanking new one

GatorCandie: Wearing one is an incredibly unique experience. It's definitely been a very long time.

BDR 529 IL: sorry, brb

BDR 529 IL: k

GatorCandie: OK but I'm not discussing intimate stuff with you anymore because you keep leaving, haha.

BDR 529 IL: no nooooo

BDR 529 IL: I'm here to stay.

GatorCandie: don't worry, if you're busy, be busy. It's okay with me and I understand.

BDR 529 IL: no, I'd much rather talking about intimate things with you!

BDR 529 IL: take a picture of yourself right now. What do you look like at this very moment?

GatorCandie: My camera is in my car, sorry. But I'm wearing a white ribbed t-shirt, my bell bottomed carpenter jeans and my boots. No makeup

BDR 529 IL: "in my car, sorry"… like it's on the moon or something

GatorCandie: I live on the third floor and I parked halfway down the street last night. so…

BDR 529 IL: I wish you were here right now… ooohhh the fun we could have!

GatorCandie: Well, if you had played your cards right, there could have been a possibility of something for later tonight, but…

BDR 529 IL: I know, don't remind me

BDR 529 IL: now I'm daydreaming about what could have been

GatorCandie:	Kris is so suspicious (in general). She called me yesterday and asked if I was still meeting you and she was like uh-oh, maybe you'll never meet him; maybe he's making up how cool he is…
BDR 529 IL:	hahaha "making up how cool he is"
GatorCandie:	So I was like, well if that's the case then I haven't lost anything but sleep, so fahgetaboutit
BDR 529 IL:	hahaha
GatorCandie:	I know, "making up how cool he is"
GatorCandie:	You can't make that stuff up!
BDR 529 IL:	you know I'm the coolest
GatorCandie:	Close enough.
BDR 529 IL:	hahaha
BDR 529 IL:	come over so I can undress you!
GatorCandie:	huh?
BDR 529 IL:	you heard me… get over here right now!
BDR 529 IL:	post haste!
GatorCandie:	what can I do?
BDR 529 IL:	I could think of quite a few things
GatorCandie:	You come here!!
BDR 529 IL:	I'm going to
GatorCandie:	and maybe we can negotiate about these "things"
BDR 529 IL:	negotiate, ya say? Be careful… I'm a pretty good negotiater.
GatorCandie:	ooh, then we'll be deadlocked forever, haha.
BDR 529 IL:	we can't have that, now can we?

GatorCandie: no. What will we do about that?

BDR 529 IL: well, if it comes up a stalemate, then I'll just have to force myself on you

GatorCandie: wow, I never thought of that

BDR 529 IL: see, there's a solution to everything.

GatorCandie: you're really turning me on right now. You know how I wan't you to force yourself on me.

BDR 529 IL: yes, I'm feeling quite amorous myself.

GatorCandie: I really don't want it to stop either

BDR 529 IL: visions in such graphic detail… I should slap MYSELF

GatorCandie: I know, and when you meet me you won't want to hurt me, so my rape fantasy will never happen, guaranteed, and you'll have to slap yourself again

BDR 529 IL: do exactly as I say…

BDR 529 IL: unbutton your pants

GatorCandie: now?

BDR 529 IL: now

GatorCandie: okay. And?

GatorCandie: what do I do now?

BDR 529 IL: you are going to think of me pulling your hair and biting your neck

GatorCandie: if I were you I wouldn't put up with any more questions from me. ☒

BDR 529 IL: I wasn't going to

BDR 529 IL: you get on your knees while I hold your hair in my hand to prevent you from getting away

BDR 529 IL:	you look up at me and I yell at you to look away
BDR 529 IL:	I then pull you up by your hair and pull you close to me
BDR 529 IL:	I turn you around; your back facing me while you feel my fingers glide over your panties and my warm breath on your neck
GatorCandie:	you're so bad. I am SO turned on!!
GatorCandie:	Too bad you're not coming.
BDR 529 IL:	in more ways than one!
GatorCandie:	by the way, if you want to say things like "do exactly what I say" you have to be careful with me.
BDR 529 IL:	why is that?
GatorCandie:	because if I'm in the mood to listen to you, then I will do exactly what you say, and that is all. So precision is the key there.
BDR 529 IL:	wow, this could work out very well
BDR 529 IL:	very well indeed
GatorCandie:	oh, this is good?
BDR 529 IL:	yes its good. I could think of many instructions that I would want you to follow with remarkable precision.
GatorCandie:	well like I said, if I felt like listening...
BDR 529 IL:	did you feel like listening when I told you what to do earlier??
GatorCandie:	well I did, but you don't have the power over me that you would in person.
GatorCandie:	technically speaking

BDR 529 IL: oh this would be much more fun in person

GatorCandie: I think so too. You're a natural dominant.

BDR 529 IL: sometimes, yes

GatorCandie: and sometimes you're just a sweetie and/or cold-blooded killa?

BDR 529 IL: hahaha

BDR 529 IL: mostly a sweetie, except when we're playing

GatorCandie: well, eye contact is really, really important for me

GatorCandie: I cannot over stress that

BDR 529 IL: the thought of you on your knees, looking up at me standing over you

GatorCandie: wow you're pretty cool. I've never heard anything like that. You think that would be sweet?

BDR 529 IL: sweet? Not exactly sweet, but definitely sexy.

GatorCandie: I'm not totally like this in public, by the way. Just letting you know... but I can be deferential if the situation calls for it. I'm pretty outgoing.

BDR 529 IL: I didn't think you were like this in public... but public and private are two very very different situations

GatorCandie: Unless you had your hands very close to my throat, that is. Then I'd be whatever you wanted, ha.

BDR 529 IL: I think everyone is a bit of a sexual devient. They just don't have the nerve to admit or know how to express it

BDR 529 IL:	grab you by the neck in a restaurant and force you down under the table
BDR 529 IL:	think anyone would mind?
GatorCandie:	You think I'm joking, but start turning me on in public and see what happens
BDR 529 IL:	I will definitely give that a try
GatorCandie:	Be careful. You need to make sure you have control of the situation before you get me going on that path.
BDR 529 IL:	so if we were in a restaurant, and you felt my hand on your thigh, and I whisper in your ear "do you want to cum"?
BDR 529 IL:	what answer or reaction would I get?
GatorCandie:	If you had me all turned on, and you thought it would be okay, I'd say yes.
GatorCandie:	But I wouldn't want to have to worry.
BDR 529 IL:	about what?
GatorCandie:	about anything... people, restaurant... anything
GatorCandie:	I'm usually extremely aware of my surroundings.
BDR 529 IL:	those things would be the last thing on your mind
GatorCandie:	as long as they were on yours, I would have an awesome time.
BDR 529 IL:	good
BDR 529 IL:	Pamela, what's a boy to do? I am sooooo turned on right now and I want you to be here with me!

GatorCandie: JFK is right down the street!

BDR 529 IL: wheres that 16 year old kid from yesterday?!?!?! hahaha

GatorCandie: hey!!

BDR 529 IL: haha

BDR 529 IL: just kidding silly

GatorCandie: Please don't end up in jail!

GatorCandie: You're not finished yet, not by a long shot!

GatorCandie: So let me get this straight.

BDR 529 IL: you already did

BDR 529 IL: hehe.... go on

GatorCandie: You have a good job, you're smart, funny, handsome, perverted and you're not gay. What's wrong with you?

BDR 529 IL: hooks for hands, remember

GatorCandie: lol

BDR 529 IL: I might ask you the same question

GatorCandie: Actually, I don't fit all those.

BDR 529 IL: replace handsome with pretty

BDR 529 IL: and you're right there

GatorCandie: I'm bi-sexual, and I have a gig that keeps my life pretty easy, but I don't make lots of money.

BDR 529 IL: minor details

GatorCandie: haha, ok, if you say so.

BDR 529 IL: don't you think they are minor details?

GatorCandie: well, money has never been an issue, and I guess with you they are minor. So sure, minor details.

BDR 529 IL: wen was the last time you were with a girl?

BDR 529 IL: was it Kris?

GatorCandie: no, she and I never slept with each other, believe it or not, ha. She's gay.

GatorCandie: She doesn't like girls who like men.

BDR 529 IL: so who and when?

GatorCandie: I think the very last time was last year when Eri's husband was away and we hung out and got drunk and slept together. She and I don't get together very often though.

BDR 529 IL: how was it?

GatorCandie: Good. She and I have been hanging out on and off for um... 12 years! Haha, I never thought about it before. We slept together when I was about 18.

GatorCandie: We did it at a party in front of our boyfriends

BDR 529 IL: ever with two girls and a guy or with two guys?

GatorCandie: Yes, I've been with Eri and James before.

GatorCandie: That's a funny story when we did it at that party

BDR 529 IL: tell me... details

GatorCandie: Well, she came to me at the party and asked me if I wanted to make out and let the boys watch for James Bday present, so I said sure.

GatorCandie: So she told them to wait 15 minutes and then come up so we could kind of figure out what we were doing.

BDR 529 IL: k

GatorCandie: Anyway, we really got into it and didn't notice when they entered the room. They sat and watched us for AN HOUR and we never noticed, haha. When we were kind of finished, they were actually holding up "10.0" signs. haha, I loved those guys.

BDR 529 IL: haha

GatorCandie: The four of us were awesome friends.

BDR 529 IL: and when did James join in?

GatorCandie: not then… another time. Actually two other times. After that, sometimes it just happend when Eri and I were both in the mood.

BDR 529 IL: lucky James

GatorCandie: you're not kiddin

GatorCandie: he was lucky

GatorCandie: I was always kind of curious about being with two guys but it never happened.

BDR 529 IL: oh my God… I had no idea how late it was

BDR 529 IL: I have to go for a while

GatorCandie: me too. K, ttyl

BDR 529 IL: k sweetie. Talk to you in a bit

GatorCandie: I'll miss you. And I really, really, really, really like you!

BDR 529 IL: I'll miss you too and the feeling is mutual. Take care honey. Talk to ya a little later on.

THE END

And that was it. That's all of the conversations that I have recorded. Unfortunately (or fortunately), however you look at it, Pamela and I never did meet in person. In fact, we only spoke over the internet a few more times after this last conversation. It became clear to both of us that the distance was going to be a major issue. Moving to Buffalo permanently was not really an option for me at the time. I had lived in Buffalo before and it just wasn't for me, not my kind of town. Don't get me wrong, it's actually a very cool town with an interesting cross section of people. There is a decent music and art scene there, but I'm the type of person that must be within driving distance to New York City. That is a "must have" for me. As for Pamela, she kind of felt the same way in that she really couldn't uproot her entire life and come live downstate. For one, she didn't have the money to do so nor did she have any kind of prospects for a job down here. We both came to the conclusion that this long-distance relationship was not going to come to fruition, and that it would be better to break it off, quickly and cleanly like a Band-Aid, rather than drag it out longer and longer while both of us fell deeper and deeper in love with each other.

Here is it, many years later, and I still think about her from time to time. Since then, I've gotten married and I now have two children, and believe it or not, I'm married to a girl that I met on Match years after meeting Pamela. After Pamela, I gave up on Match for a while. Looking back on it, I don't know if Pamela and I would have worked out in the long run. We might have been too similar. I'm not exactly sure why, but something tells me that it wouldn't have lasted. Wherever she is, I certainly hope that she is doing well, feeling healthy and most of all *happy*. Happy with her life and happy with her family and/or significant other.

I'm glad that things turned out the way that they did; for if they didn't, I never would have met my Gia who is, indeed, the love of my life. I have two beautiful little girls that I wouldn't trade for anything in the world. It just goes to show you that things really do happen for a reason. It makes me wonder if there truly is some sort of master plan. Could all these twists and turns in our lives that lead to certain events really just happen by chance? That's a question that I am in no way qualified to answer, but the romantic part of me wants to think that it was all meant to be. And with that, I'll let you; the reader, reflect on some of the events that have taken place in your own lives. Give some thought to fate versus chance. Whatever answer you come up with might change some of the decisions that you are about to make at this very moment.